Praise for the First Edition of *Finnish Lessons*

"Like other professionals, as Pasi Sahlberg shows in his book *Finnish Lessons*, Finnish teachers are driven by a sense of intrinsic motivation, not by the hope of a bonus or the fear of being fired."

—Diane Ravitch in the *New York Review of Books*

"*Finnish Lessons* provides valuable evidence that investing in teachers and instruction—rather than in tests and inspections—can bring about admirable, even excellent, results."

— ...ers College Record

"This book is an eye-opener ... the development of school systems in Sweden ... able."

... n *Dagens Nyheter*

"Simply put the one must rea... ...g... to understand how Finland has built perhaps the world's most successful educational system over the past few decades."

—Kenneth Bernstein for *Daily Kos*

"*Finnish Lessons* kills 99.9% of GERMs."

—Niall MacKinnon in the *Times Education Supplement*

"The story of Finnish educational success as told by Sahlberg in the slim volume *Finnish Lessons* is remarkable. . . . *Finnish Lessons* is an important book and educators need to read it."

—Gaea Leinhardt in *Educational Researcher*

"Sahlberg's book contains important lessons for a broad range of academics, educators, politicians, and the public. I especially appreciated its demonstration that top academic performance can be achieved with low inequality, comprehensive school for all students, low dropout rates, low school-related anxiety, and a high degree of freedom for teachers. In fact, Finland teaches that all these aspects need to be considered when giving directions for effective and sustainable educational reform."

—Henrik Saalbach in *Science*

"I know many reformers and politicians will not want to read this book because it will negate all the 'reform' that has been embraced by our country, but we will all miss out on some very important opportunities if they don't. Neither the size of Finland nor the country's demographics should be used as an excuse by any state or by the United States not to pay attention to what works. This book will give hope, vision, and strategies to anyone who is sincere in bringing a great education to every child. Pick it up and read it."

—John Wilson in *Education Week*

Finnish Lessons 2.0

WHAT CAN THE WORLD LEARN FROM EDUCATIONAL CHANGE IN FINLAND?

SECOND EDITION

PASI SAHLBERG

Forewords by Diane Ravitch
and Andy Hargreaves

Afterword by Sir Ken Robinson

Teachers College
Columbia University
New York and London

Published by Teachers College Press, 1234 Amsterdam Avenue, New York, NY 10027

Lyrics from "Rumblin'" by Neil Young are reprinted with permission from Hal Leonard Corporation. Copyright © 2010 by Silver Fiddle Music.

Library of Congress Cataloging-in-Publication Data

Sahlberg, Pasi.
 Finnish lessons 2.0 : what can the world learn from educational change in finland? / Pasi Sahlberg; foreword by Sir Ken Robinson ; afterword by Diane Ravitch. — Second edition.
      pages cm
  ISBN 978-0-8077-5585-3 (pbk. : alk. paper) —
  ISBN 978-0-8077-7329-1 (ebook : alk. paper)
   1. Educational change—Finland. 2. Education—Finland. I. Title.
  LA1013.7.S34 2015
  370.94897—dc23   2014033085

ISBN 978-0-8077-5585-3 (paper)
ISBN 978-0-8077-7329-1 (ebook)

Printed on acid-free paper
Manufactured in the United States of America

22 21 20 19 18 17 16 15   8 7 6 5 4 3 2 1

For Einar Frithiof Sahlberg (1895–1977)

I can feel the weather changing
I can see it all around
Can't you feel that new wind blowing?
Don't you recognize that sound that sound?
And the earth is slowly spinning
Spinning slowly, slowly changing.

— Neil Young, "Rumblin'"

Contents

Foreword to the Second Edition
An Alternate Universe

Pasi Sahlberg's *Finnish Lessons* was published exactly when it was most needed. When it appeared, the so-called education "reform" movement was ascendant in the United States and elsewhere and growing stronger.

President Barack Obama and Secretary of Education Arne Duncan were enthusiastic supporters of "reform." Their program, called Race to the Top, was launched in 2009, and it contained the key ingredients of the reform paradigm: testing, accountability, and choice. Educators were caught by surprise, as they had been led to expect that President Obama would end President George W. Bush's much-hated No Child Left Behind (NCLB). But the Obama program was built directly on the shaky foundation of NCLB. Instead of jettisoning high-stakes testing, Race to the Top increased the importance of testing. Now, not only would students and schools be held accountable for student test scores, but teachers would be given a bonus or fired based on test scores.

The reform movement moved into high gear in 2010. *Newsweek* magazine ran a cover story that spring declaring "we must fire bad teachers," as though the schools were overrun by "bad" teachers. That fall, the film *Waiting for "Superman"* was released with massive publicity. Its message: our public schools are failing, and the only hope for children stuck in "failing" public schools is escape to a privately managed charter school. The then-chancellor of the District of Columbia public schools, Michelle Rhee, became a media sensation, with her tough talk about the schools and the pleasure she took in firing teachers and principals.

Some of the nation's richest foundations—the Bill and Melinda Gates Foundation, the Eli and Edythe Broad Foundation, the Walton Family Foundation, and many others—poured millions into this reform movement, encouraging high-stakes testing, Teach for America, charter schools, and even (in the case of the Walton Foundation) vouchers for religious schools.

Several states, including Wisconsin, Michigan, and Indiana, rolled back collective bargaining rights, and teachers' unions became scapegoats, blamed for low test scores and for driving up the cost of education because of their health care and pensions. Surveys showed that teachers were demoralized—as well they should be—by the attacks upon them and upon their profession.

Thus it was that when Pasi Sahlberg's *Finnish Lessons* was published, it injected a new dimension into education debates. Finland had high test scores in international student assessments, and it was not doing anything that our American reformers demanded. It had a strong public school system. It did not have charters or vouchers. It had very high standards for entry into teaching; there was no such thing as Teach for Finland that would allow inexperienced young college graduates to teach in Finnish schools. Sahlberg described a 5-year teacher preparation program that all teachers must complete to teach in Finnish schools.

Teachers and principals belong to the same union, which not only negotiates wages and working conditions, but advocates on behalf of children and schools. Although Finland has a national curriculum, teachers have wide latitude to shape it to their own needs and strengths. Best of all, Finland does not subject students to standardized tests until the end of their high school years. As Sahlberg writes, the schools are a standardized testing–free zone.

What many American educators loved about *Finnish Lessons* is that it portrays an alternate universe, one that respects educators and enables them to do their best work, one that recognizes that society has an obligation to ensure the health and well-being of children. Sahlberg knew that the Finnish story stood in sharp contrast with what was happening in the United States and other countries. He refers to this movement for testing and choice as GERM: the Global Educational Reform Movement.

Yes, indeed, the United States, Britain, and many other countries are infected with GERM. *Finnish Lessons 2.0* is a disinfectant. It reminds us that a nation can consciously build an admirable school system if it pays close attention to the needs of children, if it selects and prepares its educators well, and if it builds educational communities that are not only physically attractive but conducive to the joys of teaching and learning.

—Diane Ravitch

Foreword to the First Edition
UnFinnished Business

In the 1960s, the Russian launch of Sputnik propelled a massive drive to develop science and mathematics innovation in U.S. schools. In the 1980s and 1990s, the rising sun of Japan and other Asian tiger economies prompted calls to copy Japanese educational methods—making schoolwork more rigorous, extending the impact of standardized testing, and increasing the number of hours of schooling over the school year. In the past decade, the burgeoning economies of India and China have provoked United States commissions and initiatives to advocate the teaching of 21st-century skills, tougher curriculum requirements, common national standards, yet more testing, increased competition between teachers and schools, and harder work for everybody. Nevertheless, over the past quarter-century, the standards and performance of American teachers and schools have steadily declined in relation to international benchmarks. In spite of this, across more than 2 decades of educational reform, the United States, like many other Anglo-American nations, has epitomized Einstein's definition of madness: keep doing the same thing while expecting to get a different result. Force, pressure, shame, top-down intervention, markets, competition, standardization, testing, easier and quicker passages into teaching, closure of failing schools, the firing of ineffective teachers and principals, and fresh starts with young teachers and newly established schools—the very reform strategies that have failed dismally over 2 decades in many Anglo-Saxon nations—are being reinvented and reimposed and with even greater force and determination.

THE LEMMING RACE TO THE TOP

The critics are already out in force. International change adviser Michael Fullan predicts that President Obama's Race to the Top strategy, with its intention to turn around the nation's 5,000 worst-performing schools, lift limits on establishing charter schools, and introduce measures such as performance-related pay to raise teacher quality, will end in failure (Fullan, 2010). The strategy, Fullan says, pays little or no attention to developing the capacity of leaders and teachers to improve together or as a system; it is based on a failed theory that teacher quality can be increased by a system of competitive rewards, and it rests on a badly flawed model of management where everyone manages their own unit, is accountable for results, and competes with their peers—creating fiefdoms, silos, and lack of capacity or incentives for professionals to help one another.

Former Assistant Secretary of Education Diane Ravitch also condemns Barack Obama's "awful education plan," which she regards as even worse than its much-derided predecessor, No Child Left Behind (Ravitch, 2010a). The plan promotes charter schools even though the evidence indicates that they do not consistently or even on average outperform their public school district alternatives, and that they simply "skim the best students in poor communities," leaving the rest to flounder (Ravitch, 2010b). Meanwhile, performance-based pay ties teacher rewards to results on appallingly designed tests of dubious validity and "destroys teamwork" among professionals who instead "need to share what they know." The reform, she concludes, is "mean-spirited, punitive, and deeply indifferent to the real problems that teachers face."

Yong Zhao, the leading American expert on educational reform in China and Southeast Asia, points out that China, the leading economic competitor of the United States, is actually decentralizing its curriculum, diversifying assessment, and encouraging local autonomy and innovation. Meanwhile, Zhao concludes, while China is decentralizing and Singapore is promoting a creative environment characterized by the principle of "Teach Less, Learn More," U.S. education has been stubbornly "moving toward authoritarianism, letting the government dictate what and how students should learn and what schools should teach" (Zhao, 2009).

In culture, politics, and business—as well as in educational reform—too many Anglo-American cultures and societies have developed an unhealthy obsession with all that is bigger, harder, tougher, faster, and stronger. Companies that sacrifice customer safety to short-term shareholder value; businesses that wreak ecological havoc with excessively bold and risky efforts to increase profitability; financial collapses that result from astronomical levels of unrepayable debt; turnaround specialists who create arbitrary disruption by setting unrealistic targets for growth and equally arbitrary quotas for staff dismissals—these are the consequences of the impatience, hubris, arrogance, and greed that characterize the worst kinds of business. Failure, firings, competition, and closures are the educational equivalent of unsustainable change in business. What they offer is oversized, pumped-up, artificially enhanced school reform on steroids.

Even in business, these larger-than-life strategies of turnaround and improvement do not produce sustainable improvement. Companies may be broken up, assets sold off, and employees fired with impunity, and all this might increase short-term shareholder returns, but few strategies of these sorts survive in the long term, and many turnaround companies eventually become casualties of their leaders' reckless behavior. Indeed, management expert Manfred Kets de Vries explains how many so-called turnaround specialists are little more than psychiatrically disturbed narcissists, sociopaths, and control freaks (Kets De Vries, 2006).

THIRD AND FOURTH WAYS AHEAD

The worst of the steroidal school reform movement has been tempered by lighter, less punitive alternatives in other Anglo-American contexts. Here, the political targets and goals for test-driven improvement in the fundamentals of literacy, mathematics, and science are still imposed with insistent inflexibility, but they are now moderated by a less harsh improvement discourse and by higher levels of professional support in the form of improved materials, increased resources, and better training.

About a decade ago in England, and more recently (and somewhat differently) in Ontario, Canada, and Australia, a model has been advanced and advocated that stands between and beyond the complete professional autonomy of the 1970s, and the mean-spirited, miserly, market-driven, and standardized reforms that characterized England in the early 1990s, and other places after that.

The "Third Way" of educational change reflected in the models offers a double twist on more blatantly steroidal reform efforts:

- a clear emphasis on the moral purpose of education
- a commitment to capacity building

These components sound more professionally plausible and inspiring than their reform counterparts that hounded and hectored the teaching profession into submission. Yet in reality, they are still highly problematic.

First, the admirable advancement of moral purpose in Third Way reforms repeatedly turns out, in practice, to be *the same* moral purpose irrespective of culture, country, or context—*Raise the bar and narrow the gap* to improve tested achievement scores in literacy and mathematics (linked to imposed system-wide achievement targets). Whether it is Ontario, Australia, Bermuda, or Greater Manchester in England, the goal or moral purpose is almost identical. The countries and cultures may differ, but the consultants' PowerPoint slides remain pretty much the same. In the Third Way, people aren't defining or developing their own shared visions or moral purposes. They don't *own* their visions. They *rent* them from other people.

Second, while the Third Way has an admirable commitment to capacity building, it has often distorted the meaning of "capacity people" and diverted people from the noble purposes that underpinned its origins. The idea of capacity building first emerged in the context of developing countries. Much like the concept and strategy of community organizing, capacity building meant helping a community help itself. It was a humanistic and empowering concept directed toward assisting people to fulfill their own personally compelling purpose. In Third Way policies, though, capacity building has often turned into something else—training people in prescribed strategies to deliver accountability goals and targets imposed by others.

In the Third Way, capacity building is about training for policy delivery. In the Fourth Way of inspiration, innovation, and collective responsibility, as set out by Dennis Shirley and myself as a result of our direct work in high-performing jurisdictions like Finland and Alberta, Canada, capacity building is more about self-directed growth and development (Hargreaves & Shirley, 2009). In short, and to be very clear: The Third Way is about renting and delivering the policies of others, while the Fourth Way is about shared ownership and development of a community's own compelling purposes.

THE NORTHERN LIGHT APPROACH

Into all this policy mix has come the unlikeliest exemplar of educational success—Finland. With its unexpectedly and consistently superlative performance on international tests of student achievement, its possession of the narrowest achievement gaps in the world, and its equally high rankings on ratings of economic competitiveness, corporate transparency, and general well-being and quality of life, this little Nordic country of barely 5.5 million people has illuminated a different path to educational and economic goals from those being forged by the Anglo-American groups of nations.

Curious about and intrigued by Finland's unusual example, educators and policymakers from all over the world have visited this Scandinavian country to try to discover the secrets of its success. I have been fortunate enough to be among them. In 2007, I had the rare opportunity to take a small team from the Organisation for Economic Co-operation and Development (OECD) to Finland to examine the relationship between the country's achievement record and its strategies of school improvement and leadership development (Hargreaves, Halasz, & Pont, 2008).

Unlike many other commentators on the Finnish experience, we did not rely solely on secondary sources, on a few interviews with senior policymakers, or on the available educational research literature. We observed and interviewed students, teachers, school and district administrators, university research experts, and Ministry of Education staff up to the very highest level. We read material on the history and organization of Finland as a society and of its dynamic leading company, Nokia. We wanted to understand the country and its history as well as its schools, and to grasp what explained its dramatic economic and educational turnaround after the fall of the Berlin Wall and the collapse of Finland's protected Soviet markets in 1990. In all this research, it quickly became evident to us that the leading authority on Finland's distinctive educational reform strategy was and still is Pasi Sahlberg.

Sahlberg grew up in a Finnish educational family. He taught in the Finnish school system and then at the university level. From there, he went on to oversee the professional development strategy for the Ministry of Education. Like all the best researchers and commentators, Sahlberg was and remains both an insider and outsider. As a loyal and trusted insider who now heads up one of Finland's leading organizations in the field of innovation, Sahlberg possesses a rich and authentic grounding in and understanding of the inner workings of the country's educational and societal system that are often so mysterious to outside visitors.

Leaving Finland for a significant position with the World Bank, Pasi Sahlberg quickly developed the capacity to understand, interpret, and provide systemic support for countries in Eastern Europe, Central Asia, North Africa, and the Middle East. In addition to publishing a range of key scholarly articles on Finland, he also wrote the definitive country report on Finland for the World Bank.

Pasi Sahlberg's insider status here is critical. He is not only interested in systemic educational reform in a cerebral sense. He cares passionately about and remains deeply connected to the students, teachers, and communities that reforms ultimately serve. One of the distinguishing features of his character is that upon entering a new country anywhere in the world to provide systemic evaluation and support, one of his first professional acts is always to teach a mathematics lesson and converse with the students in one of the country's everyday secondary schools.

Pasi Sahlberg helped our OECD team understand, as he will help readers of this book understand, what makes Finnish reform distinctively successful, and why it has proved inconvenient to the Anglo-American group of nations as an exemplar of educational change. Finland, he shows,

- has developed and owned its own vision of educational and social change connected to inclusiveness and creativity, rather than renting a standardized vision that has been developed elsewhere;
- relies on high-quality, well-trained teachers, with strong academic qualifications and master's degrees, who are drawn to the profession by its compelling societal mission and its conditions of autonomy and support—compared with the rapid entry strategies of short-term training and high teacher turnover advanced in countries such as England and the United States;
- has an inclusive special educational strategy where nearly half of the country's students will have received some special education support at some time before completing 9-year basic school, rather than the special education strategy of legal identification, placement, and labeling of individuals favored by Anglo-American nations;
- has developed teachers' capacity to be collectively responsible for developing curriculum and diagnostic assessments together rather than delivering prescribed curricula and preparing for the standardized tests designed by central governments; and
- has linked educational reform to the creative development of economic competitiveness and also the development of social cohesion, inclusiveness, and shared community within the wider society.

Pasi Sahlberg urges us not to follow the educational reform strategies (which he calls GERM) advanced by Anglo-American political leaders and their educational advisers who dismiss the potential lessons of Finnish educational reform because of their ideological inconvenience. Nations that have become committed to and stuck with high rates of economic inequality respond only to public impatience for tough talk and short-term gain. He shows how those who dismiss Finland (in favor of their own preferred models, of course) on the grounds of its modest size as a nation overlook how its population of 5.5 million is close to the average of most U.S. states, where the bulk of educational policy decisions are made. Against the argument that Finland is just too different from America, England, or Canada (as if India, China, and Japan are not!), Sahlberg reveals how Finland has dramatically changed its identity and orientation as a nation, and how other countries can and must do so as well.

There are unresolved questions in Anglo-American educational reform that pumped-up steroidal reform strategies and the "lemming" Race to the Top will never be able to answer but that Sahlberg's work profoundly can. This is not just because Pasi Sahlberg is the most credible indigenous expert on his own country's exemplary reforms. It is also because, as a world-ranking scholar, and former World Bank expert on a host of countries and their educational systems, Sahlberg has developed an international perspective on educational reform in general as well as the outsider's advantage in being able to make all that is familiar in Finland fresh to others.

One of the ways that teachers improve is by learning from other teachers. Schools improve when they learn from other schools. Isolation is the enemy of all improvement. We have spent decades breaking down the isolation of teachers within and between our schools. It is now time to break down the ideology of exceptionalism in the United States and other Anglo-American nations if we are to develop reforms that will truly inspire our teachers to improve learning for all our students—especially those who struggle the most. In that essential quest, Pasi Sahlberg is undoubtedly one of the very best teachers of all.

—Andy Hargreaves

Preface to the Second Edition

At the turn of this millennium, the global education landscape looked very different than it does today. There were many countries and jurisdictions that believed they had the best education system in the world. Vast financial investments in national education reforms loaded with promises of excellence and quick fixes carried the hope of global lead positions in the international rankings. At that same time, there were education systems that were building equity and equality of opportunity to ensure successful learning for all of their children. These countries didn't aim to be among the best in the world but instead were trying to offer the best for their own children and the parents of those children. The irony is that today none of the countries that have aimed to be the best has succeeded in becoming the best, and none of the current successful school systems ever intended to be on the top.

Finnish Lessons was born from this new emerging global educational landscape. Researchers around the world began to search for common factors that would explain the unexpectedly good educational performance of Finland, Korea, Canada, Japan, and later Singapore and Estonia. The question that was bothering me even more than that was what these successful school systems *don't* do that the others do. I soon realized that Finland was, in many ways, an outlier among all countries. Finland seemed to have many central school policies that were almost the opposite of those introduced in the United States, England, Australia, New Zealand, and much of the rest of the world. *Finnish Lessons*, which was published in late 2011, was a story of the alternative education solutions behind Finland's surprisingly good educational performance.

When I am invited to speak about *Finnish Lessons*—and I have done that since the book first was published on all the continents of the world—I always begin with three points of warning that I want to mention here. First, my intention in this book and in my presentations of the Finnish school system is not to convince my audiences that Finland has the best education system in the world. International media and some pundits have created the incorrect impression that there exists a global metric to determine what are the best—and the worst—education systems in the world. Current international education rankings only include a small number of academic subjects in their indices—typically literacy, mathematics, and science. Therefore, when the first results of the Programme for International Student Assessment (PISA) became public in December 2001 showing Finland as being ranked number one, some Finns said to themselves: "We must have done something wrong to be the best in a standardized test–based assessment that measures students' achievement in three academic areas." There are few, if any, educators in Finland who would say that the Finnish school system is the best in the world.

Second, I am not claiming in this book or in my talks that if only other countries would imitate Finland's model in reforming their education systems, then things would get better. Some education improvement experts before me have noted that school reforms are poor travelers. This means that what seems to make an education system perform beyond expectations in one place may not have the same positive effect on school systems elsewhere. Too often, I must admit, I have met people who have visited Finland or studied its education system believing that if they only had Finland's curriculum, school buildings, and teachers, their own educational challenges would disappear. This book and my work with it around the world are meant to emphasize that we can learn from one another. Finland may offer inspiration to educators in other countries to think more deeply about their own schools and cultures. There are many lessons, as I share in this book, that others can learn from us, just as Finland has been inspired by educators and school systems around the world.

Finally, it is important to keep in mind that much of the pedagogical innovation in Finnish classrooms and the inspiration for education policies has its origins in other countries. In the early 20th century after Finland became an independent nation and its education system began to shape up, Germany and Switzerland served as a model for the first Finnish schools. Then the idea of an equitable, comprehensive school system came from neighboring Nordic countries, especially from Sweden. More recently, England, Scotland, Canada, and the United States have served as places where Finnish educators have found good ideas to enrich teaching and learning in their schools. Curriculum theories, teaching methods, student assessments, and school leadership models are examples of the positive influence that American educational research and development has had in Finland since the 1980s.

This second edition of *Finnish Lessons* includes comprehensive updates on Finland's education scene as well as updates on international statistics measuring educational performance. This new edition uses data from all the international studies and surveys in which Finland has participated since 2011. Based on this updated evidence, this edition of the book also discusses how things are changing in Finland and what the possible responses to these trends may be. Also included are an illustration of the early childhood education component that is now part of the Finnish education system, a description of the renewed special-needs education system, and a more detailed narrative of the upper-secondary matriculation examination.

Finnish Lessons has had a successful journey so far. I have presented the ideas in this book at Parliament houses in Scotland, England, Sweden, Australia, New Zealand, and the European Union. It has given me scores of new friends and colleagues. In 2013, *Finnish Lessons* received the Grawemeyer Award, a prestigious prize given by the University of Louisville in Kentucky that recognizes important ideas in education that have the potential to change the world. Indeed, this book has brought me invitations to guest-lecture at leading universities around the world. I am grateful to all those hundreds of people who have sent me their comments and opinions on the first edition. Many of these suggestions are now incorporated into the pages of this renewed edition.

I hope that *Finnish Lessons 2.0* inspires you and convinces you that there is a way to build good public school systems that serve all of our children well. The Finnish recipe for good education is simple: Always ask yourself if the policy or reform you plan to initiate is going to be good for children or teachers. If you hesitate with your answer, don't do it.

—Cambridge, Massachusetts, autumn 2014

Acknowledgments

Before writing this part, I went to my neighborhood bookstore and read the acknowledgments in several other authors' books. Many of them include lengthy lists of names—colleagues, friends, students, and sometimes opponents—who are given credit in the book. Some texts made me wonder if all those mentioned really deserved to be thanked. With this book, I can assure you that everyone named below has had a role to play in developing or writing this book. Some contributions were smaller than others, but they were all important.

Writing a book about a topic so close to your own life and work is difficult without occasionally soliciting an outsider's perspective. For the writing of this book, I have depended on the knowledge, wisdom, and experience of some close colleagues and friends. Their confidence that the story of Finland is worth sharing with others was an important kickoff to write this book. But to listen to only those who agree with you won't make a good story. This is when I remember my grandmother's wisdom: "If we all think the same way, none of us probably thinks very much." In this regard, I am particularly thankful to those trusted ones who have dared to disagree with me or raise their concerns, but always in eloquent and respectful terms.

Special thanks to following colleagues and friends: Erkki Aho, Lisa Belzberg, David Berliner, CIMO, Jean-Claude Couture, Linda Darling-Hammond, Carrie Fuller, Slavko Gaber, Howard Gardner, Kauko Hämäläinen, Andy Hargreaves, Tom Hatch, Jarkko Hautamäki, Hannah Hayman, Henry Heikkinen, Olli-Pekka Heinonen, Martti Hellström, Stephen Heyneman, Peter Johnson, Ben Levin, Henry Levin, Stephen Murgatroyd, Cera Murtagh (for inspiring me to find the name for this book), Nicholas Negroponte, Hannele Niemi, David Oldroyd, Lyda Peters, Diane Ravitch, Sir Ken Robinson, Veera Salonen, Laura Servage, Robert Schwartz, Dennis Shirley, Tony Wagner, and Win Wiencke. I want to thank Sam Abrams for his critical friendship and thoughtful assistance in more ways than one to make my writings more understandable to readers.

An important source of inspiration to write this book has been the tens of thousands of people around the world whom I have met at hundreds of conferences, seminars, and symposia. They have taught me to understand better and to respect more deeply the complexity of educational change. As a consequence, I am humbled by the question of why some nations do better at educating their people than others. It is easy to overlook contextual differences and give simple explanations about why Finnish students do better on international tests than most others. Questions, discussions, and critical concerns in this light have been essential for me in giving shape to the story of educational development in Finland. My international students at the University of Helsinki have also been a source of inspiration when we have explored the secrets of the Finnish education system from perspectives that often include very different experiences and expectations from those of Finnish students. I am grateful to all my audiences and students, who have made writing this book an exciting journey and a process of personal growth for me. The Ministry of Foreign Affairs of Finland has generously disseminated *Finnish Lessons* at their events and to their guests, and for that I am thankful.

This book has been developed from earlier versions of various parts of my analyses, research, and arguments that can be found in the References section. Reviewers and editors of the journals and edited volumes in which my previous works have appeared have also played a significant role in enhancing my own argumentation and clarity in telling the story of Finland.

I am forever grateful to Petra for her enduring support and wisdom to show me the way forward when my power and will have been low. Our son, Otto, deserves a big kiss for giving me a new reason to write about the education that all children deserve.

Yes, We Can
(Learn from One Another)

During the next 10 years about 1.2 billion young 15-to-30-year-olds
will be entering the job market and with the means now at our disposal
about 300 million will get a job. What will we offer these young, about a
billion of them? I think this is one of the greatest challenges if we want to
achieve peaceful development and hope for these young.

—Martti Ahtisaari, former president of Finland, 1994–2000,
and Nobel Peace Prize laureate

It has become clear everywhere that the schools we have today will not
be able to provide opportunities for students to learn what is necessary
in the future. The demand for better-quality teaching and learning and
more equitable and efficient education is universal. Indeed, educational systems are facing a twin challenge: how to change schools so that
students may learn new types of knowledge and skills required in an
unpredictably changing knowledge world, and how to make that new
learning possible for all young people regardless of their socioeconomic
conditions. To be successful with these challenges is both a moral and
economic imperative for our societies and their leaders. It is a moral obligation because each person's well-being and ultimately happiness arises
from knowledge, skills, and worldviews that good education provides. It
is also an economic imperative because the wealth of nations depends as
never before on know-how. The aftermath of the recent global economic
crisis is showing how unemployed young people are becoming hopeless
to an extent that is bringing governments down. Many of these young
people lack relevant education and training that would help them to
help themselves.

This book is about Finland and how the Finns transformed their
educational system from mediocre in the 1980s to one of the models of

educational excellence and equity today. International indicators show that Finland has one of the most educated citizenries in the world, provides educational opportunities in an egalitarian manner, and makes efficient use of resources. Finnish education has recently attracted attention from many international scholars. Linda Darling-Hammond (2010) writes extensively about it in her book *The Flat World and Education*. Marc Tucker (2011) included Finland as one example of a high-performing model for the United States in the book *Surpassing Shanghai* that he edited. Andy Hargreaves and Dennis Shirley (2012) chose Finland as an example of a nation that has successfully transformed its education system in their book *The Global Fourth Way*. Diane Ravitch (2013) refers to Finland in her book *Reign of Error* as an example for Americans that shows why preserving public education helps bring about better education for all. A chapter on Finnish education has become an integral part of any international handbook or volume that reports contemporary thinking and practice in the field. International development agencies, consulting firms, and media houses refer to Finland as a good model and "a witness" of successful transformation of public education.[1] Monographs on Finnish schools and teachers have been published in China, Korea, Japan, France, Slovenia, Mexico, and Germany, to mention just a few countries. The first edition of this book was translated into 20 languages—clearly, there is a global interest in Finland's experience.

In leading the way toward educational reform in Finland in the early 1990s, Dr. Vilho Hirvi, then director general of Finland's National Board of Education, said in a speech to his staff that "an educated nation cannot be created by force." He acknowledged that teachers and students must be heard, and that the way forward called for active collaboration. In Finland, teachers and students were insisting on more flexibility and more freedom in deciding how to design instruction, what to study, and when. "We are creating a new culture of education and there is no way back," Hirvi said. Basic to this new culture has been the cultivation of trust between education authorities and schools. Such trust, as we have witnessed, creates reform that is not only sustainable but is also owned by the teachers who implement it.

NORTHERN EXPOSURE

In the 1990s, education in Finland was nothing special in international terms. All young Finns attended school regularly, the school network was wide and dense, secondary education was accessible for all Finns, and higher education was a realistic option for an increasing number of upper-secondary-school graduates. However, the performance of Finnish students on international assessments was close to international averages, except in reading, where Finnish students did better than most of their peers in other countries. The unexpected and jarring recession of the early 1990s brought Finland to the edge of a financial breakdown. Bold and immediate measures were necessary to fix national fiscal imbalances and revive the foreign trade that disappeared with the collapse of the Soviet Union in 1990. Nokia, the main global industrial brand of Finland, with its mobile communication products, became a critical engine in boosting Finland out of the country's biggest economic dip since World War II. Another Finnish brand not yet known to many people abroad at that time, *peruskoulu*, or the 9-year comprehensive basic school, was the other key player in this turnaround of the Finnish economy and society.

There are countries around the world where education leaders find their own educational systems in a situation very similar to what Finland faced in the 1990s. The global economic downturn has hit many schools, universities, and entire education systems hard. Take Ireland, Greece, England, or the United States, for example—student achievement is nowhere close to what it should be in these knowledge-based economies, where productivity and innovation are necessary conditions for competitiveness and a sustainable way of life. Students seem to find the teaching offered in schools and universities increasingly boring and irrelevant to their needs in a rapidly changing world. The story of Finland's educational journey in this book brings hope to all those who are worried about whether improving their educational systems is even possible. It also provides food for thought to those who are looking for ways to adjust education policies to fit the realities of economic recovery. The lessons from Finland should be refreshing because they depart from the ideas commonly presented in books or journals on educational development. Moreover, these lessons show that systemic improvement is indeed possible if only policies and strategies are designed in smart and sustainable ways and teachers and school leaders are involved in planning, implementing, and reviewing all aspects of intended changes.

Although these lessons hold great promise, they also call for patience. In this age of immediate results, education requires a different mindset. Reforming schools is a complex and slow process. To rush this process is to ruin it. The story told in this book makes this clear. Steps must be grounded in research and implemented in collaboration by academics, policymakers, principals, and teachers.

This book is about how such a process evolved in Finland since World War II. It is the first book written for international readers that tells the story of how Finland created a system praised as much for its equity as for its high quality. Many of the world's great newspapers and broadcast services—the *New York Times*, *Washington Post*, CNN, *Times of London*, *Le Monde*, *El País*, National Public Radio, NBC, *Deutsche Welle*, and BBC—have covered this Finnish educational miracle. Filmmaker Morgan Spurlock became intrigued by Finnish schools and included them in his education episode of *Inside Man* on CNN. Thousands of official delegations have visited Finnish authorities, schools, and communities to learn about what drives their excellence in education. This story, however, has until now not received the book-length treatment necessary for enumerating, linking, and explaining the many players, institutions, and impersonal forces involved.

My approach in this book is both personal and academic. It is personal because of my intimate relationship with education in Finland. I was born in northern Finland and raised in a village primary school, where both of my parents were teachers. Most of my childhood memories are in one way or another linked to school. I had the privilege of looking beyond the secrets of the classroom after everybody else was gone, and I found that world to be rich. It was my home—and it was an enchanted one. It is perhaps no surprise, then, that I went on to become a teacher myself. My first teaching position was at a junior high school in Helsinki. I taught mathematics and physics there for 7 years. Later, I spent enough time in educational administration and in university teacher education to understand the difference between education in school and out. As a policy analyst for the Organisation for Economic Co-operation and Development (OECD), an education specialist for the World Bank, and an education expert for the European Commission, I gained the global perspective necessary for a deeper appreciation of Finland's distinct place in education.

As a representative of Finland in these different capacities, I have also been forced to develop a keener understanding of what distinguishes Finnish methods by answering questions from audiences and media around the world. During the past 10 years, I have given more than 400 keynote addresses and 200 interviews about the Finnish educational system around the world. I have had conversations with thousands of people, which has taught me to be sensitive to the complexity of educational change. These conversations with people who are interested in education, as I am, have greatly advanced the writing of this book. The following are some of the questions that I have been asked over and over again: "What is the secret of Finnish educational success?" "How do you get the best young people into teaching in Finland?" "How much does lack of ethnic diversity have to do with good educational performance there?" "How do you know that all schools are doing what they should when you don't test students or inspect teachers?" "How did Finland save its education system during the economic downturn in the 1990s?" For such questions and also for critical remarks related to my thinking, I am grateful. Without them, I would never have been able to hone my assessment of Finnish differences.

This book also has an academic orientation because it stems from research that I have been part of over the past 2 decades as an author, coauthor, or critic. This book is thus not a typical monograph, written as the result of a research project or a particular event. It is a synthesis of a decade of policy analysis, experience as a teacher and administrator, and dialogue with thousands of educators around the world. I have been privileged to spend enough time outside of Finland and to work with a number of foreign governments to better understand the true nature and peculiarity of Finnish education and life in Finnish schools.

For many years I taught a course titled "Introduction to the Finnish Education System" at the University of Helsinki. My students came from all over the world. Most of them came to study for a full year in Finland because they wanted to better understand the structure and spirit of the Finnish school system. Teaching at Harvard University's Graduate School of Education has introduced me to American students who are interested in education around the world. The opportunity to teach students in academic institutions has been the best way to enhance my own understanding of the Finnish education system. I have improved and updated this second edition of *Finnish Lessons* through listening to my students, audiences, and colleagues and learning from them.

FINLAND AS AN INSPIRATION

Public education systems are in crisis in many parts of the world. The United States, England, Sweden, Norway, and France, to mention just a few advanced nations, are among those countries where public education is increasingly challenged because of an endemic failure to provide adequate learning opportunities for all children. Tough solutions are not uncommon in these countries: Tougher competition between schools, stronger accountability for student achievement, performance-based pay for teachers, and closing down troubled schools are all part of the recipe to fix failing education systems. This book does not suggest that tougher competition, more data, abolishing teacher unions, opening more charter schools, or employing corporate-world management models in education systems will bring about a resolution to these crises—quite the opposite. The main message of this book is that there is another way to improve education systems, one that is different from the market-based reform ideology mentioned above. This other way includes improving the teaching force, limiting student testing to a necessary minimum, placing responsibility and trust before accountability, investing in equity in education, and handing over school- and district-level leadership to experienced education professionals. These are common education policy themes in some of the high-performing countries—Finland among them—in the 2012 Programme for International Student Assessment (PISA) of the OECD (2013b; 2013d). The chapters of this book offer five reasons why Finland is an interesting and relevant source of inspiration for other nations that are looking for ways to improve their own education systems.

One, Finland has a unique educational system because it has progressed from mediocrity to being a model contemporary educational system and a "strong performer" in about 2 decades since late 1970s. Finland is special also because it has been able to create an educational system where students learn well and where equitable education has translated into little variation in student performance between schools in different parts of country, as shown in all PISA studies since the year 2000. This internationally rare status has been achieved by using reasonable financial resources and less effort than other nations have expended on reform efforts.

Two, because of this proven steady progress, Finland demonstrates that there is another way to build a successful education system using solutions that differ from the market-driven education policies that have become common in many parts of the world. The Finnish way of change, as described by Andy Hargreaves and Dennis Shirley (2009) in *The Fourth Way*, is one of trust, professionalism, and shared responsibility. Indeed, Finland is an example of a nation that lacks school inspection, reliance on externally collected data, standardized curriculum, high-stakes student testing, test-based accountability, and a race-to-the-top mentality with regard to educational change.

Three, as a consequence of its success, Finland can offer some alternative ways to think about solutions to existing chronic educational problems in the United States, England, and other Nordic countries, such as high school dropout rates, early teacher attrition, and inadequate special education. The Finnish approach to reducing early school leavers, enhancing teacher professionalism, implementing intelligent accountability, and employing smarter student assessment in schools can offer inspiration to other school systems looking for a path to success.

Four, Finland is also an international high performer in commerce, technology, sustainable development, good governance, prosperity, gender equality, and child well-being, thus raising interesting questions concerning interdependencies between education and other sectors in society. It appears that other public policy sectors, such as health and employment, seem to play a role also in long-term educational development and change. In Finland, this holds true as well regarding income parity, social mobility, and trust within Finnish society, as the chapters that follow will show.

Finally, we should listen to the story of Finland because it gives hope to those who are losing their faith in public education and whether it can be improved. This book reveals that the transformation of educational systems is possible, but that it takes time, patience, and determination. The Finnish story is particularly interesting because some of the key policies and changes were introduced during the worst economic crisis that Finland has experienced since World War II. This suggests that a crisis can spark the survival spirit that leads to better solutions to acute problems than a "normal situation" would bring about. This book speaks against those who believe that the best way to solve chronic problems in many education systems is to take control away from school boards and give it to those who might run schools more effectively, by charters or other means of privatization. Although there are limits to the ideas that can be transferred from Finland to other nations, certain basic lessons may have general value for other educational systems, such as the practices of building on teacher strengths, securing relaxed and fear-free learning for students, and gradually enhancing trust within educational systems.

As this book illustrates, there is no single reason why any educational system succeeds or fails. Instead, there is a network of interrelated factors—educational, political, and cultural—that function differently in different situations. I would, however, like to cite three important elements of Finnish educational policies since the early 1970s that appear to transcend culture.

The first is an inspiring vision of what good public education should be: Finland has been particularly committed to building a good, publicly financed, and locally governed basic school for every child. This common educational goal, which placed equity in education as the key priority, became so deeply rooted in politics and public services in Finland that it survived opposing political governments and ministries unharmed and intact. Since the introduction of *peruskoulu* in early 1970s, there have been 20 governments representing different political colors and 27 ministers of education in charge of educational reforms in Finland. This commitment to having a great public school for every child has been so strong that some call it the Finnish Dream. This name provides a hint for other nations when it comes to educational transformation: It is better to have a dream of your own than to rent one from others.

The second aspect of educational change that deserves attention is the way Finland has treated advice offered by friends and neighboring countries. Much of the inspiration in building independent Finland since 1917 has come from its allies, especially Sweden. The welfare state model, health-care system, and basic education are good examples of borrowed ideas from our western neighbor. Later, Finnish education policies were also influenced by guidance from supranational institutions, especially the OECD (which Finland joined in 1969) and the European Union (which Finland joined in 1995). In this book, I launch an argument that, despite international influence and borrowing educational ideas from others, Finland has in the end created its own way to build the educational system that exists today. I call this the Finnish Way because it is different from what much of the rest of the world has done in educational improvement during the past 25 years. The Finnish Way of change preserves the best of Finland's own traditions and present good practices, and combines these with innovations received from others. Cultivating trust, enhancing autonomy, and tolerating diversity are just a few of the examples of the reform ideas found in Finnish schools today. Many pedagogical ideas and educational innovations are initially imported from other countries, often from North America or the United Kingdom. These include curriculum models from England, California, and Ontario; cooperative learning from the United States and Israel; portfolio assessment from the United States; the teaching of science and mathematics from England, the United States, and Australia; and peer-assisted leadership from Canada and the Netherlands, to mention just a few. At the same time, the Finnish Dream of education is "made in Finland" and therefore is owned by Finns rather than rented from others.

The third aspect of change is a systematic development of respectful and inspiring working conditions for teachers and principals in Finnish schools. This book raises an important question that is repeated when whole-system educational reforms are discussed: How do we get the best and brightest young people to choose teaching as their career? Experience from Finland, as illustrated in Chapter 3, suggests that it is not enough to establish world-class teacher education programs or to pay teachers well. Finland has built world-class teacher education programs. And Finland pays its teachers well. But the true Finnish difference is that teachers in Finland are expected to exercise their full professional knowledge and judgment both independently and collectively in their schools. They control curriculum, student assessment, school improvement, and community involvement. This is called teacher professionalism. Much as teachers around the world enter the profession with a mission to build community and transmit culture, Finnish teachers, in contrast to their peers in so many countries, have the latitude and the power to follow through.

LEARNING FROM OTHERS

Can Finland be a model for educational change in other countries? Many people are fascinated by the fact that Finland has been able to transform its educational system from something elitist, unknown, and inefficient into a paragon of equity and efficiency (Schleicher, 2006). Finland is also one of the few nations among the 34 OECD countries that has been able to improve educational performance as measured by international indicators and student achievement tests. Furthermore, many foreign visitors have been particularly surprised to find out that teaching has become the number-one profession among young Finns—above medicine and law—and that primary teacher education in Finnish universities is one of the most competitive choices of study. All these aspects of the Finnish educational system are explored further in this book.

There are, however, those who doubt that Finland has much relevance to other educational systems because of its special characteristics. The most commonly presented argument is that because Finland is so exceptional, it hardly provides anything meaningful to the United States, England, Australia, France, or other much larger nations, or that it is "too different to serve as models for whole-system reform for North America as a whole," as Michael Fullan (2010, p. xiv) writes. Two points are often emphasized when the relevance of Finland as a model for educational change is considered.

First, Finland is culturally and ethnically still rather homogeneous and thus too unlike the United States, for example. Fair enough, but the same holds true for Japan, Shanghai, Korea, Estonia, or Poland. The proportion of foreign-born citizens in Finland was 5.2% in 2013 and the number of non-Finnish-speaking citizens was just over 10% (Statistics Finland, 2014a). It is noteworthy that Finland is a trilingual country, where Finnish, Swedish, and Sami are all official languages. The largest language and ethnic minorities are Russian, Estonian, and Somali. The diversification of Finnish society since the mid-1990s has been the fastest in Europe, at a rate of 800%. When I began my teaching career in Helsinki in the mid-1980s, it was rare to have anybody in my classroom who looked or sounded different from the others. The number of foreign-born citizens in Finland has nearly tripled during the first decade of the 21st century. Finland is not that homogeneous anymore, but, of course, it still doesn't compare to the United States or Australia as a multicultural nation as far as ethnic diversity is concerned.

Second, Finland is considered too small to be a good model for system-wide reform for North America. This is a trickier argument to defend. When the size factor in educational reforms is considered, it is necessary to note that in many federal nations, states, provinces, or regions are to a large extent autonomous in terms of educational management and the running of their schools. This is the case in the United States, Canada, Australia, Brazil, and Germany, for example. The population of Finland today is 5.5 million. This is about the population of Minnesota in the United States or Victoria in Australia, and just slightly more than the size of the population of Alberta in Canada or Nord-Pas-de-Calais in France. Indeed, about 30 states of the United States have a population that is close to or smaller than Finland's. These include the states of Maryland, Colorado, Oregon, and Connecticut. The populations of the states of Washington, Indiana, and Massachusetts are also smallish and are close to Finland in size. In Australia, only New South Wales has a slightly larger population than Finland's; all other Australian states are smaller. In France, Île-de-France is the only region that surpasses Finland in population size. In Canada, only Ontario is significantly larger in population (and land area) than Finland; all other provinces are similar in size. If these jurisdictions have the freedom to set their own educational policies and conduct reforms as they think best, then the experiences of an educational system the size of Finland's should be particularly interesting and relevant to them.

France is the only country mentioned above that employs centralized educational management, and therefore the French education policymakers could argue for the irrelevance of smaller education systems as models for their reforms.

Finally, there are some who doubt that international comparisons are relevant or reliable in what they claim to show. One point of view is that academic achievement tests, such as the OECD's PISA, Trends in International Mathematics and Science Study (TIMSS), and Progress in International Reading Literacy Study (PIRLS), focus on areas that are too narrow to capture the whole spectrum of school education, and thus they ignore social skills, moral development, creativity, or digital literacy as important outcomes of public education for all (see Chapter 2 for references to this argument). There is also a growing concern that these comparisons are influencing educational policies and endorsing the culture of "governing by numbers" (Grek, 2009; Meyer & Benavot, 2013; Zhao, 2014). Another skeptical group simply argues that the chosen measurement methodologies in current international tests favor Finland because they match better with the culture of teaching in Finland; this group includes both Finnish and foreign scientists and experts.[2] Recently, Harvard's Howard Gardner warned his audience in Finland to treat these current student assessment studies with caution,[3] contending that results in studies like these always depend on the subject-area knowledge tested and the respective methodologies of the studies used. In addition, these studies do not measure interpersonal, spatial, or creative skills, and these skill sets are increasingly important in our contemporary world. There seems to be a growing group of people who question the credibility of PISA, and who challenge the new educational world order created in a large degree by this one measurement.

Although Finland has persistently outperformed other nations, its achievements have been downplayed in numerous accounts of recommended policy. In an influential report by McKinsey and Company (Mourshed, Chijioke & Barber, 2010), for example, Finland was not even listed as a "sustained improver" in the listing of potential model countries for education reformers. The consequence is that policymakers in many contexts will not consider Finnish strategies as they develop their repertoire of school improvement practices. Recent national education strategies and policy guidelines, such as the 2010 *Schools White Paper* in England (Department for Education, 2010), *Lessons from PISA for the United States* (OECD, 2013f), and the World Bank Education Strategy 2020 (World Bank, 2011), often refer to common features of high-performing education systems as desired criteria for improvement. Focuses on teacher effectiveness, school autonomy, accountability, and data are all central elements of education systems in Korea, Singapore, Alberta, and Finland, but in very different ways. As this book will show again and again, Finland is unique in terms of how these very aspects of education policy are employed. The Finnish experience shows that consistent focus on equity and cooperation—not choice and competition—can lead to an education system where all children learn well. Paying teachers based on students' test scores or converting public schools into private ones through charters or other means are ideas that have no place in the Finnish repertoire for educational improvement.

The size of Finland's population and the relative homogeneity of its society obviously make many aspects of setting education policies and implementing reforms easier than would be the case in larger, more diverse jurisdictions. But these factors alone don't explain all the progress and achievements in Finnish education that are described in this book, and they should not stop us from learning from one another as we strive to improve education for all students. Finland is, however, very unique among nations in terms of its values, cultural determinants, and social cohesion, as Andre Noel Chaker eloquently describes in his book, *The Finnish Miracle* (2014). Fairness, honesty, and social justice are deeply rooted in the Finnish way of life. People have a strong sense of shared responsibility, not only for their own lives, but also for the lives of others. Fostering the well-being of children starts before they are born and continues until they reach adulthood. Day care is a right of all children before they start school at age 7, and public health service is easily accessible to everyone during childhood. Education in Finland is widely seen as a public good and is therefore protected as a basic human right to all in the constitution. Adages such as "Small is beautiful" and "Less is more" are typical descriptors of everyday culture in Finland.

In this book, I describe how Finns have built a functional, sustainable, and just country with an equitable public education system by doing things in their own way. The Finnish Government's Country Brand Delegation that was chaired by ex-CEO of Nokia Jorma Ollila wrote in 2010 that "in Finland, people do not aspire to do everything the same way as the others, to dress or to live like others. Rather than the 'done thing,' Finns do what they think is the rational thing to do" (Ministry of Foreign Affairs, 2010, p. 59). The intense individuality of

Finns, blended with a low degree of hierarchy and a traditional willingness to work with others, has opened pathways to endless creative potential. The inspiration and vision to create a society with an education system that is good and accessible to all was drawn from this pool of creative potential.

Data for this book come not from one source alone, nor does this book claim that educational excellence could be justified by any single international study. Evidence is drawn from the available international databases, such as PISA and TIMSS, from global education indicators, and from versatile official statistics in Finland.

THE PLAN OF THIS BOOK

The first edition of *Finnish Lessons* offered me access to rich and detailed conversations about educational change in general and about the Finnish education model in particular. This second edition includes updates to international performance data, more detailed descriptions of equity in Finnish education, and a revised outline of the structure of Finland's education system after reforms made in 2013. I will also answer the question that many have asked since the PISA 2012 results became public: What explains Finland's decline in the global PISA league tables?

This book draws from the following 10 notions, which are explained in detail in the pages of this volume:

1. Finland has an education system in which young people learn well and where performance differences among schools are small—and all with reasonable cost and human effort.
2. This has not always been so.
3. In Finland, teaching is a prestigious profession, and many young Finns aspire to be teachers.
4. Therefore, the Finns probably have the most competitive and academically challenging teacher education system in the world.
5. As a consequence, teachers in Finland have a great deal of professional autonomy and access to purposeful professional development throughout their careers.
6. Finnish education policies since the 1970s have aimed at having a good school for every child rather than ranking high on international education tables.

7. Almost half of Finnish 16-year-olds, when they leave compulsory education, have had some sort of special education, personalized help, or individual guidance during their time in school.
8. In Finland, teachers teach less and students spend less time studying, both in and out of school, than their peers in other countries.
9. Finnish schools lack the census-based standardized testing, test preparation, and private tutoring common in the United States and much of the rest of the world.
10. All of the factors that are behind Finnish success seem to be the opposite of what is taking place in the United States and much of the rest of the world, where competition, test-based accountability, standardization, and privatization seem to dominate.

After this Introduction, the book has five chapters. Chapter 1 explains both the political and historical realities in Finland after World War II and how they shaped the move toward the idea of common basic school for all by the end of the 1960s. In telling the story of educational change in Finland to scores of foreign visitors, I have learned that it is important to go back further in time than the birth of *peruskoulu* (I use this Finnish term because there isn't an English equivalent to it) in 1970. Chapter 1 illustrates the process of reforming the old school system, which divided pupils into two tracks and relied heavily on privately governed and cofinanced grammar schools, into a comprehensive, publicly managed and funded system. It also outlines the main features of post-compulsory education that emerged soon after implementing the *peruskoulu* reform in the late 1970s. The main characteristics of the iconic Finnish Matriculation Examination, a test students take when they leave general upper-secondary education in Finland, are also described in this chapter.

Chapter 2 tackles a fundamental question: Was Finland also a high performer in education in the past? The answer provided in this chapter is as expected: no. This answer immediately invites a corollary question: What constitutes a good educational system and which educational reforms have made such impressive progress possible in Finland? The core of this chapter is the insight that Finnish educational success in international comparisons can, at least to some extent, be understood through paradoxes. We can crystallize this notion with a simple principle in educational reform: Less is more. Chapter 2 provides evidence-based examples of how this paradoxical idea appears in the Finnish educational system today.

Chapter 3 is about teachers and the teaching profession in Finland. It examines the crucial role that teachers play in Finland and describes the main features of the teaching profession, teacher education, and teacher responsibilities in Finland. This chapter suggests that whereas high-quality, university-based teacher education and continuous professional development are necessary conditions for attracting the most talented and committed young people into teaching, they are not sufficient alone. Teachers have to be provided with a professional working environment so that they feel dignified and are able to fulfill their moral purposes in schools. This chapter also looks at teacher leadership and its manifestations among Finnish teachers, including the findings from the OECD's Teaching and Learning International Survey (TALIS) 2013 regarding the teaching profession in Finland.

Since Finland's amazing recovery from a grave economic recession in the early 1990s—and more recently from the global financial crisis of 2008—many have spoken about the Finnish model of building an inclusive information society and a competitive knowledge economy (Castells & Himanen, 2002; Dahlman, Routti, & Ylä-Anttila, 2006; Halme et al., 2014). What is significant in Finland's process of economic recovery is that at the same time when the Finnish economy and especially the public sector was adjusting to tougher competition and better productivity, the performance of the education system was steadily improving. Chapter 4 illustrates some interdependencies between Finnish educational policy and other public sector policies that are at the heart of the economic comeback. Furthermore, it suggests that progress in the educational sector has happened in tandem with changes in government that have improved economic competitiveness, transparency, and welfare policy.

Finally, Chapter 5 asks a question that is, surprisingly, not often asked of Finns by their visitors: What is the future of Finnish schooling? Being in the global limelight takes its toll. Although Finns have hosted thousands of foreign education pilgrims since late 2001, they have had only a little time and energy to think about what their own education system should look like in the future. The first signs of the impact of this were reported in the PISA 2009 study and were reconfirmed in the PISA 2012 analysis. Chapter 5 culminates by insisting that an important lesson for Finland from its own past is that it needs to be clear about what to do next. I conclude that being at the center of the education reform debate has prevented Finns from thinking about what kind of education will be needed in the future. The chapter closes with a discussion about the need to change, in spite of the fact that the current system is praised for its excellence and seems to be working well.

There is an important note that the reader of this book should keep in mind. In my research I have used data primarily from the databases of OECD and Statistics Finland, which are publicly available for interested readers. I have constructed graphs showing correlation, or absence of it, between two variables—for example, the relationship between cost of education and educational performance in different countries. Old wisdom in statistics and in science states that correlation does not imply causation; this must be remembered also while reading this book. What this means is that even if there is a correlation between two variables, it does not automatically mean that one causes the other. Correlation is *necessary* for linear causation, and often suggests that indeed one variable causes the other. Figures 2.8, 2.10, 4.1, and 5.1 present such linear correlations.

CHAPTER 1

The Finnish Dream
A Good School for All

> God mend us! The fact is that we don't even know the first letter of the alphabet, and that knowing how to read is the first duty of every Christian citizen. The power of law, of church law, may force us to it. And you know what kind of contraption the State has watching, eager to snap us up in its jaws if we don't obediently learn to read. The stocks are waiting for us, my brothers, the black stocks; their cruel jaws gaping wide like those of a black bear. The provost has threatened us with those hellish pincers, and he is bound to carry out his threat unless he sees us eagerly studying every day.
>
> —Aleksis Kivi, *Seven Brothers*

The story of Finland is a story of survival. It is eloquently captured by Aleksis Kivi in the first Finnish novel, *Seven Brothers*, which was published in 1870. It is a story of orphan brothers who realize that becoming literate is the key to happiness and a good life. Since those days, reading has been an integral part of Finnish culture. Education has served as the main strategy for building a literate society and a nation that is today known by the world for its cultural and technological achievements. Therefore, *Seven Brothers* belongs to the list of core texts in most Finnish schools today.

Being a relatively small nation situated between much larger powers of the East and the West has taught Finns to accept existing realities and take chances with available opportunities. Diplomacy, cooperation, problem solving, and seeking consensus have thus become hallmarks of contemporary Finnish culture. These traits all play an important part in building an educational system that has enjoyed global attention due to its equitable distribution of good teaching and learning throughout the nation.

This chapter describes how Finland has progressed from being a poor, agrarian, and only modestly educated nation to a modern, knowledge-based society with a high-performing education system and a world-class innovation environment. Expanding access to education from early childhood education all the way to the highest academic degrees and adult learning has been a long-term ideal in Finnish society. This chapter first provides a historic and political context for realization of this Finnish Dream. It then describes the evolution of the unified comprehensive basic school, or *peruskoulu* as it is called in Finnish, and some principles of upper-secondary education that are an important part of Finnish educational success.[1] Present structures and policies of the Finnish education system are briefly outlined at the end of the chapter.

POSTWAR FINLAND

War ranks among the most serious of imaginable crises for any democratic nation. Except for a short period of ceasefire, Finland was at war from December 1939 to the spring of 1945. The cost of war for that young, independent democracy with a population of fewer than 4 million was enormous: 90,000 dead and 60,000 permanently injured. In addition, 25,000 were widowed and 50,000 children were orphaned. A peace treaty with the Soviet Union was signed in Moscow on September 19, 1944, but military campaigns to remove German troops from Finland continued until April 1945. The conditions that the Finns accepted were severe. Finland had to hand over 12% of its territory to the Soviets and had to relocate 450,000 people—11% of Finland's total population. The Finnish concessions to the Soviets were estimated to reach 7% of its Gross Domestic Product (GDP). A peninsula near Helsinki had to be rented to the Soviet army as a military base, political prisoners had to be released, and wartime leaders were judged in war tribunals. Several political associations were prohibited, and the Communist Party was established as a legal Finnish political entity. These concessions led to such fundamental political, cultural, and economic changes in Finland that some have identified the postwar era as the emergence of a "Second Republic."[2]

Most important, Finland had fought for its freedom and survived. External threats experienced during and after World War II united Finns, who still felt the wounds of the previous 1918 civil war. The post–World War II era was one of political instability and economic transformation, but it also gave rise to new social ideas and social policies—in particular the idea of equal educational opportunities. It is difficult to understand why education has become one of the trademarks of Finland without examining these post–World War II political and social developments. Even among Finns, there are those who argue that the search for key success factors in the Finnish educational system has to extend much earlier than 1970, a year often recognized as a historical milestone in Finnish education for reasons explained later in this chapter.

History is often easier to understand when it is segmented into periods or phases of development, and the recent history of Finland is no exception to this strategy. Although there are many ways to recount Finland's history depending on the purposes and perspectives of its authors, in this case it is helpful to illustrate congruencies between the development of Finland's education system and three stages of economic development following World War II:

- enhancing equal opportunities for education by way of transition from a northern agricultural nation to an industrialized society (1945–1970)
- creating a public comprehensive school system by way of a Nordic welfare society with a growing service sector and increasing levels of technology and technological innovation (1965–1990)
- improving the quality of basic education and expanding higher education in keeping with Finland's new identity as a high-tech, knowledge-based economy (1985–present) (Sahlberg, 2010a)

The 1950s were already a time of rapid changes to Finland's economic structure, but the 1960s have been characterized as phenomenal by international standards (Aho, Pitkänen, & Sahlberg, 2006; Dahlman, Routti, & Ylä-Anttila, 2006). The decade of the 1960s saw Finnish society, in more general terms, relinquish many of its old values, and traditional Finnish institutions began to transform. Public services—especially basic education—were among the most visible sites of change. When the time for decisive change arrived, its speed and thoroughness took many Finns by surprise.

The end of World War II prompted such radical changes to Finnish political, social, and economic structures that immediate changes to education and other social institutions were required. Indeed, education soon became the main vehicle of social and economic transformation in the postwar era. In 1950, educational opportunities in Finland were unequal in the sense that only those living in towns or larger municipalities had access to grammar or middle schools. Most young people left school after 6 or 7 years of formal basic education. Where private grammar schools were available, pupils could apply to enroll in them after 4, 5, or 6 years of state-run basic school, but such opportunities were limited. In 1950, for example, just 27% of 11-year-old Finns enrolled in grammar schools consisting of 5-year middle schools and 3-year high schools. An alternative educational path after the compulsory 7 years of basic education was 2 or 3 years of study in one of the so-called civic schools, offered by most Finnish municipalities. This basic education could be followed by vocational training and technical education, but only in larger municipalities and towns that housed these institutions.

In 1950, there were 338 grammar schools offering further educational opportunities after the 6-year basic school in Finland (Kiuasmaa, 1982). The Finnish state operated 103 of these schools, and municipalities ran 18. The remaining 217 grammar schools, about two-thirds of the total, were governed by private citizens or associations. The major burden of the rapid expansion of education following basic schooling was absorbed by these private schools. A significant social innovation in 1950 was issuance of legislation that guaranteed state subsidies to private schools, and simultaneously extended the government's control over these schools. This change made it possible to respond to the public's growing interest in education by opening new private schools, as their financial risks were diminished through state funding.

In the early years after Finland's independence, teaching in primary schools was formal, teacher-centered, and focused more on moral than cognitive development. Although pedagogical ideas aimed at social gains and more holistic interpersonal development were known in Finland as early as the 1930s, school education was not greatly influenced by them (Koskenniemi, 1944). Three dominant themes in Finnish national education policy between 1945 and 1970 would come to change this traditional model:

- The structure of the education system would provide access to better and more education for all.
- The form and content of curricula would focus on development of individual, holistic personalities of children.
- Teacher education would be modernized to respond to needs arising from these developments. The future dream of Finland

was built on knowledge and skills; thus, education was seen as a foundation for establishing the future (Aho, Pitkänen, & Sahlberg, 2006).

Finland's economic structure in 1950, comparable to Sweden's economy in 1910, was in transition. Key industries were shifting from farming and small business to industrial and technological production. The new political environment in the postwar era had also activated working-class families, who insisted that their children should have opportunities to benefit from extended public education. Consequently, a model for comprehensive schools offering universal access and a unified curriculum, first proposed in the 1920s, was revived and entered education policy discussions soon after the end of World War II. It was clear that to become a recognized member of the community of Western democracies and market economies, Finland needed a better-educated population. This was a vision for the entire nation.

UNIVERSAL BASIC EDUCATION

The first 2 decades after World War II were politically turbulent in Finland. The Communist Party returned to the main stage of daily politics in the first postwar elections in 1944, and identified education as one of its primary strategies for building a Finnish socialist society. In the 1948 elections, three political parties received nearly equal seats in the Finnish national Parliament: the Social Democratic Party (50 seats), the Agrarian Centre Party (49 seats), and the Communist Party (49 seats). The rebuilding of Finland began; political consensus was a precondition for reforms, including renewing the Finnish educational system. The Conservative Party increased its popularity in the 1950s and became a fourth political force to be reckoned with in Finnish parliamentary negotiations. The political education committees played particularly important roles as the groundwork for comprehensive basic schooling for all Finnish students was laid, and the vision finally realized in 1970.

Three politically oriented education committees are particularly worth mentioning. First, in June 1945, the government established the Primary School Curriculum Committee. The secretary of that committee was Matti Koskenniemi (1908–2001), who had, a few years earlier, written a seminal book on primary school didactics (Koskenniemi, 1944). Through his contributions, perspectives on curriculum in Finland shifted from focusing on syllabi (the German term *lehrplan*) to describing educational objectives, process of education, and evaluation. These reforms were the first to modernize the Finnish curriculum by international standards, and they still resonate in contemporary curriculum thinking.

There are several reasons why this committee holds a central place in the history of Finnish education. First, the members devoted special attention to formulating new objectives for education, thereby deviating from German tradition in Finnish education. The committee put forth the idea that school should aim at educating young people to realize themselves as holistic individuals, possessing intrinsic motivation for further education. The content of education that would lead to this general aim was grouped into five thematic, cross-curricular areas, which later became a model for the Comprehensive School Curriculum Committee in 1970.

Second, curriculum reform was grounded in empirical studies conducted in 300 field schools involving 1,000 teachers. In this way, research became part of education policymaking. Third, and as a corollary of the previous two reasons, the quality of the committee's work was regarded as exceptionally high. The Final Memorandum of the committee, published in 1952, has merit in its systematic formulation of educational objectives, broad child-centered perspective, modernized presentation and richness of educational content, and emphasis on the primacy of social cohesion as one important goal in education. Significant milestones in the postwar history of Finland were realized in 1952: hosting the Summer Olympics in Helsinki, the coronation of Miss Finland Armi Kuusela as the first-ever Miss Universe, and completion of heavy reparations to the Soviet Union. It is appropriate, also, to include in Finland's 1952 milestones the new, internationally comparable curriculum for Finland's primary school system, which paved the way to educational success some half a century later.

A second committee of significance, the Education System Committee, launched its work in 1946 to establish regulations for compulsory education and a common framework of principles for determining how different parts of the education system should be interlinked. The committee included representatives of all of the leading political parties of that time and was chaired by the National Board of Education's director general, Yrjö Ruutu, ally of the Finnish Communist Party. Less than 2 years after commencing its work, this committee proposed that the foundation of the Finnish educational system should be an 8-year compulsory basic school that would be common to all children regardless of their socioeconomic situation. The committee advised that this school system ought to avoid tracking more able students to "academic" subjects and to "vocational" studies those preferring to learn manual skills, as was done in the then-current parallel education system.

However, the committee retained the standard that only those students who had learned foreign languages during basic school would be allowed to enter upper-secondary school or *gymnasium*—which represented the only pathway to higher education. Although the idea of comprehensive school was clearly formulated, it was not acted upon due to bitter criticism from universities and the Grammar School Teachers' Union. However, the committee's proposal stimulated further debate within Finnish society about social justice and equal educational opportunities—tenets that, 2 decades later, would be realized and entrenched as foundations of Finnish education policy.

Development of different sectors of education continued in the 1950s. The baby boom after World War II led to rapid expansion in the number of schools. New laws stipulated that compulsory education was to consist of 6 years of primary school and 2 years of civic school for those who didn't advance further to grammar schools. The new curriculum launched in 1952 began to change work and life in schools. Vocational education became part of the education sector. Finland's dream of common schooling for all was alive, but, in practice, parallel schooling structures remained. Consequently, a third committee of key significance, the School Program Committee, was established in 1956 to unify the Finnish education system and bring coherence to changes in various subsectors of education. The establishment of this committee under the leadership of Reino Henrik Oittinen, director general of the National Board of Education and a Social Democrat, was one further step toward the big dream of Finnish education.

The work of this committee was built on an unprecedented analysis of international education policies. Particularly significant was the committee's observation that Nordic countries shared much in common regarding their education policies at that time. Increasing equality of educational opportunities—a priority at the time in England and the United States—became a central theme in the committee's strategic thinking. The period from 1956 to 1959, during which this politically broad-based committee conducted almost 200 meetings, was particularly turbulent: Global economic recession, tough political conflicts both domestically and with the Soviet Union, and the launch of *Sputnik* soon impacted educational reforms around the world. Nevertheless, the committee persevered, and its work became a cornerstone in the history of educational reforms in Finland.

The School Program Committee published its recommendations in the summer of 1959. The committee suggested that future compulsory education in Finland should be based on a 9-year municipal comprehensive school with the following structure:

- The first four grades would be common to all pupils.
- Grades 5 and 6 would constitute a middle school where pupils could choose to focus on either practical subjects or foreign languages.
- Grades 7 through 9 would have three streams: vocational and practical orientation, an "average" track with one foreign language, and an advanced stream with two foreign languages.

The committee was unable to unify political will around this structure of comprehensive school; indeed, strong disagreement arose even within the committee about main policy principles. The proposed system would, however, gradually merge private grammar and public civic schools into a new municipal structure, and diminish the role of private schools. Overall, the work of this committee initiated deep and significant debate about core values in education in Finnish society. The key question was: Is it possible, in principle, that all children can be educated and can achieve similar learning goals? Answers to this question created divided opinions, even within families. Primary school teachers believed all students could learn equally well, universities typically doubted the proposition, and politicians remained divided. At that time, given its need to advance both politically and economically on the world stage, Finland had no choice but to accept the proposition that anyone—if given adequate opportunities and support—could learn foreign languages and advance to higher levels of education than had previously been believed. It was more difficult for many politicians to accept that the educational architecture of the day, which maintained and actually more deeply entrenched inequality in Finnish society, would be unable in the long run to ensure that Finland would achieve its goal of becoming a knowledge society. Figure 1.1 illustrates the characteristics of the parallel educational system until the early 1970s, which divided pupils at the age of 11 or 12 into one of two separated streams. There was practically no possibility to move between these streams once students had decided which pathway to follow.

Figure 1.1. Structure of the Education System in Finland Before 1970

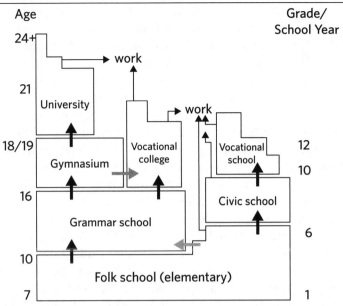

The original 1959 proposal of the School Program Committee was further elaborated by the National Board of General Education in the early 1960s, and then finally taken to Parliament on November 22, 1963. The ensuing debate was harsh. Some predicted a gloomy future for Finland if the new ideas related to common unified public school for all were approved: declining level of knowledge; waste of existing national talent; and Finland, as a nation, being left behind in the international economic race. In the final vote, the proposal for the new educational system in Finland passed, with 123 voting in favor and 68 against. The celebration of the birth of the new school in Finland was disturbed by an announcement by the speaker of the Parliament: U.S. President John F. Kennedy had been assassinated in Dallas, Texas, just minutes earlier.

It would be inappropriate to claim that the birth of the new Finnish comprehensive school or *peruskoulu* system, which is frequently identified as a structural foundation for Finland's educational fame today, was created by politicians and authorities alone. Many other people, including both school practitioners and academics, contributed to the process of defining Finland's new school system. Particularly significant was the role played by some of Finland's civil society organizations. It is beyond the scope of this chapter to conduct deeper analysis of the influence that many of these groups exerted on Finnish educational reform. However, a good example of civil society involvement in education policy development is the role played by the Finnish Primary School Teachers' Association (FPSTA). As early as 1946, FPSTA had expressed its support for the idea of a unified basic school system. In the mid-1950s, the association published its own education development program accompanied by a detailed, well-argued proposal for a unified, comprehensive school system. What was unusual about this proposed program was that, unlike the appeals of union-based teachers' associations, it was progressive and future-oriented. It was widely supported by the FPSTA members, representing nearly 90% of all Finnish primary school teachers. The FPSTA's proposal took 5 years to complete and stimulated a national discussion that was clearly focused on the need to enhance equality and social justice in Finnish society through a more equitable education system. Perhaps most important, the publication of the FPSTA's program proposal was a clear sign that schools and teachers were ready for radical change.

In 1955–1956, the nation's grammar schools enrolled approximately 34,000 pupils. Five years later, enrollment had swelled to 215,000 and it continued to soar, rising to 270,000 in 1965 and to 324,000 in 1970 (Aho, Pitkänen, & Sahlberg, 2006). Finland's old system could barely hold together as parents demanded an improved and more comprehensive basic education for their children in the hope of securing better lives for them. Such social pressure introduced a new theme in the education policy debate: the individual's potential for growth. Researchers then argued that an individual's abilities and intelligence always rose to the level required by society, and that education systems merely reflected these limits or needs.

THE NEW SCHOOL IS BORN

New legislation (1966) and a national curriculum (1970) were prepared in the second half of the 1960s. The social policy climate at the time had consolidated the values of equality and social justice across the social classes of Finnish society. The expenditures incurred by the ideal of a welfare state were seen, as argued by prominent Finnish political scientist Pekka Kuusi, as an investment in increasing productivity rather than a necessary social cost of maintaining an industrial society (Kuusi, 1961). The new comprehensive school system was poised for implementation in 1972. According to the plan, a wave of reform was to begin in the northern regions of Finland, and would reach the southern urban areas by 1978.

A fundamental belief related to the old structure was that *everyone cannot learn everything*; in other words, talent in society is not evenly distributed in terms of one's ability to be educated. In Finland, there were echoes of the Coleman Report published in the United States, favoring the view that a young person's basic disposition and characteristics were determined in the home, and could not be substantially influenced by schooling (Coleman et al., 1966). It was important that the new *peruskoulu* shed these beliefs and thus help build a more socially just society with higher education levels for all.

The central idea of *peruskoulu*, as shown in Figure 1.2, was to merge existing grammar schools, civic schools, and primary schools into a comprehensive 9-year municipal school. This meant that the placement of students after 4 years of primary education into grammar and civic streams would come to an end. All students, regardless of their domicile, socioeconomic background, or interests would enroll in the same 9-year basic schools governed by local education authorities. This

Figure 1.2. Structure of the Education System in Finland Since 1970

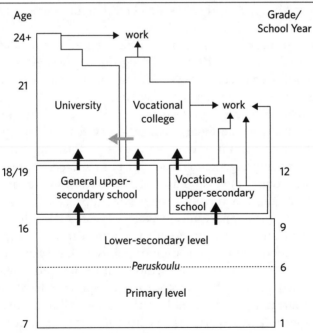

implementation was revolutionary, although as noted previously, the idea behind it was not new. Critics of the new system maintained that it was not possible to have the same educational expectations for children coming from very different social and intellectual circumstances. Opponents argued that the entire future of Finland as a developed industrial nation was at risk because overall education attainment would have to be adjusted downward to accommodate less talented students.

As planned, the wave of implementation began in the northern parts of Finland in 1972. The National Curriculum for the Comprehensive School steered the content, organization, and pace of teaching throughout the country. Although the structure of the comprehensive school was similar for all students, the National Curriculum provided schools with tools to differentiate instruction for different ability groups and personalities. Foreign languages and mathematics teaching, for example, were arranged in a way that offered students options for three levels of study in grades 7 through 9: basic, middle, and advanced. The syllabus of the basic study program corresponded to what had previously been offered in civic schools, and the advanced study program was equivalent to that offered by the old grammar schools. The reasoning behind these differentiated syllabi was that if learning foreign languages was made a requirement for all, then there had to be different courses of study for different kinds of students.

The last of the southern municipalities shifted to the new comprehensive school system in 1979. Ability grouping was eventually abolished in all school subjects in 1985. Since then, all students have studied according to the same curricula and syllabi.

Comprehensive school reform triggered the development of three particular aspects of the Finnish education system, which would later prove to be instrumental in creating a well-performing education system. First, bringing together a wide variety of students with often very different life circumstances and aspirations to learn in the same schools and classes required a fundamentally new approach to teaching and learning. The equal opportunity principle insisted that all students be offered a fair chance to be successful and enjoy learning. From early on, it was understood that the education of pupils with special needs would only be successful if learning difficulties and other individual deficits were identified early and promptly treated. Special education quickly became an integral part of school curricula, and all municipalities and schools soon housed experts trained to support special-needs pupils. Special education is discussed in more detail in the following chapter.

BOX 1.1: WHAT IS THE FINNISH CONSENSUS?

The Finnish Parliament reached a decision-in-principle for comprehensive school reform in November 1963. The decision was not unanimous; the basis of the majority consisted of the Agrarian Party and the leftists. This decision, perhaps the most important single consensus in the history of Finnish education, would not have been possible without the support of the Agrarian Party and wider national consensus for the common good.

The Agrarian Party had for a long time resisted the idea of a comprehensive school system. The youth wing of that party understood that restructuring of the Finnish economy and related urbanization required the development of the old-fashioned education system existing at that time. It was particularly important to secure access to good education in rural parts of Finland that were suffering from rapid migration to urban centers and to Sweden. The interesting question is: Why did the Agrarian Party support education reform that was based on the idea of common comprehensive school for all? A new generation of politicians who were close to the Primary School Teachers' Association became convinced that all children could have similar learning goals and that they could be taught in the same schools. The president of Finland and former Agrarian Party member Urho Kekkonen was one of the supporters of this reform.

The dream of a common public school for all Finnish children had existed since the birth of the Finnish Folk School in the 1860s. The process that led to Parliament's decision in 1963 was strictly a political one. It guaranteed that the political elite of Finland would be strongly committed to the comprehensive school reform. Political support for the reform was important because it made it possible to proceed swiftly without being halted by the new government. The foundation for a sustainable education policy was created. This same principle of the Finnish consensus has carried throughout the decades until today.

The implementation of comprehensive school reform required several other political compromises. Professor Pauli Kettunen has said that the Nordic welfare state was constructed using three political ideals: the legacy of liberated peasants, the spirit of capitalism, and the utopia of socialism. Equality, efficiency, and solidarity—the essential principles of these three political ideals—merged into a consensus where they all enriched one another. I think this is the root of the solid ground on which Finnish education policy has been established.

Erkki Aho, Director General (1973–1991)
National Board of General Education

Second, career guidance and counseling became a compulsory part of the comprehensive school curricula in all schools. It was assumed at the time that if all pupils remained in the same school until the end of their compulsory education, they would need systematic counseling on their options after completing basic school. Career guidance was intended to minimize the possibility that students would make inappropriate choices regarding their future. In principle, students had three options: to continue education in upper-secondary general school, to go on to vocational school, or to find employment. Both types of upper-secondary education offered several internal options. Career guidance and counseling soon became a cornerstone of both lower- and upper-secondary education, and has been an important factor in explaining the low rates of grade repetition and dropout in Finland (Välijärvi & Sahlberg, 2008). Career guidance has also served as a bridge between formal education and the world of work. As part of the overall career guidance curriculum, each student in *peruskoulu* spends 2 weeks in a selected workplace.

Third, the new *peruskoulu* required that teachers who were working in very different schools—namely, the academic grammar schools and work-oriented civic schools—had to begin to work in the same school with students with diverse abilities. As Jouni Välijärvi explains, comprehensive school reform was not just an organizational change but a new philosophy of education for Finnish schools (Hautamäki et al., 2008; Välijärvi et al., 2007). This philosophy included the beliefs that all pupils can learn if they are given proper opportunities and support, that understanding and learning through human diversity is an important educational goal, and that schools should function as small-scale democracies, just as John Dewey had insisted decades before. The new *peruskoulu*, therefore, required teachers to employ alternative instructional methods, design learning environments that enable differentiated learning for different pupils, and perceive teaching as a high-status profession. These expectations led to wide-scale teacher education reform in 1979: a new law on teacher education, emphasizing professional development and focusing on research-based teacher education, that is discussed in detail in Chapter 3.

Another concrete consequence of the emergence of *peruskoulu* was a rapid expansion of upper-secondary education. Parents expected their children to study further, and young Finns themselves also hoped to reach higher in their self-development. Let us now take a look at how upper-secondary education provided pathways to improving human capital in Finland.

EXPANDING UPPER-SECONDARY EDUCATION

The general upper-secondary school had a traditional school-like organization until 1985 when the new Act on General Upper-Secondary Education abolished the old system and introduced a modular curriculum structure. Two annual semesters were replaced by five or six periods per school year, based on how schools planned their teaching. This meant that teaching and studying were reorganized into 6- or 7-week periods during which students would complete the courses they had chosen. This change enabled schools to rearrange teaching schedules, and, in turn, affected local curriculum planning because schools had more flexibility to allocate lessons into these periods differently (Välijärvi, 2004). The next phase of development was to replace age cohort–based grouping of students with a nonclass organizational system in the mid-1990s. This new general upper-secondary school organization is not based on fixed classes or grades (previously called 10th, 11th, or 12th grades). Students thus have greater choice available to them in planning their studies in terms of both the content and the sequencing of their courses. The new curriculum framework places a stronger emphasis on understanding students' cognitive development and also invites schools to make the best use of their own and their community's strengths. Although students now have more freedom to plan and choose their studies, all students are still obliged to study the basics of the 18 compulsory subjects. Students have to successfully complete at least 75 courses of 38 lessons each. About two-thirds of these are compulsory and the rest are freely chosen by students for their general upper-secondary education diploma. Normally, students exceed this minimum limit and study more, typically taking between 80 and 90 courses.

Student assessments and school evaluations are additional important factors affecting the nature of teaching and learning in general upper-secondary school. Teachers assess the achievement of each student at the end of each period (of 6 or 7 weeks), which means students are assessed five or six times per school year. The National Matriculation Examination that students take after successfully completing all required courses is a high-stakes external examination (for students), and therefore it has a notable effect on curriculum and instruction. A frequently expressed criticism by teachers and school principals in Finland is that the matriculation examination results in "teaching to the test" and thus narrows curriculum and increases stress among students and teachers. As a former mathematics and science teacher, I concur.

Vocational upper-secondary education also underwent significant adaptations to better suit new economic and political situations. Structures, curricula, and methodology of vocational education were renewed to meet the expectations of a knowledge-based economy and provide required labor knowledge and skills. One of Finland's key policy targets has been to increase the attractiveness of vocational education at the upper-secondary level (Ministry of Education, 2004; Sahlberg, 2006b). Currently, about 42% of students who transit from *peruskoulu* to upper-secondary education start their studies in vocational schools.

The *structure* of vocational education was simplified and all initial vocational qualifications today consist of 120 credits, equivalent to 3 years of full-time study. One-quarter of the study time is allocated to general or optional courses. The number of vocational qualifications was reduced from more than 600 to 52, and related programs of study to 113. In principle, vocational school students are eligible to take the matriculation examination, although very few do. Moreover, providers of upper-secondary education are required to promote transferability, ensuring that students have access to general upper-secondary schools from vocational schools, and vice versa, if they wish to include courses from other schools in their learning plans.

Curriculum and study programs in vocational schools were revised to match the changes made in upper-secondary education, especially the modular-based structure, as well as the needs of labor markets in a knowledge society. The new curriculum was designed to balance the need for more general knowledge and skills and specific professional competences required in each vocational qualification. Performance assessments of achieved professional knowledge and skills are developed via collaboration among three key stakeholders: schools, employers, and employees' representatives.

Methods of instruction and training have been gradually changing in vocational secondary schools. At least one-sixth of the training has to be arranged as on-the-job learning, and this is an integral part of the curriculum. Alternative workshops, apprenticeship training, and virtual learning have become commonplace in upper-secondary education. A results-based component of the funding system for vocational schools allocates a factor of 6% at the top of the school's core funding for staff development. Vocational schools are increasingly investing these funds to upgrade their teachers' pedagogical knowledge and skills.

Two key factors appear to influence the efficacy of students' choices at the critical point of transition to upper-secondary education. First, when they enter upper-secondary education, Finnish students have no experience with high-stakes standardized testing in school, unlike their peers in many other countries where testing has become an integral element of school life. In a comparative study of teachers' experiences under different accountability regimes, we concluded that "the pressure of a structured instructional model of teaching and external assessment of pupils' achievement is having dramatic consequences according to some teachers" (Berry & Sahlberg, 2006, p. 22). Consequences of the high-stakes testing environment include avoidance of risk taking, increased boredom, and fear. The study also suggested that in Finland, most lower-secondary school teachers teach in order to help their students learn, not pass tests. The PISA studies provide further evidence for this argument: Finnish students experience less anxiety in learning mathematics compared with their peers in other countries (Kupari & Välijärvi, 2005; OECD, 2013c).

A second contributing factor to the successful transition to upper-secondary schooling is that students are well prepared to make decisions about post-compulsory education, because counseling and career guidance are widely available in basic school. During their 3-year lower-secondary school, all students are entitled to 2 hours a week of educational guidance and counseling. This reduces the risk that students will make ill-informed decisions regarding their further studies. It also helps students put more effort into those areas of their studies that are most important for their anticipated route in upper-secondary school.

Finnish students today enter the transition point between lower- and upper-secondary education with a more effective set of knowledge, skills, and attitudes than in the past. Implemented reforms to upper-secondary education in Finland have had a fundamental impact on school organization, especially with respect to teaching and learning. Traditional school organization based on presentation-recitation models of instruction, age grouping, fixed teaching schedules, and the dominance of classroom-based seatwork has been gradually transformed to provide more flexible, open, and interaction-rich learning environments, where an active role for students comes first. Ongoing school improvement has therefore been facilitated by the implementation of structural changes in upper-secondary school and by the enrichment of schools and classrooms with alternative instructional arrangements and teaching methods.

IMPROVING EDUCATIONAL ATTAINMENT

Comprehensive school reform has generated obvious consequences. As the number of graduates from these schools has increased, so too has the demand for upper-secondary education. Annually, about 94% of students who graduate from *peruskoulu* immediately continue their studies in one of the two types of upper-secondary education settings or enroll in an additional 10th grade of *peruskoulu*. Some students who do not continue their formal education immediately after *peruskoulu* enroll in nonformal educational programs, and will return later to adult educational programs. For example, about half of those who enroll in vocational upper-secondary schools are graduates of *peruskoulu* of that same year. Figure 1.3 illustrates the choices made by students leaving *peruskoulu* between 2000 and 2012, who were given the option of participating immediately after completing *peruskoulu* in general or vocational upper-secondary education, taking an additional 10th grade,[3] or exiting formal education. Vocational education has become a true alternative for many students because of its more generally oriented curricula and also because there are more opportunities to continue studies in higher education after receiving a professional qualification from vocational school.

As shown in Figure 1.3, in 2012 about 94% of those who completed compulsory basic education immediately continued their studies at the upper-secondary level or undertook an additional 10th grade of *peruskoulu*. In 2012, the number of students enrolled in general and vocational upper-secondary education stood at 50.0% and 41.5%, respectively. In absolute numbers, the 2009–2010 school year marked the first time when more young people enrolled in vocational upper-secondary schools than in general upper-secondary schools when all students were counted (gross enrollment rate includes those who enroll in vocational schools after the age of 16). In 2012, about 6.5%, or 4,000 of the students leaving basic school, opted not to continue studying in upper-secondary education or 10th grade of *peruskoulu*. Some of these students enrolled in other post-compulsory educational programs, such as arts, crafts, or manual trades.

The relatively large number of students leaving basic school who don't continue their formal education immediately after graduation has become a social and political problem in Finland. Although the total number of young Finns who don't even apply to upper-secondary education is less than 1,000 annually, those who leave the education system

Figure 1.3. Transition from *Peruskoulu* to Upper-Secondary Education as a Percentage of Age Cohorts Between 2000 and 2012

Source: Statistics Finland (n.d.a).

are, in the long run, becoming an economic burden for the society. It is estimated that each young person who doesn't complete upper-secondary school will, on average, cost 1.4 million U.S. dollars to the society in lost tax revenues, increased health and social costs, and often chronic unemployment. The current coalition government therefore launched a campaign in 2011 to guarantee a study place or apprenticeship to all students leaving *peruskoulu* and others under 25 years of age. One part of this initiative was to enhance youth education and employment opportunity by extending compulsory education from age 16 to age 17, but a majority of politicians and key stakeholders were not convinced that one obligatory year of schooling for those who are not inspired to go to school would be a good idea. As a consequence, compulsory education in Finland ends at the age of 16.

It is noteworthy that in Finland upper-secondary education remains noncompulsory after a person turns 16. Rather than making upper-secondary education compulsory, Finnish education policies have relied on developing equal opportunities for everyone to participate in upper-secondary education as a matter of individual choice, while at the same time creating incentives for young people to stay in the education system after completing their compulsory education. Since the introduction of the comprehensive school in the 1970s, the aims of education policy have been to provide a place of study for all young people in post-compulsory educational institutions (Aho, Pitkänen, & Sahlberg, 2006). Most general and vocational upper-secondary schools today are under municipal (and in some cases regional) administration, and municipalities therefore determine policies regarding provision and accession for post-compulsory education. However, this does not mean that local authorities have complete freedom; curricula, teachers' professional requirements, and expectations regarding overall pedagogical environments are fairly unified throughout the country and create a common culture of schooling in Finland.

An important indicator of the success of post-compulsory education is the completion rate. As part of the newly introduced education efficiency system in Finland, state authorities have, since 1999, been collecting systematic data and analyzing completion rates in upper-secondary education. If an ideal completion time for vocational or general upper-secondary studies is set at 3.5 years, then about three out of four students successfully completed their studies in the desired time. Table 1.1 shows how many students terminated their upper-secondary and higher education in Finland in the academic year 2011–2012. Overall, graduation rates in Finland are internationally high. Only 0.2% of the age cohort did not complete their compulsory education as planned. Less than 4% of those who graduated *peruskoulu* in 2012 received their diploma from an institute other than school (students living abroad and home schooled, for example). The first-time graduation rate in upper-secondary education in Finland in 2012 was 93%, compared with 88% and 79% in Canada and the United States,

Table 1.1. Termination of Upper-Secondary and Higher Education in Finland in Academic Year 2011–2012 as a Percentage of the Total Number of Students

Type of Education	Academic Year 2011–12
General Upper-Secondary	3.5
Vocational Upper-Secondary	8.7
Polytechnic	8.5
University	6.4

Source: Statistics Finland, 2014b

respectively. The OECD average upper-secondary education graduation rate is 84% (OECD, 2014a).

Because personalized learning plans in upper-secondary school are not tied to age groups or classes, some students will take more time to complete their studies than others. Some will leave the education system without a qualification or diploma. Early school-leaving rates thus provide a further measure of the quality and efficiency of secondary education. According to national statistics in Table 1.1, in recent years about 3.5% per annum of general upper-secondary school students terminate their studies without moving on to some other form of upper-secondary education or training. Approximately the same number of students moves from general to vocational secondary education and completes studies there. In vocational secondary education, the situation is a bit worse. For example, in the school year 2011–2012, 8.7% of vocational school students terminated their initial studies; of these about 2% continued their education in some other school or institution.

Dropouts from formal education and training in Finland are slowly declining, and in upper-secondary education, dropout rates are substantially lower than those of most other countries. As far as all upper-secondary education is concerned, about 5.5% of students terminated their studies during the academic year 2011–2012 without immediately continuing their studies in some other degree program. The need to prevent educational failure and dropouts is greatest in upper-secondary and higher vocational education. Keeping students in education has become a particular incentive for schools through a results-based central government funding scheme, which was introduced in upper-secondary vocational education in the early 2000s and will be extended to all upper-secondary education by 2015. When the results-based financing index for education and training providers is calculated, reduced dropout rates and improved completion rates have a positive effect on the overall issued budget. Although the financing index concerns only a small part of overall education budgets, it has been a sufficient incentive to rapidly focus the attention of schools and teachers on measures to improve the early recognition and prevention of problems that might lead to dropout and on improved direct supports for students' learning and overall well-being in school. Moreover, because the basic funding of schools is tied to student numbers, success in preventing dropout has a positive impact on the school budget. Vocational schools in particular have developed innovative solutions for those students whose learning styles work best with a more practically oriented curriculum. For example, practice-oriented workshops where students can design and build concrete forms have become a popular way to increase the attractiveness and relevance of secondary education for many students who are at risk of leaving school.

Matriculation Examination

Students who have passed the required courses in upper-secondary general school are eligible to take the National Matriculation Examination. The examination is organized by the Matriculation Examination Board and is administered at the same time in all schools nationwide. There is no national examination for students graduating from upper-secondary vocational schools. Instead, vocational schools assess the form and content of certification examinations. Students who successfully complete either track can apply to institutions of higher education, namely polytechnics or universities. However, vocational school graduates make up a lesser share of total enrollment in higher education.

The Matriculation Examination first debuted in 1852 as an entrance test for the University of Helsinki. Students had to show sufficient evidence of general academic knowledge and be proficient in Latin. Today, the purpose of the examination is to discover whether students have assimilated the knowledge and skills required by the national core curriculum, as well as whether they have reached a level of maturity that is in line with the goals of upper-secondary general school. Students take tests in at least four subjects. Passing the matriculation examination, which is given only in upper-secondary general schools, entitles candidates to continue their studies at higher education institutions.

The Matriculation Examination is administrated by an external board appointed by the Ministry of Education and Culture. The board has about 40 members, who include university professors, high school teachers, and education policymakers. Exams are prepared and marked by separate subject committees that have altogether some 330 associate members, most of them current or previous schoolteachers. The secretariat of the board that is responsible for technical matters related to employing, safeguarding, and managing the examination has a staff of 22 people. The typical examination fee per student for five exams is about 200 U.S. dollars. The entire administration of the examination, which costs about 10 million U.S. dollars annually, is financed from these student-paid fees.

What is the structure of this exam and what does it measure? First, students must pass at least four individual tests in order to be awarded the Matriculation Examination certificate. An exam assessing students' competency in their mother tongue (Finnish, Swedish, or Sami) is compulsory for everybody. Second, each student chooses three additional tests from the following pool: a second domestic language (for example, Swedish), foreign language (most often English), mathematics, and one test from the humanities and sciences category. Students may also add optional exams in the following subjects: various foreign languages, history, civics, biology, geography, physics, chemistry, health education, psychology, philosophy, ethics, and religious studies. Students have a maximum of 6 hours to complete each exam.

Exams are offered twice a year, in September and March–April. Students must complete all required tests of the examination within three consecutive exam periods—in other words, within 1 year from the time they sit for their first exam. All tests, except listening and reading comprehension in second domestic and foreign languages, are pencil-and-paper tests, which typically require extensive writing in open-ended tasks. The examination process will become digital in 2016.

Teachers whose students are taking the exam in school first read the test papers and give their initial marks. Then the board's subject committee members give their final marks independently, not regarding what teachers have marked on each exam. This combined process then leads to a final grade. Subjects are graded using a seven-point scale that is adjusted to normal distribution. This means that the number of top grades and failed grades in each exam is approximately 5%. Students can have one failed exam if they perform well in the other exams. The exams and their grades are included in the Matriculation Examination Certificate that is awarded to students who successfully pass the mandatory exams and sufficiently complete the required high school studies.

The Finnish Matriculation Examination is a measure of students' general academic maturity, including their readiness to continue their studies in higher education. Students' successful performance on the Matriculation Examination becomes an asset to their university application. The nature of these individual exams is to try to test students' ability to cope with unexpected tasks. Whereas the California High School Exit Examination (CAHSEE),[4] for example, is guided by a list of potentially biased, sensitive, or controversial topics to be avoided, the Finnish examination does the opposite. Students are regularly asked to show their ability to deal with issues related to evolution, losing a job, dieting, political issues, violence, war, ethics in sports, junk food, sex, drugs, and popular music. Such issues span across subject areas and often require multidisciplinary knowledge and skills.

Here are some examples from the spring 2014 Matriculation Examination:

Sample essay topics in mother tongue:

"Some politicians, athletes and other celebrities have publicly regretted and apologized for what they have said or done. Discuss the meaning of the apology and accepting it as a social and personal act."

"Has your body become your hobby?"

"Media is competing for audiences—what are the consequences?"

"Choose three world religions and compare the role and use of a holy image within them."

Sample health education questions:

"What is the basis of dietary recommendations in Finland and what is their aim?"

"Compare chlamydia and condyloma."

Sample psychology question:

"Design a study to find out how personality affects individuals' behavior on Facebook or other social media. Discuss the ethical considerations for that type of study."

Sample history question:

"Karl Marx and Friedrich Engels predicted that a socialist revolution would first happen in countries like Great Britain. What made Marx and Engels claim that and why did a socialist revolution happen in Russia?"

Sample philosophy question:

"In what sense are happiness, good life, and well-being ethical concepts?"

Sample ethics question:

"High school students often require that they are served a particular diet as their school lunch. Reasons may be medical, religious, ethical or moral. Describe students' requirements and their reasons; and assess the righteousness of having any particular diet in school."

Instead of a national examination, vocational students take a school-level assessment of learning outcomes and skills. The principle behind the assessment is to develop a positive self-image and personal growth in students with different kinds of competencies. Students are gauged according to their own self-assessments, as well as through interviews with their teachers. In addition, their on-the-job training instructors participate in workplace assessments. Performance is graded from 1 (satisfactory) to 3 (excellent). In the absence of a national vocational education examination, the National Board of Education issues recommendations to ensure equality in school-based performance assessments.

A current topic of debate in vocational education is how to ensure the quality of certification from school to school. Parliament passed an act on this issue in 2005, and certification will now include both the teachers' assessment and a demonstration of skills to prove that a student has achieved the vocational proficiency set out in the curriculum. These skills demonstrations will take place, wherever possible, at work sites, mostly in conjunction with periods of on-the-job learning. Representatives of employers and employees will also take part in assessment. Depending on the program, students can expect to undergo from 4 to 10 demonstrations of proficiency during the course of their studies.

A GENERATION OF EDUCATIONAL CHANGE

Because the terrain of educational change has not been explored much in Finland, it is safe to suggest theories of change and conceptual models to organize the thinking about what has happened and why. After the comprehensive school reform in the 1970s, educational change in Finland can be described in terms of three phases (Sahlberg, 2009):

- Rethinking the theoretical and methodological foundations of teaching and learning (1980s)
- Improvement through networking and self-regulated change (1990s)
- Enhancing efficiency of structures and administration (2000–present)

This process is illustrated in Figure 1.4. Each phase conveys a certain policy logic and theory of change. By the early 1980s, the structural reforms that led to creating *peruskoulu* were completed. After that, attention was focused on *conception of knowledge* and *conception of learning* in the school practices that were embedded into the philosophy of *peruskoulu*. The second phase emerged from the liberalization of Finnish education governance, a period characterized by the self-directed networking of schools and collaboration among individuals. The third and ongoing phase was initiated by a need to raise productivity in the public sector, and was accelerated by publication of the initial PISA results in December 2001 and later by the 2008 economic downturn. This phase focuses on reforming the structures and administration of education and is careful to avoid disturbing the sensitive balance of a well-performing education system in the pursuit of enhanced efficiency.

Phase 1: Rethinking the Theoretical and Methodological Foundations (1980s)

Several research and development projects launched within the new comprehensive school system in the late 1970s and early 1980s led

Figure 1.4. Three Phases of Educational Change in Finland Since the 1980s

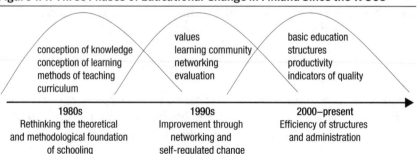

1980s	1990s	2000–present
conception of knowledge conception of learning methods of teaching curriculum	values learning community networking evaluation	basic education structures productivity indicators of quality
Rethinking the theoretical and methodological foundation of schooling	Improvement through networking and self-regulated change	Efficiency of structures and administration

to criticism of then-current pedagogical practices, especially teacher-centered methods of teaching in Finnish schools. The new school system was launched with philosophical and educational assumptions that insisted that the role of public education must be to educate citizens to think critically and independently. One of the main themes of school development then was the realization of a more dynamic *conception of knowledge*. As a result, renewed approaches to teaching would lead to meaningful learning and understanding, teachers believed (Aho, 1996). A significant driver of this change was emerging information and communication technologies in schools at that time. Some feared, quite correctly, that the expansion of computers in classrooms would lead to problems, including isolated knowledge, unnecessary information, and technological determinism.

Technological development corresponded with the revolution in learning sciences. The dominance of cognitive psychology, along with the emergence of constructivist theories of learning and the advances in neurosciences on the horizon, attracted Finnish educational researchers to analyze existing conceptions of knowledge and learning in schools. Several influential and teacher-friendly readers were published and sent to schools. They included *Conception of Knowledge* (1989), *Conception of Learning* (1989), and *About Possibilities of School Change* (1990). Questions like "What is knowledge?," "How do pupils learn?," and "How do schools change?" were common themes for teachers' inservice training and school improvement until the end of the 1990s (Lehtinen et al., 1989; Miettinen, 1990; Voutilainen, Mehtäläinen, & Niiniluoto, 1989).

From an international perspective, this first phase of educational change in Finland was exceptional. At the same time that Finnish teachers were exploring the theoretical foundations of knowledge and learning and redesigning their school curricula to be congruent with them, their peers in England, Germany, France, and the United States were struggling with increased school inspection, controversial externally imposed learning standards, and competition that disturbed some teachers to the point that they decided to leave their jobs. In England and the United States, for example, deeper analysis of school knowledge and implications of new research on learning mainly remained issues among academics or reached only the most advanced teachers and leaders. Perhaps it was due to these philosophical aspects of educational change that Finland remained immune to the winds of market-driven education policy changes that arose in many other OECD countries during the 1990s.

Although the nature of educational development in Finland during this phase was genuinely Finnish work, it is important to give credit to the knowledge and ideas that were brought from abroad, especially from the United States, Canada, and the United Kingdom, as well as other Nordic countries. Particularly significant was the role of teaching and student assessment methods—especially those published by the Association for Supervision and Curriculum Development (ASCD)—that were developed in the United States and then adopted into Finnish culture and educational practice. Two examples deserve to be mentioned here. First, Finland was one of the first countries to launch a large-scale implementation of cooperative learning in select Finnish universities and later in schools. Research and development work done at the University of Minnesota (David and Roger Johnson), Stanford University (Elizabeth Cohen), Johns Hopkins University (Robert Slavin), and Tel Aviv University (Shlomo Sharan and Yael Sharan) had an important role to play in the transformation of teaching and learning in schools according to the philosophical principles described in the Finnish readers mentioned above. Second, in the late 1980s, the National Board of General Education in Finland launched a national initiative to diversify teaching methods in science teaching. *The Models of Teaching* by Bruce Joyce and Marsha Weil (later with Beverly Showers) was the main source of inspiration and ideas for this work (Joyce & Weil, 1986). Bruce Joyce visited Finland in the late 1980s, and his work has left a permanent impression on the history of Finnish school improvement that still exists today in hundreds of Finnish schools through expanded repertoires of teaching methods. Work by David Berliner in educational psychology, Linda Darling-Hammond in teacher education, and Andy Hargreaves and Michael Fullan in educational change has been closely studied and implemented in developing Finnish education since the 1970s. The secret of the successful influence of these educational ideas from the United States, United Kingdom, and Canada is that there was fruitful ground in Finnish schools for such pragmatic models of change. Interestingly, the Finns themselves have developed only a little novel pedagogical practice that would have had more international significance.

There is surprisingly little reliable research on how this first phase of educational change actually affected teaching and learning in Finnish schools. Erno Lehtinen (2004), one of the key figures in Finland of that time and author of some of the readers mentioned earlier, was cautiously reserved about the impact:

Discussion on conceptions of knowledge and learning has clearly affected how teachers talk about learning and teaching. Earlier discourse that was characterized by traditional values of socialization and teaching of facts and automated ideals of mastery has been replaced by understanding, critical thinking, problem solving, and learning how to learn. Expanding the conceptions of knowledge and learning was also reflected in implementation of the new curriculum in the mid-1990s at all levels of schooling, and also in the national curriculum reforms in this new decade. (p. 54)

This phase of educational change in Finland has been characterized as a time that challenged conventional beliefs, searched for innovation, and increased trust in schools and their abilities to find the best ways to raise the quality of student learning. Deeper understanding of knowledge and learning strengthened schools' moral foundations. A recent evaluation of education in Finnish comprehensive schools concluded that "teachers pay conscious attention to diversifying teaching and learning environments. Teachers think that the use of versatile teaching methods is important both to planning and classroom work" (Atjonen et al., 2008, p. 197). This suggests that schools have made progress in teaching and learning, at least modestly.

Phase 2: Improvement through Networking and Self-Regulation (1990s)

The National Curriculum Reform of 1994 is often regarded as the major educational reform in Finland, along with the Comprehensive School Reform of the 1970s. The main vehicle of change was the active role of municipalities and schools in curriculum design and the implementation of related changes. Schools were encouraged to collaborate with other schools and to network with parents, businesses, and nongovernmental organizations. At the level of central administration, this new collaborative and self-directed movement culminated in the Aquarium Project, a national school improvement initiative enabling all Finnish schools, principals, and teachers to network with one another.[5] The aim of the Aquarium Project was to transform schools into active learning communities. According to Martti Hellström (2004), this project was "a unique self-directed school improvement network that was open to all active educators" (p. 179). As a form of practice, this was previously unheard of in Finnish educational administration, and only rarely found elsewhere.

The Aquarium Project offered schools a new context for improvement—something that combined traditional community work with modern social networking. It has close links to the ideas of the Alberta Initiative for School Improvement (AISI), a unique long-term government-funded school and teacher development program in Alberta, Canada (Hargreaves et al., 2009). Research has shown that school improvement through networking and self-regulation has positively impacted the engagement level of schools in development in Finland and Alberta. Particularly important is the fact that the majority of schools involved in these initiatives reported that during a time of economic downturn and decreasing resources, teachers believed they had succeeded in improving their schools. Despite different educational governance systems, the Aquarium Project and AISI have stimulated local innovations and research activity among principals and teachers who pursued advanced educational studies in universities. They also have demonstrated that it is the school, not the system, that is the locus of control and capacity—a point reinforced by Hellström (2004) and Murgatroyd (2007). Alberta's government terminated funding for AISI in 2013 as part of the province's fiscal adjustment procedures.

At the beginning of 1997, there were more than 1,000 projects in 700 schools and 163 municipalities participating in the Aquarium Project. My best estimate is that this included about 5,000 teachers and 500 principals who were directly involved in this school improvement initiative. The project was in accord with new ideas of decentralization, increased school autonomy, and stronger school identity in the 1990s. As a strategy for school improvement, this project stressed shared responsibility in schools, personalization, and collaborative efforts to enhance the quality of learning. In this sense, the Aquarium Project incorporated features consistent with neoliberal education policies, and occasionally, these characteristics were seen as signals of increased competition among schools in the education sector. It is true that school choice creates a competitive environment, but the school improvement network transformed bold competition into mutual striving for better schools. The strong social aspect of the Aquarium Project valued sharing ideas and solving problems together, thus preventing schools from viewing one another as competitors. In this respect, the project relied on earlier values of equal educational opportunities and social responsibility, rather than competition and administrative accountability. Perhaps this political duality served as the Achilles' heel of the Aquarium Project. The project was terminated by a political decision in early 1999 at the dawn of the era of enhanced efficiency of administration and structural reforms.

Phase 3: Enhancing Efficiency of Structures and Administration (2000–the present)

The first PISA results, published on December 4, 2001, took everyone by surprise. In all three academic domains—reading literacy, mathematics, and science—Finland was the highest-performing nation of the OECD countries as measured by standardized tests. This new international study revealed that earlier student performance gaps with Japan, Korea, and Hong Kong were closed. Finns seemed to learn all the knowledge and skills they demonstrated on these tests without private tutoring, after-school classes, or the large amounts of homework that are particularly prevalent among students in East Asia. Furthermore, the relative variation of educational performance between schools in the sample was exceptionally small in Finland.

Initial reactions after the first PISA results within the education community were confusing. Some Finnish educators wondered if there was something wrong because the test scores in academic school subjects were so high. Since the 1970s, education in Finland had had as strong a focus on music, arts, crafts, social studies, and life skills as there was on reading, mathematics and science. The world media immediately wanted to know the secret behind good Finnish education. Within the first 18 months after the PISA results were published, several hundred official foreign delegations toured Finland to learn how Finnish schools operate and how their teachers teach. Questions from the foreign visitors regarding the "Finnish miracle" were often such that Finns themselves were not prepared to respond with reliable answers. The next two PISA cycles, in 2003 and 2006, advanced and consolidated Finland's reputation even further, thus elevating the world media's interest in Finnish education. PISA 2009 and 2012 showed some decline in Finnish students' academic performance, which will be discussed further in the next chapter. Overall, PISA data show that Finland, Canada, Japan, and Korea produce consistently high learning results regardless of their students' socioeconomic status (OECD, 2013b). England, Germany, France, and the United States, among other countries, have both average achievement scores and a wide performance variance.

What PISA surveys, in general, have revealed is that education policies that are based on the principle of equal educational opportunities and equity in education and that have brought teachers to the core of educational change have positively impacted the quality of education systems. Further analysis of PISA data in Finland indicates that factors related to domicile and place of living also play visible roles in Finland in explaining the variations in assessed student learning and students' future career paths as well (Välijärvi, 2008). Apparently, the variations in student performance caused by students' socioeconomic factors are increasing. There is growing skepticism among teachers and researchers in Finland regarding limitations that international student assessments impose on their definition of student performance and educational success.

Combining PISA results with other global education indicators and national surveys of people's satisfaction with schools, it is safe to conclude that Finland's education system is in very good condition by international standards. This is obviously a challenge to Finnish education policymakers and to the school improvement community—after all, it is difficult to renew a system that is already performing well. Perhaps this explains the rather conservative mode when it comes to reforming primary and secondary schools in Finland recently. Structural reforms have focused on regulatory changes related to the length of compulsory education, administration of postsecondary education, and the efficiency of the entire education system. In the Finnish school system, multiculturalism, special education, and abolishing the administrative line between primary and lower-secondary schools have been the main areas of development since the year 2000. Another significant change since the beginning of 2013 has been to move early childhood education away from social issues administration to make it an integral part of the Finnish education system. The National Curriculum Frameworks for comprehensive and upper-secondary general education were revised in early 2000s but no significant changes were introduced. The next renewed National Curriculum Framework for Basic School and General Upper-Secondary School will be put into effect during the 2016–2017 school year. A focus on enhanced efficiency and productivity has led to shrinking school budgets in many parts of the country, which means there is now a need to do more or the same as before with fewer resources. Many practitioners, among them school leaders and teacher leaders, have been waiting for new directions in school improvement to make up for these negative developments in resourcing. Some of the possible trends for Finnish primary and secondary education will be discussed in Chapter 5.

THE FINNISH EDUCATION SYSTEM IN 2015

One of the key messages of this book is that unlike many other contemporary systems of education, the Finnish system has not been infected by market-based education reform models, such as tougher competition between schools over enrollment, standardization of teaching and learning in schools, and high-stakes testing policies. The main reason for this is that the education community in Finland has remained unconvinced that these globally fashionable directions in improving education would be good for Finnish schools. The ultimate success of a high-stakes testing policy is whether it positively affects student learning, not whether it increases student scores on a particular test (Amrein & Berliner, 2002). If student learning remains unaffected, or if testing leads to biased teaching as it increasingly does nowadays in many parts of the world, the validity of such high-stakes tests must be questioned. Finnish education authorities and especially teachers have not been convinced that frequent external census-based testing and stronger accountability for teachers would be beneficial to students and their learning.

Education policies are necessarily intertwined with other social policies, and with the overall political culture of a nation. The key success factor in Finland's development of a successful knowledge economy with good governance and a respected education system has been its ability to reach broad consensus on most major issues concerning future directions for Finland as a nation. The conclusion is that Finland seems to do particularly well in implementing and maintaining the policies and practices that constitute *sustainable leadership and change* (Hargreaves & Fink, 2006). Education in Finland is seen as a public good and therefore has a strong nation-building function.

Education policies designed to raise student achievement in Finland have put a strong accent on teaching and learning by encouraging schools to craft optimal learning environments and establish instructional content that will help students reach the general goals of schooling. This is the opposite of policies in many other countries where externally designed directives are imposed upon schools, such as the Common Core State Standards in the United States, the National Standards in New Zealand, or the New Education Standards in Germany. It was assumed very early in Finland's reform process that teachers and teaching are the key elements that make a difference in what students learn in school, not standards, assessment, or alternative instructional programs. As the level of teacher professionalism gradually increased in Finnish schools during the 1990s, the prevalence of powerful teaching methods and pedagogical classroom and school designs increased. A new flexibility within the Finnish education system enabled schools to learn from one another and thus make their best practices universal by adopting innovative approaches to organize schooling. It also encouraged teachers and schools to continue to expand their repertoires of teaching methods, and to individualize teaching in order to meet the needs of all students. The structure and the internal dynamics of the education system in Finland are illustrated in Figure 1.5.

Since the beginning of 2013, early childhood education has been part of the Finnish education system. Until then, it fell under the umbrella of social and health administration. In Finland, early childhood education refers to the education and care children receive before they start primary school at the age of 7. Before they go to school, all children have the subjective right to day care, either family-based or in kindergarten. Finnish education system offers, as Figure 1.5 shows, all children an opportunity to attend voluntary preschool at the age of 6. Let's take a closer look at what Finnish children do before they enter primary school.

Figure 1.5. The Education System in Finland in 2015

The Finnish social welfare system provides parents of newborns the right to parental leave to be at home with the baby. Mothers normally start maternity leave about 2 months prior to their due date and are entitled to continue that leave for about 5 months after the child's birth. Maternity leave is followed by parental leave, which should be shared by both parents and can last about 8 months. Parents will continue to receive their normal monthly salaries during these leaves through the State Insurance Institution of Finland (Kela). Fathers are continuously encouraged to take part in parental leave and to spend time at home with family.

The vast majority of children stay home during their first year. The child's right to day care means that the municipality where the family lives is responsible for offering the child a place in kindergarten or family-based day care. There are three types of day care options for the child: municipal day care, privately provided day care, and private family-based day care. According to the National Institute for Health and Welfare in 2012,[6] about 40% of 1- to 2-year-olds and 75% of 3- to 5-year-olds are in day care. Optional preschool at the age of 6 is very common, and some 98% of children are enrolled. Preschool hours are normally only held in the morning, which means that 70% of 6-year-olds are in day care in the afternoons. Sixty-three percent of all 1- to 6-year-old children in Finland are in day care, with 92% of these in public kindergartens or family-based day care and 8% in publicly subsidized private day care.

The new administrative system that makes early childhood education part of the education system will help provide better-coordinated and higher-quality services to children and families. Probably most important, there will be a more seamless transition from early childhood to preschool and primary school for those children who require special support. In 2014, one-third of the teaching staff working in kindergartens in Finland has a higher education degree. Most of them study in the departments of teacher education where all other teachers are educated in Finland. There is a shortage of qualified kindergarten teachers at the moment and therefore the Ministry of Education and Culture, which regulates the number of new students in the universities, is temporarily increasing the intake of new kindergarten teacher education programs.

What happens in kindergartens and preschools is steered by national frameworks for early childhood care and preschool education. The main aim of early childhood education for 1- to 5-year-olds is to enhance the health and well-being of each child. The National Framework for the Early Years of 2005 states that educators in kindergartens are responsible for:

1. enhancing the personal well-being of children;
2. enforcing behaviors and habits that take into account other people; and
3. increasing individual autonomy gradually.

These guidelines also stress the importance of the joy of learning, enriching language and communication, and the role of play in children's development and growth. The core content of early childhood education is led by six orientations: mathematical, scientific, historical, aesthetic, ethical, and religious. These are not content areas that are taught to children but, rather, broader frameworks within which action for children will be planned. Kindergarten in Finland doesn't focus on preparing children for school academically. Instead, the main goal is to make sure that all children are happy and responsible individuals. It is a common practice for all 1- to 5-year-olds to nap every day in the afternoon.

Similarly, preprimary school is guided by the National Framework for Preprimary Education, which stipulates the overall goals of preprimary education and specific educational objectives. Again, the aim of preprimary school in Finland is not "school readiness" but rather to "promote children's growth into humane individuals and ethically responsible members of society by guiding them towards responsible action and compliance with generally accepted rules and towards appreciation for other people" (National Board of Education, 2010). This framework emphasizes the development of thinking in relation to language and communication, mathematics, ethics and religion, environmental issues, physical development, and arts and culture. All these domains must be handled in a way that supports children's holistic growth and must be discussed with children's parents. "School readiness" in Finland means that all schools must be ready to receive all children just as they are. This is one reason why Finland's early childhood education, including preschool, doesn't prioritize reading, writing, and mathematics as core skills to determine children's successful entry into primary school.

What the scheme shown in Figure 1.5 is not able to reveal are the principles of individualized education and the systematic care of all children that are typical in Finnish schools today. For example, schools are encouraged to maintain strong support systems for teaching and learning—nutritious, free school meals for all pupils, health services, psychological counseling, and student guidance are normal practices in every school. Another strong element of the education system in Finland is a built-in network of schools and communities of teachers in municipalities and school improvement initiatives. These principles make the Finnish school system—as I see it—one of the most individualized school systems in the world. Andreas Schleicher (2006), who is director of the education department and the chief of PISA at the OECD, concluded in his analysis of Finnish education that building networks among schools to stimulate and spread innovation helps explain Finland's success in making "strong school performance a consistent and predictable outcome throughout the education system, with less than 5% variation in student performance between schools" (p. 9). The question is: Has Finland always had such a well-performing education system? If the answer is no, then it is worth asking another question: What factors have contributed to Finland's educational improvement?

CHAPTER 2

The Finnish Paradox
Less Is More

If everybody thinks the same way, nobody thinks very much.

—My grandmother's advice to me for succeeding in life

Today Finland is regarded as one of the world's most literate societies. As a nation of modest people, Finland never actually intended to be the best in the world in education. Finns like to compete, but collaboration is a more typical characteristic of this nation. In the early 1990s when Finnish education was known internationally as average, the Finnish minister of education visited her colleague in neighboring Sweden to hear, among other things, that by the end of that decade the Swedish education system would be the best in the world. The Finnish minister replied that the Finns' goal is much more modest than that. "For us," she said, "it's enough to be ahead of Sweden." This episode is an example of the close sibling-like relationships and coexistence between Finland and Sweden. In fact, companionship is more common than rivalry between these neighboring Nordic nations, which share many values and principles in their education systems and societies.

This chapter answers questions such as: Has the Finnish education system always been a top performer? What do we mean by a successful education system? How much does homogeneous society or culture explain Finland's good educational performance? This chapter also describes how Finland has been able to improve participation in education, creating equal educational opportunities for all, and how it has spread good-quality teaching to most schools and classrooms with modest overall cost. Rather than increasing time for teaching and learning, testing students more frequently, and insisting that students work harder on their homework, Finland has done the opposite, as this chapter illustrates. The key lesson from Finland is: There are alternative ways to build good public education systems that differ from those commonly offered in world education policy forums.

FROM PERIPHERY TO LIMELIGHT

In the 1980s the Finnish education system had only a few features that attracted any interest among international educators. Many aspects of education policy were adopted from Finland's wealthier western neighbor, Sweden. In international comparisons, Finnish education was exceptional on only one account: Finnish 10-year-olds were among the best readers in the world (Allerup & Medjing, 2003; Elley, 1992). Other than that, international education indicators left Finland in the shadows of traditional education superpowers such as Sweden, England, the United States, and Germany. What is noteworthy is that Finland has been able to upgrade human capital by transforming its education system from mediocre to one of the best international performers in a relatively short period of time. This success has been achieved through education policies that differ from those found in many other nations. Indeed, some of Finland's educational reform policies appear to be paradoxes because they depart so clearly from global educational reform thinking that often insists upon hard-hand control, more data, tougher accountability, and harder work from all involved in schooling.

When the OECD countries in the mid-1990s first discussed the need to create new metrics and measurements to compare educational performance in the most developed countries, Finnish authorities were concerned about whether this was a good idea. They questioned whether a fair single measure for such a diverse set of countries and economies as the United States, Japan, Italy, and Finland, for example, would be possible in the first place. They were also afraid that this new student assessment program would become an international league table, ranking entire education systems from the best to the worst by using one single criterion. These views were overruled and the inauguration of the Programme for International Student Assessment (PISA) was set for the year 2000. Because the massive amount of data from the 28 countries that were then OECD members and 4 partner countries took some time to process, the first results were scheduled to be released in December 2001.

PISA is a standardized assessment that measures the extent to which students at the end of compulsory education can apply their knowledge to real-life situations and how far they are equipped for full participation in society. OECD describes the essence of PISA (at pisa.oecd.org):

> Since the year 2000, every three years, fifteen-year-old students from randomly selected schools worldwide take tests in the key subjects: reading,

mathematics and science, with a focus on one subject in each year of assessment. The students take a test that lasts 2 hours. The tests are a mixture of open-ended and multiple-choice questions that are organized in groups based on a passage setting out a real-life situation.

More than 70 countries (and cities) have signed up to take part in the test for 2015 that will focus on science. It is important to keep in mind that PISA is a sample-based assessment that uses statistical methodology to analyze collected data to make generalizations. PISA is methodologically similar to other international student assessments, such as TIMSS and PIRLS, but it measures different types of learning, as mentioned above.

Prior to the first cycle of the PISA in 2000, many countries thought that their education systems were world-class and that students in their schools were better learners than those elsewhere. Educational indicators about educational attainment, spending, and college graduation rates, as well as academic competitions such as the International Olympiads in mathematics, physics, and chemistry (and later in subjects such as computer science, biology, and philosophy), had given these nations reason to celebrate the respective performances of their school systems. In academic scholarly competitions, high school–aged students compete to demonstrate advanced-level knowledge in their fields. Naturally, those education systems that have established effective selection systems to identify talents and special abilities early on and then provide gifted students with optimal learning opportunities have succeeded well in these games. Population-rich nations with large numbers of students, such as China, the United States, and the former Soviet Union, have acquired reputations as high-performing education nations on the basis of academic Olympiads. Interestingly, several Central and Eastern European countries—among them Hungary, Romania, and Bulgaria—are ranked high in the overall league tables of these Olympiads. Table 2.1 illustrates the top 12 countries in mathematics Olympiads and the position of Finland and some of its neighbors among them between 1959 and 2013.

Success in these academic Olympiads was often used as a proxy for the quality of national educational systems. Even if Finnish students' performance in mathematics is adjusted for population size, the relative position of Finland has fluctuated between 25th and 35th in the overall global rank list. Until 2001—and in some circles, for quite some time after that—a common conception in Finland was that the level of mathematical and scientific knowledge and skills of Finnish students was internationally modest, at best.

Table 2.1. Finnish Upper-Secondary School Students in Mathematics Olympiads Compared with their Peers in Selected Countries in 1959–2013

	Medals			Number of Participations	Number of Participating Students
	Gold	*Silver*	*Bronze*		
1. China	128	27	6	28	164
2. USA	100	106	29	39	246
3. Russia	84	39	9	22	132
4. Hungary	77	149	88	53	354
5. Soviet Union	77	67	45	29	204
6. Romania	73	124	96	54	362
7. Korea	55	60	25	26	156
8. Bulgaria	53	99	100	54	366
9. Vietnam	49	92	66	37	222
10. Germany	49	86	66	36	222
11. UK	41	81	117	46	302
12. Iran	38	80	32	28	163
34. Sweden	5	25	70	46	301
36. The Netherlands	4	26	63	43	280
46. Norway	2	11	28	30	172
55. Finland	1	8	48	40	254
61. Denmark	1	5	23	23	132

Source: International Mathematical Olympiad (www.imo-official.org/)

In 2008, OECD launched the Teaching and Learning International Survey (TALIS), which explored various aspects of teaching and learning in 24 participating countries. The second cycle of TALIS was conducted in 2013 in 34 countries. Finland and the United States did not participate in 2008, but both did so in 2013. TALIS asks a representative sample of teachers and school principals in each country about their working conditions and learning environments. According to the OECD (2014b, p. 26), "[TALIS] aims to provide valid, timely and comparable information to help countries review and define policies for developing a high-quality teaching profession." This survey, OECD says, enables teachers and school leaders to provide input into educational policy and development in key areas. TALIS results are based on opinions, views, and perceptions from teachers and school principals. Data that are collected for these surveys are therefore subjective. They include teachers' and school principals' voices, which sometimes differ from the objectively collected data in research projects. Some findings of TALIS 2013 are discussed in the following chapters.

As Finland attracts global attention due to its high-performing education system, it is worth asking whether there has really been any progress in the performance of its students since the 1970s. If such progress in any terms can be reliably identified, then, consequently, the question becomes: What factors might be behind successful education reform? When education systems are compared internationally, it is important to have a broader perspective than just student achievement. What is significant from this analysis is the steady progress Finland has made during the past 3 decades within four main domains:

1. Increased levels of educational attainment of the adult population
2. Widespread equity in terms of learning outcomes and performance of schools
3. Improved student learning as measured by international student assessments
4. Efficiency in using human and financial resources, almost solely from public sources

Let us next take a look at each of these domains in more detail.

EDUCATIONAL ATTAINMENT

Finland's people remained rather poorly educated until the 1960s. Education was accessible only to those who could afford it and who happened to live close to a grammar school and university. When *peruskoulu* was launched in the early 1970s, for three-quarters of adult Finns, basic school was the only form of education they had completed. Holding an academic degree was rare, as only 7% of Finns held some kind of university degree. Overall progress since 1970 in educational attainment by the Finnish adult population (15 years and older) is shown in Figure 2.1. The current situation is congruent with a typical profile of the educational attainment pyramid in advanced societies, where about

30% of the population has higher educational attainments and about 40% are upper-secondary education degree holders.

Figure 2.1 indicates that there has been steady growth in participation in all levels of education in Finland since 1970. The growth was especially rapid in the upper-secondary sector in the 1980s and, then, within the higher and adult education sectors in the 1990s and up to the present. Policies that have driven Finnish education reform since 1970 have prioritized creating equal opportunities for all children to a good education, improving the quality of teaching and learning, and increasing participation within all educational levels across Finnish society. As a result, each year more than 99% of the age cohort successfully completes compulsory education, about 95% continue their formal education in upper-secondary schools or in the additional 10th grade of *peruskoulu* (3%) immediately after graduation, and 95% of those starting upper-secondary education eventually graduate, which is a license to higher education (Statistics Finland, n.d.a).

According to OECD, two-thirds of the Finnish adult population participated in formal or non-formal adult education programs in 2012, more than in any other country (OECD, 2014a). What is significant about this expansion of participation in education is that it has taken place without shifting the burden of costs to students or to their parents.

Figure 2.1. Level of Educational Attainment Among the Finnish Adult Population Since 1970

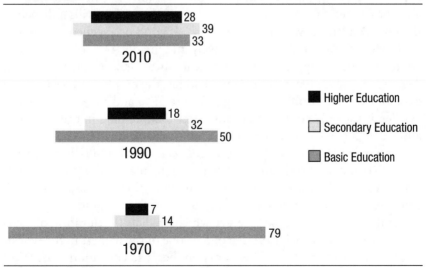

Source: Statistics Finland (n.d.a).

According to recent global education indicators, only 2.4% of Finnish expenditure on educational institutions (at all levels of education) comes from private sources, compared with an average of 16.1% of total educational expenditure (OECD, 2014a). For example, in the United States 32.1% and in Canada 23.6% of all funding for educational institutions comes from private sources.

OECD conducted the first cycle of the Programme for the International Assessment of Adult Competences (PIAAC) study in 24 countries, including Finland, in 2012 (OECD, 2013h). The study assessed selected basic skills that adults need in different life situations, including work and everyday living. Reading literacy, numeracy, and practical problem solving in technology-rich environments form the main areas of the PIAAC study. This study provides further information about the quality of educational attainment among adult Finns, and how they are likely to cope with different issues as citizens and in working life.

So, what does PIAAC 2012 tell about adult Finns' knowledge and skills related to everyday life? The average reading literacy skills in Finland are excellent. Only Japan has better overall adult competences. Two out of three adults in Finland are either good or excellent readers. In Canada, just over half and in the United States almost half of adults reach these same levels in reading literacy. The mathematical skills of Finnish adults are at the same high international level; 57% of all adult Finns have either good or excellent skills in numeracy. Again, Japan was the only country that exceeded Finland in numeracy. In both Canada and the United States, adults' everyday mathematics skills fall below the OECD average, with the proportion of good or excellent numeracy skills being 45% and 34%, respectively. In Finland, 41% of adults have good or excellent problem-solving skills in technology-rich contexts. And again, in Canada and the United States, the numbers of adults with good or excellent problem-solving skills are 36% and 31%, respectively. Sweden is the only country that did better than Finland in this aspect of adult competencies. Finland's good performance in PIAAC 2012 was in a large degree thanks to the younger segment of adults between the ages of 20 and 39. Proficiency in basic reading, mathematical, and problem-solving skills is strongly connected to educational background in all countries that participated in this survey, including Finland.

Finland's school life expectancy, which predicts the duration of a citizen's formal education at the age of 5, is one of the highest in the world, at over 20 years in 2013. This is mainly because education is publicly financed and hence available to all. The two types of higher education institutions offer a place of study for about two-thirds of the age cohort. Because studying in Finnish universities and polytechnics is tuition-fee free, higher education is an equal opportunity for all those who have successfully completed upper-secondary education. The current challenge in Finnish higher education is to encourage students to complete their studies faster than they did before and thereby enter the labor market sooner. The government of Finland is introducing new conditions for financial aid for students that are encouraging students to graduate on time. Total monthly financial aid for higher education students is about 1,000 US dollars, of which 55% is government-guaranteed bank loans and the rest is government grant. A student who graduates on time may deduct annual interest paid for her student loan from her income tax.

EQUITY OF OUTCOMES

People sometimes incorrectly assume that equity in education means all students should be taught the same curriculum, or should achieve the same learning outcomes in school. This was also a common belief in Finland for a long time following the equality-based school reform that was first launched in the early 1970s. Rather, equity in education means that all students must have access to high-quality education, regardless of where they live, who their parents might be, or what school they attend. In this sense, equity ensures that differences in educational outcomes are not the result of differences in wealth, income, power or possessions—in other words, home background.

Equity of education systems is measured in international student assessments by calculating the strength of the relationship between students' achievement in school and various aspects of their home background. OECD uses an index that includes economic, social, and cultural status (ESCS) by calculating a value for equity for each student based on parents' education, occupations, wealth, and some aspects of socioeconomic background. In more equitable education systems, students' learning in school is less dependent on their family background. Countries vary greatly in terms of how much of student achievement is associated with family background, just like they are different with regard to student achievement in reading, mathematics and science in school.

Equality of educational opportunity and equity of outcomes are important features in Nordic welfare states. They mean more than just ensuring that everybody has access to school. In Finland, equity means having a socially fair and inclusive education system that provides everyone with the opportunity to fulfill their intentions and dreams through education. As a result of the comprehensive school reform of the 1970s, education opportunities for good-quality learning have spread rather evenly across Finland. In the early 1970s, at the start of the implementation of the comprehensive school reform, there was a significant achievement gap among young adults due to very different educational orientations associated with the old parallel system (see Figure 1.1). This knowledge gap strongly corresponded with the socioeconomic divide within Finnish society at the time. Although students' learning outcomes began to even out by the mid-1980s, the streaming of pupils according to ability grouping in mathematics and foreign languages kept the achievement gap relatively wide.

After abolishing streaming in comprehensive school in the mid-1980s and raising learning expectations for all students, the achievement gap between low- and high-achievers began to decrease. This meant that all pupils, regardless of their socioeconomic conditions or interests, studied mathematics and foreign languages in the same non-streamed classes. Earlier, these subjects had three levels of curricula to which pupils were assigned based on their prior academic performance in these subjects and also often on their parents' or peers' influence.

Until the first PISA study in 2000, it was not clear if equality-based education policies and heavy investments in enhancing equity were actually any good for raising the quality of learning outcomes at the system level. Many thought that having equality and equity as the key drivers in national education policy would prevent the system from cultivating individual talent and thereby improving quality. One of the unexpected aspects of the first PISA findings was that most of the education systems with high overall student learning were also the most equitable. Since then PISA has revealed, among other things, that Finland has the smallest performance variations among schools in reading, mathematics, and science scales of all OECD nations (OECD, 2001; 2004; 2007; 2010b; 2013b).

Calculating how much of the total variation in student performance is associated with variation within schools and how much with between-school variation indicates another aspect of equity and equality in education systems. Between-school variation in performance indicates how different schools are statistically in any given country. In the Netherlands, Belgium, and Germany, for example, variation of student learning between schools is larger than within schools, which suggest that there is a big gap between schools in terms of their performance overall. Figure 2.2 shows performance variance within and between schools in the OECD countries as assessed by the mathematics scale in 2012 (OECD, 2013b). Across OECD countries, 37% of the overall performance differences are observed between schools and 63% within schools. Total variation of educational performance as a proportion of the OECD variation in Finland is 86%.

According to Figure 2.2, Finland has about 6% between-school variance on the PISA reading scale, whereas the average between-school variances in Canada, the United States, and the United Kingdom are 18%, 23%, and 30%, respectively. Performance variation between different schools in Finland in 2012 was at a level similar to what was shown in the previous PISA cycles. The fact that almost all variation (or inequality) occurs within schools, as shown in Figure 2.2, means that the remaining differences are probably due mainly to variation in students' natural talent. Accordingly, variation between schools mostly relates to social inequality. Because this is a small source of variation in Finland, it indicates that Finnish schools successfully deal with social inequalities. Furthermore, this suggests, as Norton Grubb observed in his review of equity in education in Finland, that Finnish educational reform has succeeded in building an equitable education system in a relatively short time, a main objective of Finland's education reform agenda set in the early 1970s (OECD, 2005; Grubb, 2007). Relatively small between-school variation in performance means that in Finland parents rarely are worried about the quality of their neighborhood school. While choosing a school other than the neighborhood school is an increasing phenomenon in larger urban areas in Finland, parents most often look for an ordinary, safe school for their children.

Strong emphasis on equity in education gives different meaning to *school performance* and how it is measured. Standardized testing has become the most common way to measure school performance in many parts of the world. Test-based accountability relies on data from these tests. Teachers and administrators are held accountable for their students' learning based on these data—but not in Finland. The absence of standardized tests in Finland leaves schools responsible for assessing student achievement themselves. A high-performing school in Finland is one where *all* students perform beyond expectations. In other words, the greater the equity, the better the school is according to the Finnish criterion.

An educational system that is equitable and where students learn well is also able to redress the effects of broader social and economic

Figure 2.2. Variance Within and Between Schools in Student Mathematics Performance on the 2012 PISA Study

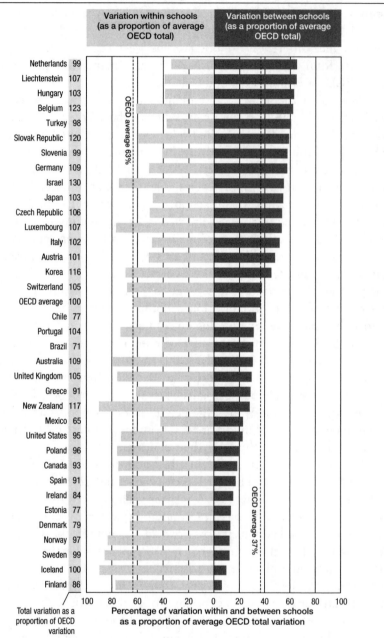

Source: OECD (2013b).

inequalities. Since the 1970s, Finnish education policies have fostered high overall levels of student achievement while limiting the influence of student backgrounds on learning outcomes and thereby attaining a high level of equity. Some have wondered why Finns think this is so important. Inequity in educational systems in Finland is seen as particularly problematic because it demonstrates a failure to utilize students' cognitive potential fully. As a small nation, Finland cannot leave any child behind. Evidence also shows that strengthening equity in education can be cost-beneficial. The OECD, after examining the four cycles of PISA data, recently concluded that the highest-performing education systems across OECD nations are those that combine quality with equity (OECD, 2012). Other research (Cunha & Heckman, 2010) demonstrates that investing as early as possible in high-quality education for all students, and directing additional resources toward the most disadvantaged students as early as possible, is a cost-effective strategy that will produce the greatest impact on improving overall academic performance.

How has Finland turned these findings into practices that enhance equity in schools? The universal right that all Finnish children have to high-quality early childhood education is one thing. The other, equally important, is the inclusion of children with special educational needs in mainstream schooling, which is an important guiding principle of Finnish education. All schools must have special education teachers and classroom assistants who can help children with special needs. There are notable differences between how special education is defined and delivered in Finland and in many other countries, including the United States. Most important, special education in Finland is for all students, based on the assumption that at some points of our lives all of us need support and help to move forward.

First, in Finland, special education is defined primarily as addressing difficulties related to learning, such as reading and writing, and learning difficulties in mathematics or foreign languages. In the United States and many other nations, students are identified as possessing special education needs if they meet criteria that often refer to a variety of disabling conditions, such as sensory and speech-language impairments, intellectual disabilities, and behavioral difficulties.

Second, in Finland special education needs are identified and addressed as early as possible; *prevention* is a common strategy within special education. This means that there is a larger number of special education children in Finland compared with the United States or other nations, especially during the early years of schooling. In Finnish comprehensive schools, corresponding to K–9 education in the United States, almost one-third of all pupils were in part- or full-time special education in 2012.

Finally, the new special education system in Finland since 2011 is defined under the title Learning and Schooling Support, and all special education students are increasingly integrated into regular classrooms. There are three categories of support provided to those pupils with special needs: (1) general support, (2) intensified support, and (3) special support. The first includes actions by the regular classroom teacher in terms of differentiation as well as efforts by the school to cope with student diversity. The second category consists of remedial support by the teacher, co-teaching with the special education teacher, and individual or small-group learning with a part-time special education teacher. The third category includes a wide range of special education services, from full-time general education to a placement in a special institution. All students in this category are assigned an Individual Learning Plan that takes into account the characteristics of each learner and thereby personalizes learning to meet each learner's abilities. As a consequence of this renewed special education policy, the number of students in intensified support has increased and in special support decreased. In school year 2013–2014 in *peruskoulu*, 6.5% received intensified support and 7.3% special support. In 2013, about 22% of all students in *peruskoulu* were in part-time general or intensified support. Total percentage of students in special education in Finnish *peruskoulu* in 2013 was 28%, according to Statistics Finland.

Many believe that Finland's special education system is one of those key factors that explain the world-class results in achievement and equity of Finland's school system in recent international studies. My personal experience, based on working with and visiting hundreds of Finnish schools, is that most schools pay very particular attention to those children who need more help to become successful, compared with other students. Many teachers and administrators who have visited Finnish schools think the same way, but they are often stuck in the middle of *excellence versus equity* quandaries due to external demands and regulations in their own countries. Standardized testing that compares individuals to statistical averages, competition that leaves weaker students behind, and merit-based pay for teachers all jeopardize schools' efforts to enhance equity. None of these factors currently exists in the Finnish education system.

At the dawn of *peruskoulu* reform, Finland adopted a strategy of early intervention and prevention to help those individuals with special educational needs of some kind. This means that possible learning and development deficits are diagnosed during early childhood development and care, before children enter school. In the early years of primary school, intensive special support—mostly in reading, writing, and arithmetic—is offered to all children who have major or minor special needs. As a result, the proportion of students in special education in Finland in the early grades of primary school is relatively higher than in most other countries. As Figure 2.3 shows, the number of students who receive special support in school in Finland declines by the end of primary school and then slightly increases as students move to subject-based lower-secondary school. The reason for the increased need for special support in lower-secondary school in Finland is that the unified curriculum sets certain expectations for all students, regardless of their abilities or prior learning. The common strategy internationally is to repair problems in primary and lower-secondary education as they occur rather than try to prevent them from happening (Itkonen & Jahnukainen, 2007). Countries that employ the strategy of repair have an increasing relative number of special-needs students throughout primary and lower-secondary education, as Figure 2.3 shows.

The highly equitable education system in Finland is not a result of educational factors alone. Basic structures of the Finnish welfare state play a crucial role in providing all children and their families with equitable conditions for starting a successful educational path at the age of 7. Extended parental leave, comprehensive and preventive health care for all infants and their mothers, and systematic monitoring of children's

Figure 2.3. Estimated Relative Number of Students in Part-Time or Full-Time Special Education in Finland and Other Countries During Primary and Lower- Secondary Education

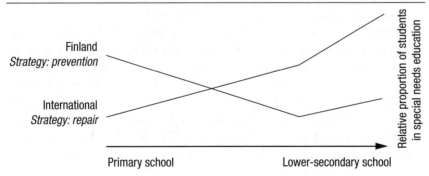

physical and mental development are accessible to everybody regardless of life circumstances or wealth. Early childhood education, voluntary free preschool that is attended by some 98% of six-year-olds, comprehensive health services, and preventive measures to identify possible learning and development difficulties before children start schooling are accessible to everyone. Finnish schools also provide each child with a free and healthy lunch every day, regardless of their home socioeconomic situation. Child poverty is at a very low level—about 5% of the child population, compared with over 23% in the United States and 13% in Canada. In order to prevent primary school pupils from being ranked according to their educational performance in schools, grade-based assessments are not normally used during the first 5 years of *peruskoulu*. This has been an important principle in developing elementary education in Finland: Structural elements that cause student failure in schools should be removed. That is why grade retention and overreliance on measured academic performance, which is discussed next, have gradually vanished in Finnish schools.

STUDENT LEARNING

The ultimate criterion of the quality of a national education system is how well students learn what they are expected to learn. International comparisons of education systems put a strong emphasis on scores in standardized achievement tests. Although it is difficult to compare students' learning outcomes today with those in 1980, some evidence of progress in student achievement in Finland can be offered using IEA (International Association for the Evaluation of Educational Achievement) studies, and from research records since the 1970s (Kupari & Välijärvi, 2005; Martin et al., 2000; Robitaille & Garden, 1989). Because it is impossible to conclude whether there has been progress in student learning in general, let us look at some school subjects individually instead.

Mathematics is often used as a proxy for general academic educational performance. The studies available include the Second International Mathematics Study (SIMS) in 1981 (8th grade, 20 nations), Trends in Mathematics and Science Repeat Study (TIMSS) in 1999 and TIMSS 2011 (4th and 8th grades), and five PISA surveys since 2000 (15-year-olds). These are the international student assessment studies in which Finland has participated since 1980. Because the nations participating in each international survey are not the same and the scope of IEA and OECD surveys are different, the international average as a benchmarking value does not always provide a fully comparable or coherent picture.

Table 2.2 shows Finland's performance in international student assessment studies since the early 1960s when the First International Mathematics Study was launched. These studies normally compare student achievement in reading comprehension, mathematics, and science at three points of education: at the end of elementary school (age 10), in lower-secondary school (age 14), and in upper-secondary school (age 17). Finnish students' performance on the Second International Mathematics Study (published in 1981) was, in all areas of mathematics, at the international average. The national average performance of Finland was clearly behind that of Hungary, the Netherlands and Japan in lower- and upper-secondary education. In 1999, the Third International Mathematics and Science Study ranked Finland 10th in mathematics and 14th in science among 38 participating countries. In TIMSS 2011, Finnish 4th- and 8th-graders were ranked eighth of all participating countries and one of the best education nations outside of East Asia. Since the first cycle of PISA in 2000, Finland has been one of the top-performing nations in mathematics among all OECD member states. Progress has been similar in science since the Second International Science Study in the early 1980s. It is noteworthy that Finnish students have always performed well internationally in reading: Finnish 4th-grade students were the best readers in the Reading Literacy Study in the late 1980s and Finnish 15-year-olds achieved top rankings in all four PISA cycles.

IEA published its 2011 results of 4th- and 8th-grade student achievement in reading (PIRLS) and mathematics and science (TIMSS) in December 2012. Finnish 4th-grade pupils took part in reading literacy tests for the first time since IEA's Reading Literacy Study in 1988. Finland had opted out of TIMSS after a 1999 repeater study because it joined PISA in 2000. In the late 1980s Reading Literacy Study, Finnish 4th-grade pupils were the best readers of all 32 participating countries. TIMSS 1999, which measured mathematics and science, included a representative sample of Finnish 7th-grade students that deviates from normal procedure of IEA, which normally includes a representative sample of 4th- and 8th-grade students. The results of the 1999 TIMSS study showed that among 38 participating countries, Finnish students were doing well above the international average, and among participating OECD countries, Finnish students were close to the OECD average.

Table 2.2. Performance of Finnish Students in International Student Assessment Studies Since the Early 1960s

Study	Population	Countries	Rank of Finland
IEA First International Mathematics Study (FIMS) 1962–1967	13-year-olds and high school completion	12	Average performer
IEA First International Science Study (FISS) 1967–1973	10- and 14-year-olds and high school completion	18	Average performer
IEA Study of Reading Comprehension 1967–1973	10- and 14-year-olds and high school completion	14	Average performer (in one area, third)
IEA Second International Mathematics Study (SIMS) 1977–1981	13-year-olds and high school completion	19 (13-year-olds) 15 (high school)	Average performer
IEA Second International Science Study (SISS) 1980–1987	At primary, middle, and high school completion	23	10-year-olds: high performer; 14-year-olds: average performer
IEA Written Composition Study 1980–1988	At primary, middle, and high school completion	14	Average performer
IEA Reading Literacy Study 1988–1994	9- and 14-year-olds	32	Top performer
IEA Third (later Trends in) International Mathematics and Science Study (TIMSS)	4th and 8th grade	1995: 45 1999: 38 2003: 50 2007: 59 2011: 63	Didn't participate Above average Didn't participate Didn't participate Near the top
IEA Progress in International Reading Literacy Study (PIRLS)	4th grade	2001: 35 2006: 45 2011: 48	Didn't participate Didn't participate Top performer
IEA International Civic and Citizenship Education Study (CIVED and ICCS)	8th grade	1999: 31 2009: 38	Top performer Top performer
OECD Programme for International Student Assessment (PISA)	15-year-olds	2000: 43 2003: 41 2006: 57 2009: 75 2012: 65	Top performer Top performer Top performer Top performer Top in OECD

The release of TIMSS and PIRLS results in 2012 received much less international media attention than when PISA studies were published in 2013.[1] One major difference in these two types of international student assessments is that all 34 OECD member countries take part in PISA, whereas only some of them are included in PIRLS and TIMSS. In 2011, PIRLS covered 48 and TIMSS 63 countries or regions around the world. Overall, Finnish students were close to the top in all PIRLS and TIMSS scales in 2011. Finnish 4th-grade pupils were second in reading and third in science. In mathematics, Finnish 4th- and 8th-grade students were eighth overall. IEA's TIMSS and PISA 2011 studies suggest that Finnish students are close to the world's top performers in all measured school subjects. However, the main concern that these studies also reveal is a low level of motivation and engagement among students in Finnish schools.

What might explain this evident improvement in student achievement in Finnish schools on the international student assessments since the 1980s? There has been some research on this question, but it has produced more speculation and qualitative analysis than reliable answers (Hautamäki et al., 2008; Linnakylä, 2004; Ofsted, 2010; Välijärvi et al., 2007). Three possible explanations appear. First, mathematics teaching is strongly embedded in curriculum design and teacher education in Finnish primary schools. For example, in the University of Helsinki each year about 15% of students in primary school teacher education programs specialize in teaching mathematics. This allows them to teach mathematics in lower-secondary schools as well. As a consequence, most primary schools in Finland have professionals who understand the nature of teaching and learning—as well as assessing—mathematics. Second, both teacher education and mathematics curriculum in Finland have a strong focus on problem solving, thereby linking mathematics to the real world. Mathematics tasks on PISA tests are based on problem solving and using mathematics in new situations rather than showing mastery of curriculum and syllabi. Third, the education of mathematics teachers in Finland is based on subject didactics and close collaboration between the faculty of mathematics and the faculty of education. This guarantees that newly trained teachers with master's degrees have a systemic knowledge and understanding of how mathematics is learned and taught. Both faculties have a shared responsibility for teacher education that reinforces the professional competences of mathematics teachers.

PISA is increasingly being adopted as a global measure to benchmark nations' student achievement at the end of compulsory education. All 34 OECD member nations participate in these triannual assessments of reading, mathematics, and science literacies of 15-year-olds. There is also an increasing number of countries and jurisdictions (e.g., East Asian cities) taking part in this study. PISA focuses on young people's ability to use their knowledge and skills to meet real-life challenges. PISA uses the concept of literacy to refer to "students' capacity to apply knowledge and skills in key subjects, and to analyse, reason and communicate effectively as they identify, interpret and solve problems in a variety of situations" (OECD, 2013a, p. 24). It is noteworthy that PISA is based on testing a sample of 15-year-old students in each participating country, not all the students. PISA results are therefore an outcome of complicated statistical calculations that are explained in the technical documents available on their website (www.pisa.oecd.org).

Finland was the top overall performer among the OECD countries in 2000 and 2003 PISA studies, and the only one that was able to improve performance. In the 2006 PISA survey, Finland maintained its high performance in all assessed areas of student achievement. In science, the main focus of the PISA 2006 survey, Finnish students outperformed their peers in all 56 countries, some of which are shown in Figure 2.4 (OECD, 2007). In the 2009 PISA study, Finland was again the best-performing OECD country, with high overall educational performance and equitable learning outcomes with relatively low cost. Significant in this national learning profile is a relatively large number of best performers (level 6) and a small proportion of low achievers (level 1 and below). More than half of Finnish students reached level 4 or higher in comparison to the United States, where approximately one quarter of all students was able to do the same. The Canadian provinces Alberta, British Columbia, Ontario, and Quebec also have more than 40% of students showing at least level 4 performance.

The fifth PISA cycle in 2012 confirmed the weak signal that the previous cycle had sent to the Finns: Student achievement in this international ranking had continued to decline. In PISA 2009, reading slid 11 points from the 2006 results, from 547 to 536; math, 7 points, from 548 to 541; and science, 9 points, from 563 to 554. National student assessments and academic research in Finland had showed already, before PISA 2012 became public, that students' knowledge and skills in reading and mathematics were not what they used to be. A study from the University of Helsinki that compared learning outcomes in *peruskoulu* in 2001 and 2012 found a significant drop in 15-year-old students' learning of skills (Hautamäki et al., 2013). PISA 2012 therefore revealed no big surprises in Finland. The score in reading dropped 12 points since the last administration of the exam 3 years earlier, from 536 to 524; in

Figure 2.4. Percentage of Students at Each Proficiency Level on the PISA 2006 Science Scale in Selected OECD Countries and Some Canadian Provinces (*)

Source: OECD, 2007

math, the score dropped 22 points from 541 to 519; and in science, it dropped 9 points, from 554 to 545 (OECD, 2013a).

Many have asked: What has gone wrong in Finland? Why are scores now dropping? Is it because something that was driving improvement earlier has disappeared from Finnish schools? Or is it due to changes in Finnish society or homes? Whatever the reasons behind the changes, Finns must adopt smart responses and avoid hasty, false recoveries; they must analyze past data again; and they must learn more from other countries, both their success stories and their failed reforms.

The unexpected position as a global educational leader and role model may have disturbed Finland's previous commitment to continuous improvement and renewal. Some argue that complacency and a focus on explaining the past to thousands of education tourists have shifted attention away from developing Finland's own school system for the future. Others contend that the high profile of PISA has led other nations to alter their curricula. Such observers point to the usage of PISA questions to shape lessons and coaching students to take PISA-like tests. As a norm-referenced test, PISA is graded on a curve. What other nations have learned from Finland and put into practice has necessarily brought down Finland's own results.

Figure 2.5 shows other divergences in Finnish students' learning performance trends as measured by the PISA mathematics and science scales in comparison with some other OECD countries over time (OECD, 2001, 2004, 2007, 2010b, 2013a). It is noteworthy that student achievement in Finland consistently demonstrated progress until 2006 in all measured subjects, according to the PISA data, which was not the case for many education superpowers. It is important to note that any effects teaching may have had on the results in a given education system primarily reflect the influence of education policies and reforms that were implemented in the 1990s—not the most recent education reforms. The reasons behind Finland's inconvenient downward trend in measured student achievement are further discussed later in this chapter and in Chapter 5.

Another intriguing question emerges from Figure 2.5: What could explain Finnish students' exceptionally good performance in science? The strength of Finland's schools, as far as its success in PISA is concerned, seems to be science education. Some factors suggested by Finnish science educators include the following: First, primary school teacher education has for the past 2 decades focused on redesigning science teaching and learning in schools so that students have opportunities for experiential and hands-on science. At the same time, more and more new primary school teachers have studied science education during their teacher education—more than 10% of graduates of the University of Helsinki have studied some science education in their master's degree programs. These university studies, as part of the normal teacher education program, have focused on building pedagogical content knowledge and an understanding of the scientific process in knowledge creation. Second, the science curriculum has been transformed from traditional academic knowledge-based to one oriented to hands-on experiments and problem solving in the classroom. This change has been followed by massive national professional development support for all primary school science teachers. Third, teacher education in all Finnish universities, including the faculties of science, has been adjusted to the needs of the new school curriculum. Today, science teacher education is coherent and consistent with the current pedagogical principles of contemporary science teaching and learning that have been inspired by ideas and innovation from the United States and England.

Figure 2.5. Student Achievement in Mathematics and Science on PISA Surveys Between 2000 and 2012 in Selected OECD Countries

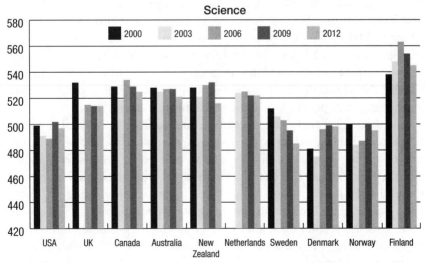

Source: OECD (2001, 2004, 2007, 2010b).

There are few international student assessments that focus on sub-jects other than reading, mathematics, and science. The IEA Internation-al Civic and Citizenship Education Study (ICCS) is one such assessment, and it is the third IEA study designed to measure contexts and outcomes of civic and citizenship education (Schulz, Ainley, Fraillon, Kerr, & Losi-to, 2010). The ICCS of 2009 that built on IEA's Civic Education Study 1999 studied the ways in which young people in lower-secondary schools (typically grade 8) are prepared to undertake their roles as citizens in 38 countries in Europe, Latin America, and the Asia-Pacific region. A cen-tral aspect of the study was the assessment of student knowledge about a wide range of civic- and citizenship-related issues. In this study, *civic knowledge* refers to the application of the civic and citizenship cognitive processes to civic and citizenship content. *Civic knowledge* is a broad term that includes knowing, understanding, and reasoning. It is a key outcome of civic and citizenship education programs and is essential to effective civic participation.

In the 2009 ICCS, Finnish 8th-grade students scored the highest av-erage score in civic knowledge, alongside their Danish peers (see Figure 2.6). As in the PISA and TIMSS results, Finland had the smallest be-tween-school variation in student performance on the ISSC 2009 study. The ICCS 2009 shows a strong relationship between the Human De-velopment Index (HDI) and civic knowledge at the country level. The variation in HDI explains 54% of the between-country variation in civic knowledge. This shows that national averages of civic knowledge are related to factors reflecting the general development and well-being of a country. This finding is similar to those from other international studies of educational outcomes, but it does not necessarily indicate a causal relationship between civic knowledge and the overall development of a nation. Paradoxically, this study also found that Finnish youth feel the least engaged in politics and civic issues in their everyday lives.

All five PISA survey cycles since 2000 indicate that Finnish educa-tional performance is consistent across all assessed educational domains, and that Finnish students on average score high in every survey across all measured subjects (reading, mathematics, and science). The quality of Finnish public education as measured by international student assess-ment studies has been steadily improving since the early 1970s. PISA 2009 was the second cycle that focused on reading literacy after 2000, and PISA 2012 was the second time mathematics was in focus. These studies therefore provide a unique opportunity to look at the trend in how well students understand and can use what they have learned in

Figure 2.6. Civic Knowledge Scores of 8th-Grade Students in the OECD Countries That Participated in the 2009 International Civic and Citizenship Education Study (ICCS)

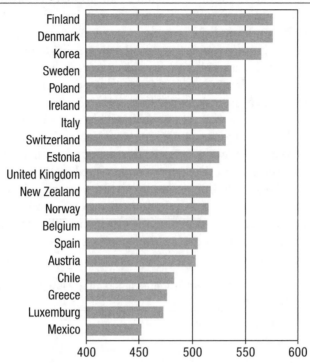

Source: Schulz et al. (2010).

reading and mathematics in school. Although the national average of student performance in 2012 declined from 2000, especially in mathematics, as Figure 2.7 shows, Finnish students' reading and mathematical literacies remain at an internationally high level. What is alarming in the most recent PISA data, however, is related to finding that Finnish young people read less for pleasure today than they did 10 years ago. Half of 15-year-old Finnish boys reported that they don't read for pleasure. This is also clearly visible in national studies of reading comprehension and habits in Finland. It appears that the observed downturn of Finland's educational performance may be associated with boys and their looser grip on school learning.

According to the OECD (2011a, p. 117), "Finland is one of the world's leaders in the academic performance of its secondary school students, a position it has held for the past decade. This top performance is also remarkably consistent across schools. Finnish schools seem to serve all students well, regardless of family background, socio-economic status or ability." The strength of Finland's educational performance is its consistently high level of student learning, which is equitably distributed across schools throughout the country.

Since its inauguration in 2000, PISA has had a huge impact on global education reforms as well as national education policies in the participating countries. It has become a significant pretext for educational development in Asia, Europe, and North America, and is gaining interest in the rest of the world. Large-scale education reforms have been initiated (in the United States, England, New Zealand, Germany, Korea, Japan, and Poland), new national institutions and agencies have been created, and thousands of delegations have visited well-performing education jurisdictions, including Finland, Alberta, Ontario, Singapore, and Korea, to discover the "secrets" of good education. In most of the more than 70 participating education systems or regions, PISA is a significant source of education policy development.

Figure 2.7. Performance of Finnish Students in Reading, Math, and Science on PISA Surveys, 2000–2012

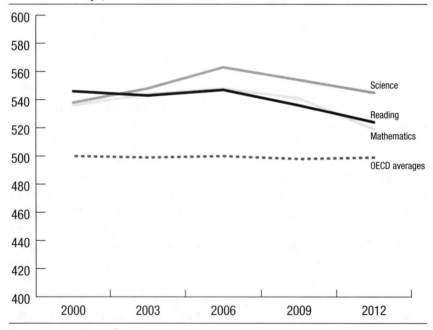

Source: www.pisa.oecd.org

Perhaps it is surprising that Finnish educators are not as excited by PISA results as many foreigners would expect. Many Finnish teachers and school principals think that PISA measures only a narrow band of the spectrum of school learning. There are also Finns who see that PISA is promoting the transmission of educational policies and practices that are not transferable. This will, they maintain, lead to a simplistic view of educational improvement. Just like in sports, too strong an emphasis on international comparisons (or competitions) may lead to unethical means of temporarily boosting performance just to get a better position in the results tables. A good education system and high educational performance are much more than just measured academic scores. Some teachers in Finland are afraid that the current movement, which judges the quality of education systems by using academic units of measurement only, will eventually lead to narrowing curriculum and the dominance of the measured subjects at the expense of social studies, arts, sports, music, and whole-child development.

There is, indeed, an increasing debate about what these international tests really measure and whether PISA alone can be used to judge the quality of education systems. Earlier critics' and defending proponents' arguments are available in the educational literature (Adams, 2003; Bautier & Rayon, 2007; Bracey, 2005; Dohn, 2007; Goldstein, 2004; Kreiner & Christensen, 2013; Mortimore, 2009; Prais, 2003, 2004; Riley & Torrance, 2003; Schleicher, 2007). More recently, commentators on PISA, most of whom are internationally recognized scholars, have insisted that politicians and the public at large (including media) must understand better what PISA can and cannot do. Among them is David Spieghalter (2013) of the University of Cambridge, who wrote in the *Guardian*, "If PISA measures anything, it is the ability to do PISA tests. Aligning policy along a single performance indicator can be damaging. We need to look at the whole picture." Yong Zhao of the University of Oregon has argued that while the East Asian systems may enjoy being at the top of PISA tests, they are not happy at all with the outcomes of their education. "They have recognized," Zhao writes in his blog post, "the damages of their education for a long time and have taken actions to reform their systems." In his book *Who's Afraid of the Big Bad Dragon* Zhao (2014) offers a comprehensive summary of the most recent critique of PISA and concludes that the core of Chinese education, including Shanghai's high PISA scores, are the three basics: "Chinese families' high expectation, hard work and diligence, and the examination system" (2014, p. 187). Howard Gardner (2010) of Harvard University wrote in his commentary titled

"The Ministers' Misconception" following the 2009 PISA results: "I am constantly surprised at the persistence, in ministerial talk and writing, of allegiance to the 'transmission theory' of education . . . and the notion that the best questions have a single correct answer and a resulting suspicion of multiple plausible answers, productive errors and creative leaps." Finally, Sam Sellar and Bob Lingard (2013) argue that "PISA, and the OECD's education work more broadly, has facilitated new *epistemological* and *infrastructural* modes of global governance for the OECD in education."

These observations are good reminders that PISA is a good servant but a bad master. Even if it may be at the moment the best international assessment for comparing school systems, it nevertheless measures the best of the past. Furthermore, there are many who are afraid that PISA, like many other social indicators, verifies Campbell's Law. Campbell's Law states that "the more any quantitative social indicator is used for social decision-making, the more subject it will be to corruption pressures and the more apt it will be to distort and corrupt the social processes it is intended to monitor" (Campbell, 1976, p. 49). OECD's own analysis shows how PISA has become an increasingly high-stakes social indicator for national policies and their implementation in several countries (Breakspear, 2012). Many Finns—myself included—would like to see lower stakes for these international student assessments among national policymakers and a broader scope of student learning reflected in assessments, including learning-to-learn skills, social competencies, self-awareness, and creativity.

COST OF EDUCATION

Until now we have seen how Finland has transformed its education system by increasing youth and adult participation in all types of education, making a publicly funded education system accessible to a large proportion of its population, and achieving internationally high learning outcomes with very small performance differences between schools across the nation. All of this has been accomplished by financing education, including higher and adult education, almost exclusively from public sources. One more question regarding successful education system remains to be addressed: How much does all this cost Finnish taxpayers?

In OECD nations for which data on comparable trends are available for all educational levels combined, public and private investment in Finnish education increased 34% from 1995 to 2004 in real terms, while the OECD average for the same period was 42%. Total public expenditure on educational institutions as a percentage of GDP in Finland was 6.5% in 2011 (OECD, 2014a). This is close to the OECD average of 6.1% and less than spending in the United States (6.9% of GDP) and Canada (6.8% of GDP). As mentioned earlier, only 2.4% of total Finnish expenditure on education institutions comes from private sources.

The Relationship Between Cost and Student Performance

Figure 2.8 summarizes students' mean performance on the PISA reading scale in relation to cumulative educational spending per student (between 6 and 15 years of age) in 2009 in U.S. dollars and adjusted to purchasing power parities (OECD, 2010, 2013f). These data, first of all, indicate that there seems to be no positive correlation between spending and measured outcomes in education. Second, Finland has accomplished world-class educational performance at a reasonable cost. For example, the United States and Norway have high levels of spending in education but their student outcome results are only moderate. This, of course, does not suggest any causal logic between education expenditures

Figure 2.8. Relationship Between PISA Performance in Reading and Cumulative Expenditure per Student Between Ages 6 and 15 in OECD Countries in 2009

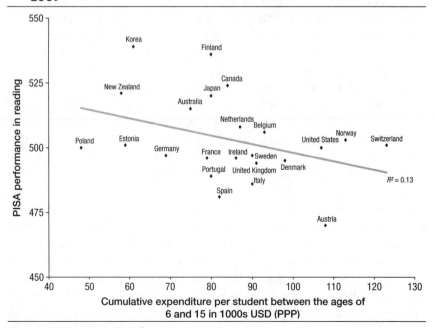

Source: OECD (2010, 2013f).

and learning outcomes, although regression indicates a small negative interdependency (R^2=0.133) between education spending and student achievement. Efficiency is therefore more important to good educational performance than level of expenditure. Money rarely is the solution to the problems in education systems.

The Cost of Grade Repetition

One of the cost factors in education is grade repetition. This means that a student is asked to repeat a grade because he or she failed to successfully master the subject(s) covered the first time. Repetition is a commonly used method of treating individual deficits and problems. Not only is grade repetition an ineffective way to help students who are in need of help, but it is also expensive for education systems. How does Finland cope with this common global phenomenon?

Grade repetition in the old Finnish parallel school system was not rare in elementary schools, and it was an integral educational principle of grammar school. In some cases, a student repeated the 3rd grade of elementary school in order to improve knowledge and skills required in the grammar school admission test at the end of the 4th grade. At the time of the introduction of the new 9-year school, approximately 12% of students in each grammar school grade did not progress from their grade. Grade repetition at that time was not evenly distributed between schools or grades. For example, in general upper-secondary school, one in six students repeated a grade. We have estimated that up to half of those graduating from upper-secondary grammar school repeated one or more grades at some point in their schooling (Välijärvi & Sahlberg, 2008). Furthermore, significant numbers of students dropped out of school before completion—often after not being able to progress from one grade to the next. Inadequate progress in mathematics or Swedish (as a second language) were the most commonly cited reasons for grade repetition, although some students had to repeat a grade because of behavioral or attendance problems.

Peruskoulu was built on the social value of equity and was driven by the idea that all students are able to achieve common academic and social goals through choice-based educational streams in the upper grades of comprehensive school. In the old school system, grade repetition was a method of differentiation for teachers. Problems related to retention were well known at the inception of the new school system in the early 1970s. The impact of being sent back to the same grade with younger students was often demoralizing and rarely paved the way for the expected academic improvements among students repeating a grade (Brophy, 2006; Jimerson, 2001). After all, repeating an entire grade was an inefficient way to promote learning because it did not focus on those specific parts of the curriculum in which a student needed targeted help. Studying for a second time those subjects that a student had already successfully completed was rarely stimulating for either students or their teachers. Students were sent to the same class without any plan to specify the areas that needed improvement, let alone the methods of achieving most effectively the required levels of knowledge and skills.

In the early days of comprehensive school reform, grade repetition was seen as an inadequate and incorrect strategy for fixing individual learning or social deficiencies. In the elementary school, grade repeaters who had difficulties in one or two subjects were often labeled "failing" students who also had behavioral and personality problems. This educational stigma normally had a dramatic negative impact on students' self-esteem and thereby their motivation and efforts to learn. It also lowered teachers' expectations regarding these students' ability to learn. Grade repetition created a vicious circle that for many young people cast a negative shadow right into adulthood. Educational failure is linked to an individual's role in society and is characterized by unfavorable attitudes toward learning and further education. Leaving this role behind was possible only for young people who had strong identities and high social capital in the form of friends, teachers, and parents. Finnish experience shows that grade repetition, in most cases, led to increased social inequality and did not help students overcome academic and social problems.

Peruskoulu changed grade repetition policies and practices. Although the new system did not completely remove the problem of repeating grades, the number of students who repeated grades in the comprehensive school decreased significantly. Personalized learning and differentiation became basic principles in organizing schooling for students across society. The assumption that all students can achieve common educational goals if learning is organized according to each student's characteristics and needs became another foundation. Retention and ability grouping were clearly against these ideals. Different students have to learn to work and study together in the same class. Diversity in students' personalities, abilities, and orientations has to be taken into account in crafting learning environments and choosing pedagogical methods in schools. This turned out to be one of the most demanding professional challenges for teachers. Even today, schools are searching for an optimal educational and economic solution to deal with the increasing diversity.

Minimizing grade repetition has been possible primarily because special education has become an inclusive and integral part of every school in Finland. Every child has the right to have personalized support provided early on by trained professionals as a normal part of schooling. This special support is arranged in many different ways today. As described earlier, special education in Finland is increasingly organized within general mainstream schooling. Special education has a key role to play in improving equity and combating educational failure in Finnish schools.

Upper-secondary schools—both general and vocational—operate using modular curriculum units rather than year-based grades. Thus, grade repetition in its conventional form has vanished from Finnish upper-secondary schools. Today, students build their own personalized learning schedules from a menu of courses offered in their school or by other education institutions. Studying in upper-secondary school is therefore flexible, and selected courses can be completed at a different pace depending on students' abilities and life situations. Rather than repeating an entire grade, a student only repeats those courses that were not passed satisfactorily. Most students complete upper-secondary school in the prescribed time of 3 years, although some progress faster while others need more time. This structure that is not tied to yearly classes has also abolished cohorts in which the same group of students moves from one lesson to another and from one grade to the next.

Finland has chosen a policy of automatic promotion combined with the principle of early intervention to help students with special needs. Such attention to dynamic inequalities in all schools, as Norton Grubb points out, is what distinguishes Finland from many other countries (Grubb, 2007). This process requires systematic counseling and career guidance as young people start to think about their educational pathways. Indeed, fewer than 2% of students who leave the compulsory 9-year comprehensive school today at the age of 16 have repeated a grade at some point in their schooling. Grade repetition is at a similar level in other Nordic countries but is much higher elsewhere in Europe: About one-third of students in France, Belgium, the Netherlands, and Spain and one-fifth of students in Germany and Switzerland repeat a grade at least once. Figure 2.9 illustrates negative correlation between grade repetition (percentage of students who have repeated a grade at least once in primary or secondary school) and equity (strength of the relationship between student achievement in school and their family background).

Figure 2.9 Grade Repetition and Equity in Education in OECD Countries in 2012

Source: OECD (2013d).

FINNISH PARADOXES OF EDUCATION

Finland has been a popular destination for many educators and politicians looking for a way to get out of lower-than-expected educational performance and education reform deadlock. Most visitors to Finland discover elegant school buildings filled with calm children and highly educated teachers. They also recognize the large amount of autonomy that schools enjoy: little interference by the central education administration in schools' everyday lives, systematic methods for addressing problems in the lives of students, and targeted professional help for those in need. Much of this may be helpful in benchmarking other countries' practice in relation to a leading education nation such as Finland. However, much of the secret of Finland's educational success remains undiscovered:

- What has the educational change process been like?
- What is the role of other public sector policies in making the education system work so well?
- What role do culture and other invisible factors play?

- How much did Finnish educators take note of global education reform movements in creating their own approaches?

In many ways, Finland is a nation of strange paradoxes. Home of the telecommunication industry and one of the highest mobile phone densities, Finland is also known for its introverted, less talkative people. Finns often prefer isolation to social interaction, but they love to dance the tango. They even select a national tango queen and king during the annual tango festival. Furthermore, with their tough, northern climate, Finns rank among the world's happiest people and live in one of the world's most prosperous nations. Finnish *sisu*, a cultural trademark that refers to strength of will, determination, and purposeful action in the face of adversity, coexists with calmness and tenderness, as Lewis (2005) and Chalcer (2014) have noted. Indeed, paradoxes are more helpful than rational logic when it comes to understanding some of the key features of the Finnish people and their education system.

Avoidance of "small talk" is a well-known cultural characteristic of the Finns, as the following traditional story illustrates. Two men met unexpectedly after a long time. Because they had been good friends since boyhood, they decided to go and celebrate their pleasant, unexpected encounter with a drink or two. They soon found a bar, looked for a quiet table, and ordered their first drinks. No words were exchanged and the drinks were soon finished. Their second drinks were ordered and enjoyed, yet there was still no talk. Their third drinks went down in silence, but when the fourth drinks were about to be sipped, one of the men raised his glass for a toast and cheerfully said, "*Kippis*" (which is equivalent to "cheers" in English). The companion gave him a puzzled look and replied, "Did we come here to drink or to talk?"

Minimalism is also favored in other walks of life in Finland. Arts, music, design, and architecture all draw their inspiration from small, clear, and simple ideas. Finnish people think that "small is beautiful." In business, politics, and diplomacy, Finns rely on straight talk and simple procedures. They want to solve problems, not talk about them. Inventions and innovations in Finland are often such that simple ideas make a big difference. It is perhaps not surprising, then, that these same principles and values are embedded in Finnish education. One of Finland's educational values is to put teaching and learning before anything else when education policies and reforms are under consideration. Most of all, Finns don't seem to believe that doing more of the same in education would necessarily make any significant difference for improvement.

Paradox 1: Teach Less, Learn More

The Finnish experience challenges the typical logic of educational improvement thinking that tries to fix lower-than-expected student performance by increasing the length of education, duration of teaching, and students' homework load. For example, when students are not learning enough mathematics, a common cure is a revised curriculum with more hours of classroom instruction and homework. In most education systems, this also requires more teaching time for teachers. Two international indicators provide a vivid picture of national differences in how much students are exposed to instruction and how much time teachers spend teaching.

First, as Figure 2.10 shows, there are big differences in the total number of intended instruction hours in public institutions between the ages of 7 and 14 in OECD countries. There appears to be very little correlation between intended instruction hours in public education and resulting student performance, as assessed by PISA. Interestingly, high-performing nations in all academic domains included in PISA rely less on formal teaching time as a driver of student learning (Finland, Korea, Estonia), whereas nations with much lower levels of academic achievement (Spain, Israel, and France) require significantly more formal instruction for their students. When these differences are converted into school years, Australian 15-year-olds, for example, have attended at least 2 more years of schooling than their Finnish peers. Moreover, in Finland, children start school at the age of 7, whereas many Australian children start school at the age of 5, which adds even more formal learning time for them (OECD, 2014a). These statistics don't tell anything about how much time students spend in private tutoring or other after-school classes on top of their formal school hours—common practice in all high-performing school systems.

There are no comparable data available regarding compulsory instruction time in the United States in the OECD database. However, estimates from some states of the United States suggest that total instruction time between 6- and 17-year-old students is about 9,500 hours; that is close to what students experience in the Netherlands and Spain, as shown in Figure 2.10. Furthermore, according to the OECD statistics, Finnish 15-year-old students spend less time on homework than do any of their peers in other nations. This is yet another difference between Finland and many other countries where "minimum homework minutes" and other means have been introduced to make sure that students are kept busy studying after school. Finnish schools seem to follow Sugata Mitra's idea of "minimally invasive education," which proposes that children can learn in unsupervised environments by themselves and by helping one another.

Figure 2.10. Total Number of Intended Instruction Hours in Primary and Lower-Secondary Schools in OECD Countries in 2012

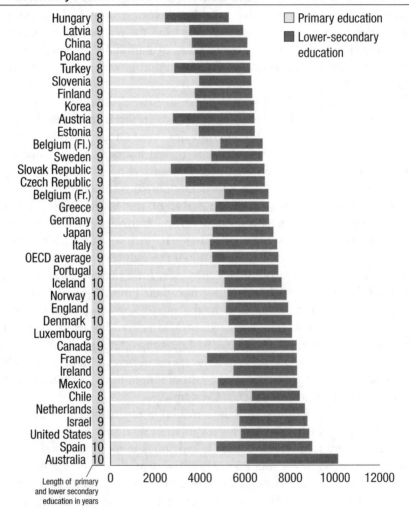

Length of primary
and lower secondary
education in years

Source: OECD (2014a).

With school days running shorter in Finland than in many other countries, what do children do when their classes are over? In principle, pupils are free to go home in the afternoon unless there is something offered to them in the school. Primary schools are required to arrange after-school activities for the youngest pupils and are encouraged to offer educational or recreational clubs for older ones. Finnish youth and sport associations play an important role in offering youth opportunities to participate in activities that support their overall learning and growth. Two-thirds of 10- to 14-year-olds and more than half of 15- to 19-year-olds belong to at least one youth or sport association. The Third Sector, as the network of these nongovernmental groups is called in Finland, contributes significantly to the social and personal development of young Finns and thereby also to the educational performance of Finnish schools.

Another way to illustrate the *quantity* versus *quality* paradox is to examine how teachers spend their working time across nations. Again, variance among countries is significant, as shown in Figure 2.11. In lower-secondary schools and primary school, on average, Finnish teachers annually teach about 590 hours and 670 hours, respectively (that is, 800 and 900 lessons of 45 minutes each, respectively). This corresponds to about four lessons daily. According to the OECD (2014a), in the United States the average annual total teaching time in primary and lower-secondary schools is 1,131 hours and 1,085 hours, respectively, which equals six or more daily lessons or other forms of instruction of 50 minutes each. Canadian teachers (the numbers vary across the provinces) teach approximately 800 hours in primary schools and 750 hours in lower-secondary schools each year. Lower teaching hours provide teachers with more opportunities to engage in school improvement, curriculum planning, and personal professional development during their working hours.

OECD's TALIS 2013 provides additional information about teachers' working time in Finland and other OECD countries (OECD, 2014b). Lower-secondary teachers' total weekly working time in Finland was 31.6 hours; that is significantly less than in Australia (42.7 hours), the United States (44.8 hours), England (45.9), Singapore (47.6 hours), Alberta (48.2 hours), or in the surveyed 34 countries on average (38.3 hours). On average, about 80% of lower-secondary teachers' working time is spent teaching and learning with students. Finnish teachers reported that they teach on average 20.6 hours a week, whereas their peers in Alberta teach 26.4 hours, in Australia 18.6 hours, in the United States 26.8 hours, and in Singapore 17.1 hours. In the OECD countries, lower-secondary teachers teach an average of 19.3 hours a week.

Figure 2.11. Number of Teaching Hours per Year in Primary, Lower-Secondary and Upper-Secondary Schools in OECD Countries in 2012

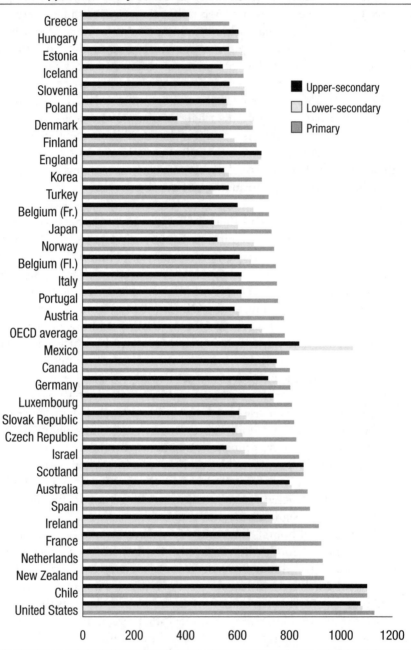

Source: OECD (2014a).

How is a typical school day different in Finnish and American upper-secondary schools (or high schools)? First of all, American teachers spend almost twice as long every week teaching or working with students as their Finnish peers. Teaching 6 hours (or four periods) daily is a tough job that leaves many teachers too tired to engage in anything professional when teaching is done. Teachers' work in the United States is therefore primarily defined as teaching in and out of classroom. In a typical Finnish upper-secondary school, on the other hand, teachers teach, on average, 4 hours a day. Despite the fact that teachers are paid by the number of lessons they teach, they also have time every day to plan, learn, and reflect on teaching with other teachers. Teachers in Finnish schools have many other responsibilities besides teaching: They assess their students' achievement and overall progress, prepare and continuously develop their own school curriculum, participate in several school health and well-being initiatives concerning their students, and provide remedial support to those students who may need additional help. Many Finnish schools are, by virtue of a unique definition of teachers' work and by their nature, professional learning communities. Of course, there are exceptions to this general image of teachers' work. Most primary schools, nevertheless, are truly professional learning communities where teaching is a holistic profession that combines work with students in the classroom and collaboration with colleagues in the staff room.

Finnish educators don't believe that more homework necessarily leads to better learning, especially if pupils are working on routine and intellectually unchallenging drills, which is unfortunately what school homework assignments often are. According to some national surveys and international studies, Finnish students in primary and lower-secondary school have the lightest load of homework of all. The *Wall Street Journal* reported that Finnish students rarely get more than half an hour of homework per day (Gameran, 2008). It is true that many primary and lower-secondary school pupils are able to complete most of their homework before they leave school for the day. According to the OECD, Finnish 15-year-old students don't take private tutoring or additional lessons other than what is offered by their school (OECD, 2013b). Seen in this light, the high achievement of Finnish students on international tests is amazing. In Korea, Japan, Singapore, and Shanghai, China—jurisdictions that are on par with or above Finland in reading, mathematics and science—most children spend hours and hours after their regular school days and on weekends and holidays in private classes and test preparation schools.

Interestingly, evidence from the most recent studies indicates that Finnish students experience less anxiety and stress in school than many of their peers in other countries (OECD, 2004, 2007). PISA concludes that only 7% of Finnish students said they feel anxiety when working on mathematics tasks at home, compared with 52% and 53% in Japan and France, respectively (Kupari & Välijärvi, 2005). Similar observations from Finnish classrooms have been reported by scores of journalists around the world. A relaxed culture of learning and a lack of stress and anxiety certainly play a role in the achievement of good overall results in Finnish schools.

Paradox 2: Test Less, Learn More

The global educational reform thinking includes an assumption that competition, choice, and more frequent external testing are prerequisites for improving the quality of education. Since the Education Reform Act 1988 was passed in England, test-based accountability policies have increased the frequency of standardized testing in many school systems around the world. Judging the annual progress of students' and schools' performance improvements is almost without exception based on these external standardized tests of reading, mathematics, and science achievements. An important question is, *Are those education systems where competition, choice, and accountability based on more frequent use of standardized tests showing progress in international comparisons?*

Using the PISA database to construct such a comparison, a suggestive answer emerges. Most notably, the United States, England, New Zealand, Japan, the Netherlands, and some parts of Canada and Australia can be used as benchmarks. Figure 2.12 demonstrates how 15-year-old students' average performances in reading literacy in five PISA surveys from 2000 to 2012 have changed in these countries (OECD, 2001, 2004, 2007, 2010b, 2013a). Trends in mathematics and science achievement in these same tests are shown in Figure 2.5 earlier in this chapter.

The trend of students' performance in all test-based accountability-policy nations is similar—it has not been improving between 2000 and 2012. Competition between schools over enrollment, increased school choice, and tougher accountability through intensified standardized testing became common policy priorities in these education systems starting in the 1990s. Although this does not constitute evidence that those market-based educational reform policies have failed (remember

Figure 2.12. Average National Reading Literacy PISA Scores in Some OECD Countries Where Competition, Choice, and Standardized Testing Have a Central Place in National Education Policies, 2000–2012

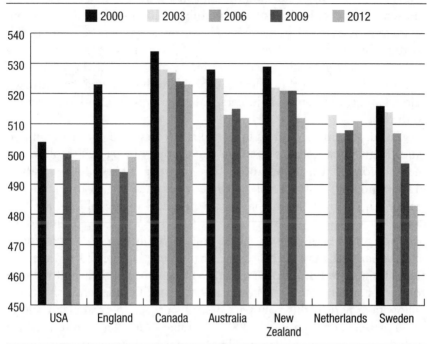

Source: OECD (2001, 2004, 2007, 2010b, 2013a).

my correlation-causation warning), it does suggest that there must be another way to improve the quality and equity of education, as has been demonstrated by more successful education systems recently.

Although students are not tested in Finland as they are in many other countries using frequent standardized tests, this does not mean that there is no assessment of students in Finland or any data about students' learning—quite the opposite. In principle, student assessment in Finland can be divided into three categories. First is classroom assessment by teachers; this includes diagnostic, formative, and summative assessment of students as part of teaching and learning. In all schools, this is solely the responsibility of teachers. All teachers are prepared to design and use various assessment methods in their work. Classroom assessment occupies a significant amount of out-of-classroom working time for teachers.

The second category of student assessment is comprehensive evaluation of students' progress after each semester. Students receive a report card that indicates their performance in academic and nonacademic subjects as well as in behavior and engagement. Students' report cards are always a collective professional judgment by their teachers. It is up to the school to decide the criteria for this evaluation, based on national student assessment guidelines. This means that report cards issued by different schools are not necessarily fully comparable because they are not based on standardized and objective measures. Many teachers, however, believe that this is less of a problem than having standardized criteria and tests that would impersonalize schools and lead to "teaching to the test."

Third, students' progress in school is also assessed externally in Finland. Regular national assessments are carried out using sample-based methodology that includes about 10% of an age cohort (6th- and 9th-grade students, for example). These assessments measure students' learning in reading, mathematics, science, and other subjects in 3- or 4-year cycles. Subjects are included in these assessments according to the needs or requests of national authorities. Schools that are not included in these samples may purchase one or more of these tests from the National Center for Education Evaluation to benchmark their performance to that of other schools. About one-fifth of all students in the grade cohort take part in this voluntary assessment. As an example, a school of 500 students pays about 5,000 U.S. dollars for each such test, which includes an analysis of results. The annual student assessment in the state budget in Finland is less than 5 million U.S. dollars for the entire school system. In an equal-size state or province in North America—for example, in Massachusetts or Alberta—the student testing budget can be 10 times higher than this.

Testing what students have learned in school is not a bad thing as long as it does not harm teaching and learning. Problems arise when tests become higher in stakes, when they are of poor quality, and when students' test scores are used to judge other things, such as the quality of teachers or schools. There are alarming reports from many parts of the world where high-stakes tests have been employed as part of punitive accountability policies in education (Amrein & Berliner, 2002; Au, 2009; Nichols & Berliner, 2007; Popham, 2007, Ravitch, 2013). Evidence suggests that teachers tend to redesign their teaching according to these tests, give higher priority to those subjects that are tested, and adjust teaching methods to drilling and memorizing information rather than understanding knowledge. It is highly questionable how much educational value such standardized tests, which are high stakes for teachers and schools (linked to teacher evaluation, promotion, salary, reputation, or accreditation) and no stakes for students, add to student learning and school improvement. Since there are no standardized high-stakes tests in Finland before the Matriculation Examination that students take at the end of their upper-secondary education, teachers can focus on teaching and learning without the disturbance of frequent tests that have to be passed.

Other signs of weakening reliance on competition and testing in education come from recent policy changes in England and Wales, and from the Canadian province of Alberta, where some of the national standardized tests have been banned and replaced by smarter ways of assessing students and schools. Alberta, for instance, had established a system of provincial achievement tests (PATs) that were used to measure pupils' performance in reading, mathematics, and science to inform decisionmakers of overall educational quality in the jurisdiction. Although the province authorities avoided using the testing data to rank schools or point out failing districts, there were some others who did so. Teachers and parents became very frustrated with the situation, in which a lot of good teaching was sacrificed in pursuit of raising test scores. In the spring of 2009, the Albertan Provincial Assembly voted in favor of removing grade 3 tests, and in 2012 the same government decided to redesign the entire provincial assessment system. As a consequence, the Accountability Department in Alberta Education (the Ministry of Education) was dissolved. This was a sign that there must be more intelligent ways to assess students' learning. A neighboring province of Alberta, Saskatchewan, has no external census-based standardized tests at all. In other jurisdictions around the world, however, winds are blowing in the opposite direction.

Paradox 3: Enhanced Equity Through Growing Diversity

The main policy principle of Finland's comprehensive school reform of the 1970s was to provide equal educational opportunities for all, as was described in Chapter 1. This also included the idea that student achievement should be evenly distributed across social groups and geographic regions. It is true that Finland long remained ethnically homogeneous. However, since it joined the European Union in 1995, cultural and ethnic diversification has progressed faster in Finland than in other European Union countries, especially in larger cities' districts and schools, where the proportion of the first- and second-generation immigrant population accounts for one-quarter of the total population. Table 2.3 shows how the number of foreign-born citizens and residents issued Finnish citizenship has grown in Finland since 1980. In 2013, approximately 5.2% of inhabitants in Finland were foreign-born citizens and thus nonnative-Finnish speakers. The low number of citizenships issued in Finland is mostly due to the requirement that all citizens must be proficient in one of the three domestic languages. All of these—Finnish, Swedish, and Sami—are not spoken anywhere outside of Scandinavia and therefore are rarely spoken by those immigrating to Finland from other places.

Finnish schools have had to adapt to this changing situation within a very short time. As a consequence, some municipalities are introducing limits to the proportion of immigrant students who attend each school to avoid segregation. For example, in the city of Espoo, there are schools with more than 40% immigrant student populations, while some schools have practically no immigrants. In 2013, for example, 4,000 new people moved to live in Espoo. Three-quarters of these new inhabitants were non-Finnish speakers. City authorities believe that a more even distribution of immigrant students in their schools would benefit both students and schools. However, school principals are doubtful about such forceful policies and their impact on communities. The proportion of immigrant children in *peruskoulu* in Helsinki is over 10% and the number of languages spoken in these schools exceeds 40. This trend is evident in all major cities in Finland.

The Finnish education system follows the principle of inclusiveness regarding the treatment of students who have differing characteristics and needs. Students are placed in regular schools unless there is a specific reason to do otherwise. Therefore, in a typical Finnish classroom, one finds teachers teaching students with different abilities, interests, and ethnicities, often with the help of assistant teachers. Cultural heterogeneity in Finnish society would suggest that variance in student learning

Table 2.3. Foreign-Born Citizens and Residents Issued Citizenship in Finland Between 1980 and 2010

Year	Foreign-born citizens	Residents issued citizenship
1980	12,853	621
1990	26,255	899
2000	91,074	2,977
2010	248,135	4,334

Source: Statistics Finland (2011).

among schools may become wider. However, as Figure 2.2 shows, a very high overall student performance in mathematics (and in reading and science) is evenly distributed throughout schools across Finland. In other words, Finland has been able to enhance equity in education while schools and classroom have become more diverse.

The Finnish sociocultural situation, which is experiencing a rapid diversification of schools and communities, offers an interesting case for research. Jarkko Hautamäki has explored the influence of increased immigration on student learning in schools. Two interesting findings emerge. First, based on the PISA data, immigrant students in Finnish schools seem to perform significantly better than immigrant students in many other countries in PISA before 2009 (Hautamäki et al., 2008). Immigrant students in Finland scored on average 50 points higher than their peers in other countries. Second, according to this same study, in the proportion of immigrant students per class there seems to be a threshold after which the learning achievement of all students in that class begins to decline. That proportion of immigrant pupils in Helsinki when notable effects of diversity on student achievement are observable is about 20%.

According to PISA 2012, pupils with immigrant background performed worse in mathematics than before. First-generation immigrant students scored up to one standard deviation lower in mathematics compared with their Finnish-born peers. Helping immigrant students catch up in learning the Finnish language is one of the biggest challenges for larger urban school systems.

Poverty is another factor that affects teaching and learning in schools. Child poverty can be defined as the percentage of children living in homes with an income that is below 50% of the national average. Based on that definition, according to the UNICEF Innocenti Research Centre, 5.4% of children in Finland live in poverty. This is the smallest child poverty rate after Iceland (4.7%). In the United States 23.1%, in Canada 13.3%, in the United Kingdom 12.1%, and in Australia 10.9% of children live in poverty (UNICEF, 2012). The equitable Finnish education system is a result of systematic attention to social justice and early intervention to help those with special needs, as well as the close interplay between education and other sectors—particularly health and social sectors—in Finnish society. It is important to note that the level of student performance has continuously increased and student performance variance has decreased, while Finnish society has become more culturally diverse and socially complex.

CHAPTER 3

The Finnish Advantage
The Teachers

You have two ears and one mouth—use them in that same proportion.

—My grandmother's advice to me for being a good teacher

Many factors have contributed to Finland's educational system's current fame, such as its 9-year comprehensive school (*peruskoulu*) for all children, modern learning-focused and teacher-designed curricula, systematic care for students with diverse special needs, and local autonomy and leadership. However, research and experience suggest that one factor is a necessary condition for all these mentioned success factors: the daily contributions of excellent teachers.

This chapter examines the central role that Finnish teachers play and describes how teacher education and a systematic focus on teacher professionalism are making major contributions to transforming Finland's educational system into a global subject of interest and an object of study. This chapter suggests, however, that it is not enough to improve teacher education or to have "the best and the brightest" teaching in schools. The Finnish experience shows that it is more important to ensure that teachers' work in schools is based on professional dignity, social respect, and collegiality so that they can fulfill their intention of selecting teaching as a lifetime career, together with their likeminded peers. Teachers' work should strike a balance between classroom teaching and collaboration with other professionals in school, as this chapter argues. This is the best way to create an image of teaching among young people that will attract young, talented professionals to choose teaching as their career. Before describing current principles and policies related to Finnish teachers and teacher education, it is useful to review some relevant cultural aspects of the teaching profession in Finland.

THE CULTURE OF TEACHING

Education has always been an integral part of Finnish culture and society. Although access to 6-year basic education became a legal obligation and right for all as far back as 1922, Finns have understood that without becoming literate and possessing broad general knowledge, it would be difficult to fulfill their lifetime aspirations. Before formal public schooling began to spread during the 1860s, cultivating public literacy was the responsibility of priests and other religious brethren in Finland as early as the 17th century. Catechist schools offered religious-oriented initial literacy education in Sunday schools and itinerant schools within villages and in remote parts of Finland. By tradition, the ability to read and write was required for legal marriage by the church for both women and men. Becoming literate, therefore, marked an individual's entry into adulthood, with its associated duties and rights. Teachers gradually assumed these responsibilities as the Finnish public school system began to expand in the early 20th century. Primarily due to their high social standing, teachers enjoyed great respect and also uncontested trust in Finland. Indeed, Finns continue to regard teaching as a noble, prestigious profession—akin to medicine, law, or economics—driven mainly by moral purpose, rather than by material interest, careers, or rewards.

Until the 1960s, the level of Finnish educational attainment remained rather low, as Figure 2.1 showed. For example, in 1952, when Finland hosted the Summer Olympics, nine out of ten adult Finns had completed only 7 to 9 years of basic education. A university degree was regarded as an exceptional attainment at that time in Finland (Sahlberg, 2010a). The Finnish educational level was close to that of Malaysia or Peru, and lagged significantly behind Scandinavian neighbors Denmark, Norway, and Sweden. In the 1960s, elementary school teachers were still prepared in 2- or 3-year teacher education seminars, not by academic institutions but rather by units that offered shorter, practical training in teaching. One graduate of a teacher preparation seminar in the late 1950s, Martti Ahtisaari, went from being a primary school teacher, to being an international diplomat, to being the president of Finland (1994–2000), and is now a Nobel Peace Prize laureate and praised global peacemaker. Today, when celebrating its educational achievements, Finland publicly recognizes the value of its teachers and implicitly trusts their professional insights and judgments regarding schooling. Stated quite plainly, without excellent teachers and a modern teacher education system, Finland's current international educational achievement would have been impossible.

The Finnish education system is distinctly different from public education in the United States, Canada, or England. Some differences are closely related to the work of teachers. For example, the Finnish education system lacks rigorous school inspection, and it does not employ external standardized student testing to inform the public about school performance or teacher effectiveness. Teachers also have professional autonomy to create their own school-based work plan and curriculum. All education in Finland is publicly financed, including teacher education in Finland's research universities.

Finnish teacher education today is fully congruent with these characteristics of educational policy in Finland. Five categories of teachers exist:

1. *Kindergarten teachers* work in kindergartens and are also licensed to teach preschool children.
2. *Primary school teachers* teach in grades 1 to 6 in 9-year comprehensive schools. They normally are assigned to one grade and teach several subjects.
3. *Subject teachers* teach particular subjects in the upper grades of basic school (typically grades 7 to 9) and in general upper-secondary school, including vocational schools. Subject teachers may teach one to three subjects—for example, mathematics, physics, and chemistry.
4. *Special education teachers* work with individuals and student groups with special needs in primary schools and the upper grades of comprehensive schools.
5. *Vocational education teachers* teach in upper-secondary vocational schools. They must possess at least 3 years of classroom experience in their own teaching field before they can be admitted to a vocational teacher preparation program.

In addition to these five teacher categories, teachers in adult education institutions are required to have similar pedagogical knowledge and skills. Each academic year, approximately 6,000 new openings become available in all teacher education programs in Finland. This chapter focuses on the education of primary and subject teachers in the K–12 part of the Finnish educational system, which constitutes about two-thirds of all teacher education students.

Teaching as a profession is closely tied to sustaining Finnish national culture and building an open and multicultural society. Indeed, one purpose of formal schooling is to transfer cultural heritage, values, and aspirations from one generation to another. Teachers are, according to their own opinions, essential players in building the Finnish welfare society. As in countries around the world, teachers in Finland have served as critical transmitters of culture. Through the centuries, Finland has struggled for its national identity, mother tongue, and its own values, first, during 6 centuries under the Kingdom of Sweden; next for more than a century under the Russian Empire; and then for another century as a newly independent nation positioned between its former patrons and the powers of globalization. There is no doubt that this history left a deep mark on Finns and their desire for personal development through education, reading, and self-improvement. Literacy is the backbone of Finnish culture, and reading for pleasure has become an integral part of the cultural DNA of all Finns.

It is no wonder, then, that teachers and teaching are highly regarded in Finland. The Finnish media regularly report results of opinion polls that document favorite professions among general upper-secondary school graduates. Surprisingly, teaching is consistently rated as one of the most admired professions, ahead of medical doctors, architects, and lawyers, typically thought to be dream professions (Liiten, 2004). Teaching is congruent with the core social values of Finns, which include social justice, caring for others, and happiness, as reported by the National Youth Survey (2010). Teaching is also regarded as an independent high profession that enjoys public respect and praise. It is particularly popular among young women—more than 80% of those accepted for study in primary teacher education programs are female (National Board of Education, 2013).

In a national opinion survey, about 1,300 adult Finns (ages 15 to 74) were asked if their spouse's (or partner's) profession had influenced their decision to commit to a relationship with them (Kangasniemi, 2008). Interviewees were asked to select 5 professions from a list of 30 that they would prefer for a selected partner or spouse. The responses were rather surprising. Finnish males viewed a teacher as the most desirable spouse, rated just ahead of a nurse, medical doctor, or architect. Women, in turn, identified only a medical doctor and a veterinarian ahead of a teacher as a desirable profession for their ideal husband. In the entire sample, 35% rated teacher as among the top five preferred professions for their ideal spouse. Apparently, only medical doctors are more sought after in Finnish mating markets than teachers. This clearly documents both the high professional and social status that teachers have attained in Finland—both in and out of schools.

BOX 3.1: WHY DO I WANT TO BE A TEACHER?

Becoming a teacher was easy for me. Actually, it was not a choice at all, but rather a process that grew from a childhood dream into a realistic goal as an adult. I have many educators in my family and teaching is in my blood. My parents have encouraged me to take this direction. They helped me find summer jobs and hobbies where I had a chance to work with children. I always found those jobs rewarding, fun, and morally fulfilling. It was that fun aspect of working with children that influenced me when I graduated high school and moved on in my career.

During my part-time teaching in school and also currently in teacher education in the university, the rosy picture of teaching has from time to time been tarnished, but every time shines again. Now, when I am about to graduate and get my master's degree to teach in primary school, I have started to think about what it is to be a teacher. Why do I do this? First is the internal drive to help people discover their strengths and talents, but also to realize their weaknesses and inadequacies. I want to be a teacher because I want to make a difference to children's lives and to this country. My work with children has always been based on love and care, being gentle, and creating personal relations with those with whom I work. I think this is the only way I will attain fulfillment in my life.

But I also understand that in my work, I will face huge responsibility for a modest salary and heavy workload. I also know that shrinking financial resources for schools will continue and will influence my work in school. In Helsinki, the social problems that children increasingly face in their lives will also be part of my work in the classroom. I need to be able to observe diverse individuals and offer help in situations for which I am probably not yet prepared. I accept that my work is not only teaching the things I like but also working out conflict situations, working with colleagues who do not necessarily think the same way I do, and collaborating with different parents in educating their children. Without a doubt, I will continue to ask myself whether this work is really worth all that.

The well-known Finnish educator Matti Koskenniemi used the term *pedagogical love*, which is also a cornerstone of my own theory of action as a teacher. Teaching is, perhaps more than any other job, a profession that you can successfully do only if you put your heart and personality into play. Each teacher has her own style and philosophy of teaching. There may be many motives for becoming a teacher. My own is that I want to do good for other people, to care about and love them. I do love them and thus I will be a teacher.

—Veera Salonen, Primary School Teacher, Helsinki

BECOMING A TEACHER

Due to the popularity of teaching and becoming a teacher, only Finland's best and most committed are able to realize those professional dreams. Every spring, thousands of Finnish general upper-secondary school graduates, including many of the most talented, creative, and motivated youngsters, submit their applications to departments of teacher education in eight Finnish universities. Thus, becoming a primary school teacher in Finland is highly competitive. It is normally not enough simply to complete general upper-secondary school successfully and pass a rigorous matriculation examination (see Chapter 1). Successful teacher education candidates must also possess high scores, positive personalities, excellent interpersonal skills, and a commitment to work as a teacher in school. Annually, only about 1 of every 10 applicants will be accepted to primary school teacher education master's programs in Finnish research universities. For example, 3,200 candidates applied to different teacher education programs at the University of Helsinki in 2013. Only 340 of them were accepted. The total annual Finnish applicants in all five categories of teacher education programs in eight universities that educate teachers number about 20,000.

Primary school teacher education candidates are selected in two phases: First, students take a written exam in early May that is the same for all eight universities that offer teacher education programs. This exam is based on a set of scientific and professional articles that are announced and made available to students in late March. In 2014, there were six articles to be read for the exam and they covered a wide range of issues, such as "Development and assessment of working memory in childhood," "Equality and justice in basic education placement and selectivity," and "Change in education policy and school's position in Europe." Based on students' performance in this exam, they are then invited to the second phase of the selection process, which varies from one university to another. It is worth noting that this first-phase exam puts all candidates behind the same line: grades or merits do not matter in getting to the second phase, only the exam mark. Therefore those who claim that Finland recruits its teachers from the top 10% of each cohort graduate from upper-secondary school are not exactly right. Nevertheless, it is safe to say that there is careful quality control at the entry into the teaching profession in Finland. It is difficult to get into teacher education without solid knowledge, skills, and moral commitment to teach.

The purpose of the second phase is to test the candidate's personality, knowledge, and overall suitability to become a teacher. Most universities require candidates to demonstrate how they can create ideas, plan, and work with other people. All candidates will go through individual interviews that, among other things, often ask candidates to explain their reasons for choosing to become a teacher. In their final selection of successful candidates, universities may take into account the results of the first phase of the exam, grades in Matriculation Examination, and a student's diploma, as well as his or her merits in arts, sports, and any other activities that they see as relevant to the teaching profession.

As these two selection phases suggest, access to Finnish teacher education is highly competitive. Normally, at least some prior experience in teaching or working with children is required for successful candidates. In 2014, total applications to primary school teacher education programs reached 8,400, with candidates competing for only 800 available student positions in eight Finnish universities. Figure 3.1 summarizes the trend in total annual applicants between 2001 and 2014, disaggregated by gender.

Two phenomena are apparent. The Finnish teaching profession in primary schools has become increasingly attractive. Also, the proportion of male primary school teachers remains relatively small. The state of the Finnish economy is reflected in the number of teacher education applicants; when the prospects of employment are dimmer, young people head toward teaching, as can be seen during the latest economic downturn in Finland that started in 2008. Although the number of Finnish students who do not complete their studies and thus fail to earn a degree is small, a relatively larger number of male students end up studying in other disciplines or working before they graduate.

Finland is one of the few nations able to select the best and most motivated young people for primary school teacher education programs year after year. A similarly good situation exists in Singapore, South Korea, Ireland, and in some other countries. This has created a strong moral and professional foundation for teaching in Finnish primary schools, where Finnish children spend their first 6 school years with able, knowledgeable professionals.

What Makes Teaching a Top Job?

If we use Finnish education as a reference, three conditions emerge for attracting the best young people into teaching and keeping them in schools. First, and most important, it is paramount that teachers'

Figure 3.1. Total Annual Applicants and Accepted Students to Finnish Primary School Teacher Education Programs in 2001-2014

Source: University of Helsinki (2014, www.helsinki.fi/vakava/koepisteet.html).

workplaces allow them to fulfill their moral missions. In Finland, as in many other countries, a teaching career is the result of an inner desire to work with people and to help both people and society through teaching. Teachers in Finland possess a strong sense of being esteemed professionals, similar to medical doctors, engineers, or lawyers. Teachers at all levels of schooling expect that they will be given the full range of professional autonomy they need to practice what they have been educated to do: to plan, teach, diagnose, execute, and evaluate. They also expect to be provided with enough time to accomplish all of these goals, both inside and outside of normal classroom duties. As described in Chapter 2, in Finland, teachers spend relatively less time teaching than their peers in many other countries do. For example, in North American schools, teachers are engaged in teaching during the vast majority of their daily working time in school, which leaves little space for any other professional activities. The concept of the professional learning community (PLC) is often applied to the way teachers work in schools, frequently on their own time. However, in Finland, Korea, and Japan, for instance, schools are regarded as professional learning communities because of the inherent nature and balance of teachers' daily professional work.

I have talked with Finnish primary school teachers in the early phases of their careers in order to understand what would prompt them to leave their chosen profession (Sahlberg, 2012). Interestingly, practically nobody cites salary as a reason for leaving teaching. Instead, many point out that if they were to lose their professional autonomy in schools and in classrooms, their career choice would be called into question. For example, if an outside inspector were to judge the quality of their work or if a merit-based compensation policy influenced by external measures were imposed, many would change their jobs. Finnish teachers are particularly skeptical of using frequent standardized tests to determine students' progress in school. Many Finnish teachers have told me that if they encountered external pressure regarding standardized testing and high-stakes accountability, similar to what their peers in England or the United States face, they would seek other jobs. In short, teachers in Finland expect that they will experience professional autonomy, prestige, respect, and trust in their work. First and foremost, the working conditions and moral professional environment are what count when young Finns decide whether they will pursue a teaching career or seek work in another field.

Second, teacher education should be sufficiently competitive and demanding to attract talented young high school graduates. Teacher education attracts many of Finland's high school graduates because it constitutes a master's degree program and is therefore challenging enough for them. In addition, due to the high quality of Finnish students entering teacher education programs, the curricula and requirements have become very demanding, comparable to other degree programs offered by Finnish academic universities. Graduates who hold a master's degree can, without further work, apply for doctoral studies. That same degree also qualifies an individual to work in government or local administration, teach in the university, or compete with other master's degree holders in private sector employment. It has been questioned in Finland now and then whether primary school teachers necessarily need master's-level academic and research-based qualifications. However, Finnish experience suggests that if the primary school teaching degree requirement were lowered, many potential teachers would seek studies in professional fields that would give them higher academic status and thus open more employment opportunities later in their careers.

Third, the salary level is not the main motive to become a teacher in Finland. Teachers earn slightly more than the national average salary. The annual statutory teacher's salary in the upper grades of *peruskoulu* after 15 years of experience (in equivalent U.S. dollars, converted by using purchasing-power parity) is about 42,600 U.S. dollars (OECD, 2014a). That is close to what teachers earn, on average, in OECD countries. The comparable annual salary in the United States is 47,000 U.S. dollars, and in Korea, 50,000 U.S. dollars.

Although making money is not the main reason for becoming a teacher, there should be a systematic way for salaries to increase. Finnish teachers climb the salary ladder as their teaching experience grows, reaching the peak after about 20 years of service. The same salary scheme is applied in all parts of the country and is determined in a national labor contract that the Trade Union of Education negotiates with the Local Government Employers that promotes the interests of Finland's municipalities and joint municipal authorities on the labor market. However, there are a number of factors that affect the paycheck.

First, teachers' pay depends on the type of school (e.g., primary or upper-secondary school). Although teachers' pay in Finland is not linked to their students' achievement in any way, the salary structure is based on merit and performance. Then, basic salary includes the base pay determined in the labor contract and an addition determined locally depending on required particular skills, responsibilities, social skills, and working conditions that may vary greatly from school to school. Next, there is a personal bonus in each teacher's salary that depends on overall job performance (including feedback from parents, colleagues, and the principal), yet it is not measured by student achievement. There is also extra pay for additional hours on top of the minimum required teaching load together with other possible compensation. Three hours a week of collaboration, school improvement, or other collegial activities are included in each teacher's basic salary. Finally, teachers may receive a performance bonus awarded to their school or cluster of schools as a collective reward for especially successful work accomplished together. As a consequence, there may be variation in teachers' earnings even within the same school depending on seniority, the nature of their work, and overall performance that is normally judged by the principal.

RESEARCH-BASED TEACHER EDUCATION

Until the end of the 1970s, primary school teachers were prepared in teacher colleges or special teacher education seminars. Lower- and upper-secondary school subject teachers studied in specific subject-focused departments within Finnish universities. By the end of the 1970s, all teacher education programs became a part of academic higher education and, therefore, were only offered by universities. A master's degree became the basic qualification for teaching in Finnish schools. Simultaneously, scientific content and educational research advances began to enrich teacher education curricula. Finnish teacher education is now *academic*, meaning that it must be based on and supported by scientific knowledge and must be focused on the thinking processes and cognitive skills needed to design and conduct educational research (Jakku-Sihvonen & Niemi, 2006; Niemi, 2008). A particular principle of research-based teacher education in Finland is the systemic integration of scientific educational knowledge, didactics (or pedagogical content knowledge), and practice to enable teachers to enhance their pedagogical thinking, evidence-based decisionmaking, and engagement in the professional community of educators. Consequently, the basic requirement today for permanent employment as a teacher in all Finnish comprehensive and upper-secondary schools is the possession of a research-based master's degree, as shown in Table 3.1.

Teacher education is an important and recognized part of higher education in Finland. In many other nations, the situation is different: Teacher preparation is frequently viewed as semiprofessional training arranged outside of academic universities. In the Acts on Teacher Education in 1978–1979, the minimum requirement for permanent employment as a

Table 3.1. Required Teacher Qualifications by Type of Finnish School

Type of school	Age of pupils	Grades	Required teacher qualifications
Kindergarten	0–6		Kindergarten teacher (BA)
Preschool	6		Kindergarten teacher (BA) Primary school teacher (MA)
Comprehensive School (*Peruskoulu*)	7–16	1–9	Comprehensive school teacher (MA)
Primary School	7–12	1–6	Primary school teacher (MA)
Lower-Secondary School	13–15	7–9	Subject teacher (MA)
General Upper-Secondary	16–18	10–12	Subject teacher (MA)
Vocational Upper-Secondary			Vocational teacher (BA) Subject teacher (MA)
University	19–		Higher academic degree (MA/PhD)
Polytechnic			Higher education degree (MA/PhD)

Source: Sahlberg (2012).

teacher was raised to a master's degree that includes an approved master's thesis with scholarly requirements similar to those in any other academic field. This legislative policy served as the impetus to transfer all teacher education programs from colleges to Finnish universities. The seeds were sown for believing that the teaching profession is based on scholarly research. An important side effect of this transition was the unification of the Finnish teaching cohort, which had become divided by the Comprehensive School Reform of the 1970s into primary school teachers and subject teachers working in lower- and upper-secondary schools.

The role of the Trade Union of Education in Finland (OAJ), established in 1973, has been both a negotiator of the terms of teachers' employment contracts and an advocate for education (www.oaj.fi). The union represents teachers at various school levels and institutes, ranging from kindergarten teachers to instructors in vocational schools, and to school principals and lecturers in universities. More than 95% of teachers in Finland are OAJ members.

As mentioned above, all Finnish teachers must hold a master's degree. The major subject in primary school teacher education programs is *education*. In subject-focused teacher education programs, students concentrate within a particular subject—for example, mathematics or foreign languages. Subject-focused teacher candidates also study didactics, consisting of pedagogical content knowledge (subject didactics) within their own subject specialty. Today, successful completion of a master's degree—which includes a bachelor's degree—in teaching takes, in theory, 5 years, but in reality the average graduation time is over 6 years, according to the Finnish Ministry of Education (Ministry of Education, 2007). There are no alternative ways to earn a teacher's diploma in Finland; only the university degree constitutes a license to teach. In the United States, for example, the Teach for America program admits college graduates, immerses them in pedagogy courses for several weeks over a summer, and then sends them to schools in need of teachers— where they often find classroom challenges to be exceedingly difficult. There are similar teacher certification initiatives in 40 countries within the Teach for All network in 2014, such as Teach First in the United Kingdom, New Zealand, Israel and Norway, Teach for India, Teach for South Africa, Teach for China, and Enseña Chile.

Academic teacher education in Finland focuses on the balanced development of a prospective teacher's personal and professional competences. Particular attention is devoted to building pedagogical thinking skills, enabling teachers to manage instructional processes in accord with contemporary educational knowledge and practice (Toom et al.,

2010; Westbury, Hansen, Kansanen, & Björkvist, 2005). In Finnish primary teacher education, this is characterized by the study of education as a main subject, composed of three thematic areas:

1. Theory of education
2. Pedagogical content knowledge
3. Subject didactics and practice

Finnish research-based teacher education programs culminate in a required master's thesis. Prospective primary school teachers normally complete their theses in the field of education. Typically, the topic of a master's thesis is focused on or is close to a student teacher's own school or classroom practice, such as mathematics teaching or learning. Subject-focused student teachers, in turn, select a thesis topic within their major subject. The level of scholarly expectations for teacher education studies is similar across all teacher preparation programs, from elementary to upper-secondary school.

Teacher education in Finland is aligned with the framework of the European Higher Education Area that is being developed under the ongoing Bologna Process.[1] Currently, Finnish universities offer a two-tier degree program. First is an obligatory 3-year bachelor's degree program that qualifies students for a 2-year master's degree program that is the minimum qualification for a license to teach in Finland. These two degrees are offered in multidisciplinary programs consisting of studies in at least two subjects. Studies are quantified in terms of credit units within the European Credit Transfer and Accumulation System (ECTS) within 46 European nations. ECTS, which will become the guiding policy for the European Higher Education Area, is a student-centered system based on the student workload required to achieve program objectives.

The objectives are normally specified in terms of the learning outcomes and competencies to be acquired. ECTS is based on the assumption that 60 credits represent the workload of a full-time student over 1 academic year. The annual student workload for a full-time study program in Europe equals, in most cases, about 1,500 to 1,800 hours. Therefore, one ECTS credit represents about 25 to 30 working hours a week. Teacher education requires 180 ECTS credits for a bachelor's degree (which doesn't meet the qualifications for a teaching diploma or enable permanent employment as a teacher), followed by 120 additional ECTS credits for a master's degree.

A broad-based teacher education curriculum ensures that newly prepared Finnish teachers possess well-balanced knowledge and skills in both theory and practice. It also implies that prospective teachers develop deep professional insight into education from several perspectives, including educational psychology and sociology, curriculum theory, student assessment, special needs education, and didactics (pedagogical content knowledge) in their selected subject areas. It is noteworthy that contemporary Finnish teacher education has been strongly influenced by research and development in this field in American, Canadian, and British universities.[2] To illustrate what teachers study during their preparation program, Table 3.2 illustrates primary school teacher education topics with required credit units, as offered by the Department of Teacher Education at the University of Helsinki. All eight Finnish universities that offer teacher education have their own nationally coordinated teacher education strategies and curricula, ensuring coherence but encouraging local initiative to make the best use of each university's resources and nearby opportunities.

Table 3.2. Summary of Primary Teacher Education Master's Degree Program at the University of Helsinki in 2014

Curriculum Component	Total credits	BEd	MEd
Communication Studies and Orienting Studies	*25cr*		
Basics of Curriculum Planning	2 cr	1 cr	1 cr
Language and Communication Skills	**14 cr**		
Mother Tongue			
Speech Communication and Interaction Skills		2 cr	
Drama Pedagogy		3 cr	
Scientific Writing			3 cr
Foreign Language		3 cr	
Second National Language		3 cr	
Education and Social Justice	3 cr	3 cr	
Information and Communication Technology in Learning	3 cr	3 cr	
Introduction to Media Education	3 cr		3 cr
Main Subject Studies in Education	*140 cr*		
Cultural Bases of Education	**16 cr**		
Introduction to Educational Sciences		3 cr	
Social, Historical, and Philosophical Foundations of Education		4 cr	
Facing Specificity and Multiplicity/Education for Diversities		6 cr	
Cultural Diversity in Schools			3 cr

Table 3.2. Summary of Primary Teacher Education Master's Degree Program at the University of Helsinki in 2014 (continued)

Curriculum Component	Total credits	BEd	MEd
Psychological Bases of Education	**11 cr**		
Introduction to Educational Psychology		5 cr	
Interaction and Awareness of Pupil		6 cr	
Pedagogical Bases of Education	**23 cr**		
Didactics		7 cr	
Theory and Didactics of Early Childhood Education		3 cr	
Evaluation and Ethics of Teaching and Learning		3 cr	
Curriculum Theory and Evaluation			3 cr
Pedagogical Knowing and Construction of Personal Practical Theory			7 cr
Research Studies in Education	**70 cr**		
Introduction to Educational Research		3 cr	
Quantitative Research Methods		4 cr	
Qualitative Research Methods		3 cr	
Bachelor's Thesis (incl. seminars 4 cr)		10 cr	
either Practicing Research Methods (quantitative)			4 cr
or Practicing Research Methods (qualitative)			4 cr
Method tray (two optional advanced method courses depending)			6 cr
Master's Thesis			40 cr
Teaching Practice	**20 cr**		
Orienting Practicum		3 cr	
Minor Subject Practicum			9 cr
Master Practicum			8 cr
Minor Subject Studies—Multidisciplinary Studies and Cross-curricular Issues Taught in Comprehensive School	*60 cr*		
Mother Tongue and Literature Education	**8 cr**	**8 cr**	
Mathematics Education	**7 cr**	**7 cr**	
Arts and Skills Education	**14 cr**		
Visual Arts Education		3 cr	
Craft Education		5 cr	
Didactics of Physical Education		3 cr	

Curriculum Component	Total credits	BEd	MEd
Music Education		3 cr	
Didactics in Humanistic Subjects	**6 cr**		
History Education		3 cr	
either Lutheran Religious Education		3 cr	
or Secular Ethics Education		3 cr	
Didactics in Environmental and Science Subjects	**12 cr**		
Geography Education		3 cr	
Biology Education		3 cr	
Physics Education		3 cr	
Chemistry Education		3 cr	
Optional Courses	**13 cr**		
One of the following:			
Visual Arts Education, Pedagogical Orientation		4 cr	
Physical Education, Pedagogical Orientation			4 cr
Music Education, Pedagogical Orientation		4 cr	
Craft Education, Pedagogical Orientation		4 cr	
One of the following:			
Visual Arts Education, Socio-cultural Orientation		3 cr	
Physical Education, Socio-cultural Orientation		3 cr	
Music Education, Socio-cultural Orientation		3 cr	
Craft Education, Socio-cultural Orientation		3 cr	
One of the following:			
History Education, Optional Studies		3 cr	
Religious Education, Lutheranism, Optional Studies		3 cr	
Secular Ethics Education, Optional Studies		3 cr	
One of the following:			
Geography Education, Optional Studies		3 cr	
Biology Education, Optional Studies		3 cr	
Physics Education, Optional Studies		3 cr	
Chemistry Education, Optional Studies		3 cr	
Optional Minor Subject and Optional Studies	*75 cr*	*40 cr*	*35 cr*
Study points in the whole degree	**300 CR**		

1 ECTS credit = 27 hours of work

As a general rule, teacher education preparing teachers for the lower grades (typically, grades 1 to 6 of comprehensive schools) includes 60 ECTS credits of pedagogical studies and at least 60 additional ECTS credits for other courses in educational sciences. An integral part of these additional educational studies is a master's thesis requiring independent research, participation in research seminars, and defending of the completed educational study. The commonly assigned credit for this research work within all universities is 40 ECTS credits.

The revised teacher education curriculum in Finland requires primary school teacher candidates to complete a major in educational sciences and earn 60 ECTS credits in minor studies within subjects included in the National Framework Curriculum for Comprehensive School, which is regularly updated by the National Board of Education and the Ministry of Education.

Most students in primary teacher education programs enter their studies with solid knowledge and skills in the range of subjects that are studied in upper-secondary school. In Finland, unlike in the United States or England, all upper-secondary school students are obliged to complete successfully a study program including up to 18 required subjects—such as physics, chemistry, philosophy, music, and at least two foreign languages in addition to two domestic languages. Normally, students accepted in Finnish primary school teacher education programs have earned higher than average grades in these subjects. For example, at the University of Helsinki, some 15% of students select mathematics as their minor subject, which earns them a license to teach mathematics as subject teachers in grades 7 to 9 (Lavonen et al., 2007). Science education is also quite popular among primary school teacher students; each year approximately 10% take basic or advanced studies in science teaching. It is clear that primary school teachers in Finland, in general, possess strong mastery of the subjects that they teach because of their broadly based upper-secondary school studies and because primary teacher education programs build upon that solid base.

Finnish subject teacher education follows the same principles as primary school teacher education but is arranged differently. There are two main pathways to becoming a subject teacher. Most students first complete a master's degree in their academic programs with one major subject, such as the Finnish language, for example, and one or two minor subjects, such as literature and drama. Students then apply to the Department of Teacher Education for their subject teacher education program. In pedagogical studies, the main focus is on subject-oriented teaching strategies equivalent to 60 ECTS credits, and requires one academic year to complete. The other pathway to becoming a subject teacher is for students to apply directly to teacher education to pursue a major subject in their selected academic program. Normally, after 2 years of subject studies, students start their pedagogical studies in their university's faculty of education. The curriculum for this second pathway is identical to that of the first route, only it is scheduled differently within the bachelor's and master's tracks, typically over four academic terms, as illustrated by the program at the University of Helsinki shown in Table 3.3.

Prospective subject teachers decide to major in fields that they will be teaching, such as mathematics or music. For major subjects, advanced studies involving 90 ECTS credits are normally required. In addition, 60 ECTS credits are required in a second subject that will be taught in schools. Generally, departments of teacher education organize courses in pedagogical studies in collaboration with subject-matter departments in their universities. Each subject-matter department is also responsible for the teacher education of students seeking certification in that particular subject. Exceptions include teacher education for some subjects that are included in the National Curriculum

Table 3.3. Structure of the Pedagogical Component of the Subject Teacher Education Program at the University of Helsinki in 2014

Bachelor's level (25 European Credit Transfer and Accumulation credits)	Master's level (35 credits)
FIRST TERM (18 CREDITS)	THIRD TERM (17 CREDITS)
Developmental psychology and learning (4)	Social, historical, and philosophical foundations of education (5)
Special education (4)	Evaluation and development of teaching (7)
Introduction to subject didactics (10)	Advanced teaching practice in teacher training school or field school (5)
SECOND TERM (7 CREDITS)	FOURTH TERM (12 CREDITS)
Basic teaching practice in teacher training school (7)	Research seminar (teacher as a researcher) (4)
	Final teaching practice in teacher training school or field school (8)
AS PART OF MASTER'S PROGRAM: Research methodology (6)	

Framework for the comprehensive school, such as textile work and crafts, special education, student counseling, and music, which are organized within departments of education. Teacher education for music, arts, and physical education usually occurs in separate departments or institutes within a university. It is also internationally unique that Finnish academic subject faculties—not the department of teacher education—issue master's degrees for subject teachers and thus play important roles in Finnish teacher education.

TEACHERS AS RESEARCHERS

Instruction in Finnish teacher education departments is arranged to support pedagogical principles that newly prepared teachers are expected to implement in their own classrooms. Although all university teachers have full pedagogical autonomy, every department of teacher education in Finland has a detailed and often binding strategy for improving the quality of teacher education programs. Subject-focused pedagogy and research in science education within Finnish universities, for example, are regarded as advanced by international standards (Lavonen et al., 2007). Moreover, cooperative learning, problem-based learning, reflective practice, and computer-supported education are now implemented—at least to some extent—in all Finnish universities. A Finnish higher education evaluation system that offers public recognition of and financial prizes for effective, innovative university teaching practice has served as an important driver of these positive developments.

Research-based teacher education means that the integration of educational theories, research methodologies, and practice all play important roles in Finnish teacher education programs. Teacher education curricula are designed so that they constitute a systematic continuum from the foundations of educational thinking, to educational research methodologies, and then on to more advanced fields of educational sciences. Each student thereby builds an understanding of the systemic, interdisciplinary nature of educational practice. Finnish students also acquire the skills of designing, conducting, and presenting original research on practical or theoretical aspects of education. An integral element of Finnish research-based teacher education is practical training in schools—a key component of the curriculum, as documented in Tables 3.2 and 3.3.

BOX 3.2: RESEARCH-BASED TEACHER EDUCATION

In my long career as a teacher educator, the most significant policy change was the requirement that all teachers must hold an academic master's degree in education or in the subject they teach in school. It launched a development chain that elevated all teachers as professionals who, among other things, are able to understand teaching holistically and improve their own work continuously. In Finland, it took more than 20 years to build common understanding among teacher educators, university professors, and practitioners about the complexity of the teaching profession. Research-based teacher education has the following three key principles:

- Teachers need a deep knowledge of the most recent advances of research in the subjects they teach. In addition, they need to be familiar with the research on how something can be taught and learned.
- Teachers must adopt a research-oriented attitude toward their work. This means learning to take an analytical and open-minded approach to their work, drawing conclusions for the development of education based on different sources of evidence coming from the recent research as well as their own critical and professional observations and experiences.
- Teacher education in itself should also be an object of study and research.

Many people ask why Finnish students perform so well in school and why many young Finns choose teaching as their career. There is no regular standardized testing, school inspection, teacher evaluation, or ranking of schools in Finland. Public education has a central role in enhancing equality and well-being in Finnish society. High-quality academic teacher education ensures readiness to work in many other areas of the Finnish labor market. Most important, in Finland teachers and schools enjoy strong public confidence. Parents trust teachers the way that they trust their dentists. Parents do not need to worry about finding a good school for their children. Many think that the nearest school in their community is good enough. I believe that because teachers—as a result of their academic education—have clear moral purpose and independent professional ethos, they are trusted. Research-based teacher education is essential in making that possible.

—Hannele Niemi, Professor of Education, University of Helsinki

There are, in principle, two kinds of practicum experiences within Finnish teacher education programs. A minor portion of clinical training occurs in seminars and small-group classes within a department of teacher education (part of a faculty of education), where students practice basic teaching skills with their peers. Major teaching practice experiences occur mostly within special teacher training schools governed by universities, which have curricula and practices similar to those of ordinary public schools. Students also use a network of selected field schools for practice teaching. In primary school teacher education, students devote approximately 15% of their intended study time (for example, in the University of Jyväskylä, 40 ECTS credits) practice teaching in schools. In subject teacher education, the proportion of teaching practice in schools constitutes about one-third of the curriculum.

The Finnish teacher education curriculum, as summarized in Tables 3.2 and 3.3, is designed to integrate teaching practice in theoretical and methodological studies systematically. Teaching practice is normally divided into three phases over the 5-year program: basic (orientation) practice, advanced (minor subject) practice, and final (master) practice. During each phase, students observe lessons by experienced teachers, complete practice teaching observed by supervisory teachers, and deliver independent lessons to different pupil groups, all evaluated by supervising teachers and department of teacher education professors and lecturers. Evaluations of Finnish teacher education have repeatedly identified the systematic nature of teacher education curricula as a key strength and a characteristic that distinguishes Finnish teacher education from that of many other nations (Darling-Hammond, 2006; Jussila & Saari, 2000; Saari & Frimodig, 2009).

The Finnish teacher education program represents a spiral sequence of theoretical knowledge, practical training, and research-oriented inquiry into teaching. Teacher education responsibilities are integrated within the activities of academic university units. At the University of Oulu, three faculties—science, humanities, and education—deliver teacher education courses for their students. They include staff (normally university lecturers and professors) who specialize in subject-oriented teaching methodologies. Their curricula are coordinated with the Department of Teacher Education, which is responsible for the overall organization of teacher education.

Although teacher training schools constitute the main portion of the network within which Finnish students complete their practice teaching, some ordinary municipal public schools (called municipal field schools, or MFS) also serve the same purpose. One-third of all teaching practice at the University of Oulu occurs in these municipal field schools. Teacher training schools where practice teaching occurs have higher professional staff requirements; supervising teachers must prove their competency to work with student teachers. Teacher training schools (but not MFS) are also expected to pursue research and development roles in teacher education in collaboration with the university's department of teacher education, and sometimes also with the academic units' teacher education staff. For example, at the University of Oulu, the Faculty of Science and the Faculty of Humanities assume teacher education roles and support appropriate staff. All teacher training schools can, therefore, introduce sample lessons and alternative curricular designs to student teachers. These schools also have teachers who are experienced in supervision, teacher professional development, and assessment strategies. There are no specific qualifications to be designated as such a teacher—it is each individual's responsibility to build the needed knowledge and skills required for employment in a teacher training school.

PROFESSIONAL DEVELOPMENT

Because teaching is a much-desired profession in Finland, most new graduates from Finnish departments of teacher education and subject-focused programs seek immediate school employment. During their studies, students develop their impressions of what school life from a teacher's viewpoint may be like. However, graduates do not necessarily acquire experience participating in a community of educators, assuming full responsibility for a classroom of students, or interacting with parents. All these considerations are part of the curriculum, but many licensed graduates discover that there is a chasm between lecture-hall idealism and school reality.

Induction of a new teacher into a first classroom assignment is relatively less developed in Finland than in the United States or England, although research and development work on teacher induction is rather active (Jokinen & Välijärvi, 2006; OECD, 2014b). It is up to each school and municipality governing these schools to incorporate new teachers' needs for induction or mentoring into their teaching responsibilities. Thus, practices regarding Finnish teacher induction are, admittedly, diverse. Some schools, as part of their mission, have adopted advanced procedures and support systems for new staff, whereas other schools merely bid new teachers welcome and show them to their classrooms. In some schools, induction is a well-defined responsibility of school principals or deputy principals, while in other schools induction responsibilities may be assigned to experienced classroom teachers. Teacher induction is an area that requires further development in Finland.

It is recognized that professional development and inservice programs for teachers are not aligned with initial teacher education and often lack focus on essential areas of teaching and school development. Perhaps the main criticism deals with weak coordination between initial academic teacher education and the continuing professional development of teachers (Ministry of Education, 2009). Municipalities, as the overseers of primary and lower- and upper-secondary schools, are responsible for providing teachers with opportunities for professional development or inservice training, based on their needs. According to the employment contract, there are 3 mandatory professional development days annually in which all teachers must take part that are offered by the local education authorities. It is up to individual teachers or school principals to decide how much time beyond those 3 days and what type of professional development is needed, and whether such interventions, in fact, can be funded.

In Finland, a significant disparity exists among municipalities' and schools' ability to finance professional development for teachers. The main reason for this situation is the way that education is financed. The central government has only a limited influence on budgetary decisions made by municipalities or schools. Therefore, some schools receive significantly more allocations for professional development and school improvement than do others, particularly during times of economic downturn when professional development budgets are often the first to vanish.

Governance of Finnish education is inconsistent throughout the nation. Some schools experience relatively high autonomy over their operations and budgeting. Others do not. Therefore, Finnish teacher professional development appears in many forms. Ideally, the school is the prime decisionmaker regarding the design and delivery of professional development. Schools may also be motivated to lower operating expenses, such as for textbooks, heating, and maintenance, and may divert those funds to teacher development priorities. However, some Finnish municipalities still organize inservice programs uniformly for all teachers and allow little latitude for individual schools to decide what would be more beneficial for them. According to a national survey conducted by the University of Jyväskylä in 2007, on average, teachers devoted about 7 working days (or 50 hours) annually to professional development; approximately half of that was drawn from teachers' personal time (Piesanen, Kiviniemi, & Valkonen, 2007).

Participation in professional development, according to a 2009 report by the Finnish Ministry of Education, is not at an adequate level among Finnish teachers (Ministry of Education, 2009). The government, therefore, is considering ways to strengthen the legal grounds for teacher professional development by requiring that all teachers must have access to adequate professional inservice support, funded by municipalities. According to the National Teacher Survey (National Board of Education, 2014), in 2013 more than 80% of Finnish teachers had participated in some type of professional development during the past year. OECD's TALIS survey confirmed that trend: The participation rate in professional development was 79% among Finnish lower-secondary teachers. In this area, Finland is lagging behind many other countries—the OECD average in that survey was 88%.

The Finnish state budget allocates normally about 30–40 million U.S. dollars each year to the professional development of teachers and school principals through various forms of university courses and inservice training. The main purpose of this investment in human capital is to ensure equal access to further training, particularly for teachers who work in more disadvantaged schools. This professional development support is contracted to service providers on a competitive basis. The government initially determines the focus of the desired training, based on current national educational development needs. Local education authorities that own the schools and also employ all the teachers make an investment of similar scale in the professional development of their education personnel each year. The Ministry of Education, in collaboration with municipalities, plans to double public funding for teacher professional development by 2016.

Finnish teachers possessing a master's degree have the right to engage in doctoral studies to supplement their normal professional development opportunities. Primary school teachers can easily begin their further studies in the faculty of education; their PhD dissertations will then focus on a selected topic in the educational sciences. Many primary school teachers take advantage of this opportunity, often while simultaneously teaching in schools. Doctoral studies in education for subject teachers who have their previous degrees in some other academic field require more work. These teachers must first complete advanced studies in the educational sciences because the main subject requires a shift from a student's initial academic major—for example, chemistry—into education, so that students are qualified to complete their research in education.

TEACHERS ARE LEADERS

Teaching is commonly viewed in Finland as a demanding profession that requires superior academic qualifications, even for teachers of very young students. Since teacher education became part of academic university studies in the 1970s, Finnish teachers' identity and sense of belonging to a highly regarded profession have gradually increased. During the course of Finland's education reforms, as explained in Chapter 1, teachers have demanded more autonomy and responsibility for curriculum planning and student assessment. The professional context of teaching in Finland differs significantly from that in other countries when it comes to the way teachers experience their work. The professionally respectful environment that teachers experience in Finland is an important factor not only for teacher education policies but also for explaining why so many young Finns regard teaching as a much-admired career.

Curriculum planning is the responsibility of teachers, schools, and municipalities, not the state. Most Finnish schools today have their own customized curriculum that is coordinated with and approved by their local education authorities. This correctly implies that teachers and school principals have key roles in curriculum development and school planning. The National Framework Curricula for comprehensive school and for upper-secondary school provide guidance and necessary regulations that each school must keep in mind in its curriculum development activities. However, there are no strict national standards for or descriptions of student learning outcomes that Finnish schools must include in their curriculum, as is true in the United States, Great Britain, or Canada, for example. That is why Finnish curriculum planning and the curricula that result from it can vary from school to school. The teachers' key role in pedagogical decisionmaking clearly requires teacher education to install in all prospective teachers well-developed knowledge and skills related to curriculum development, student assessment theory and practice, and teacher leadership. Moreover, it has shifted the focus of Finnish teacher professional development from fragmented inservice training toward more systemic school improvement that builds better ethical and theoretical grounding for effective teaching.

Another important teacher responsibility is student assessment. As mentioned earlier, Finnish schools do not employ census-based standardized tests to determine their progress or success. There are four primary reasons for this:

1. Education policy in Finland gives high priority to personalized learning and creative teaching as important components of schooling. Therefore, students' progress in school is primarily judged against their respective characteristics and abilities, rather than by a reliance on uniform standards and statistical indicators.

2. Education developers insist that curriculum, teaching, and learning are priority components in education that should necessarily drive teachers' thinking and school practice, rather than focusing on assessment and testing, as is the case in some other education systems. Student assessment in Finnish schools is embedded in teaching and learning processes and is thereby used to improve both teachers' and students' work in school.

3. Determining students' personal and cognitive progress is regarded as a responsibility of the school, not of external assessments or assessors. Most Finnish schools acknowledge some shortcomings, such as comparability or consistency, when teachers do all student assessments and grading. At the same time, there is wide acknowledgment that the problems that are often associated with external standardized testing can be even more troublesome. These problems, according to teachers, include a narrowing curriculum, teaching to the test, and unhealthy competition among schools and teachers. Classroom assessment and school-based evaluation are therefore important and valued components of Finnish teacher education curricula and professional development.

4. The Finnish national strategy for student assessment is based on the principle of diversified evidence in which test-based performance data are just one part of the whole. Data regarding student achievement in various subjects are collected using sample-based standardized tests and thematic reviews. Municipalities are autonomously designing their quality assurance practices according to their needs and aspirations.

The only external "standardized" assessment of student learning is the National Matriculation Examination that students take at the end of upper-secondary school when they are 18 or 19 years old, as described in Chapter 1. It has exerted, many Finnish education specialists argue, a discernible effect on curriculum and teaching in general upper-secondary school.[3]

Although Finnish teachers' work consists primarily of classroom teaching, many of their duties are performed outside of class. Formally, teachers' working time in Finland consists of classroom teaching, preparation (in the case of lab-based subjects such as biology), and 3 hours weekly of planning and development work with colleagues. Unlike in many other nations, Finnish teachers do not need to be present at school if they do not have classes or if the school principal has not requested that they perform other duties.

The average net teaching hours as reported by the governments to the OECD are presented in Figure 3.2. Schools in Finland are autonomous in terms of scheduling their work, but they are required to have a 15-minute recess for every 45-minute lesson, which is often a welcome break for teachers. Recently, schools have sought alternative arrangements to allow more time for teachers to collaborate—for example, combining lessons or classes into longer periods or larger groups and thereby providing more discretionary time during the school day for teachers.

Figure 3.2 reveals notable differences in the average net teaching hours of primary, lower-secondary and upper-secondary teachers between the United States and Finland in 2012. Even if teaching time is adjusted to annual school days, it appears that teachers in Finland spend less time each day in teaching. A question arises: What are Finnish teachers doing when teachers in other countries are still teaching their students? An important—and still voluntary—part of Finnish teachers' work is devoted to school improvement and work with the community. It is worth recalling that Finnish schools are responsible for the design and continuous development of their school curriculum. Students receive their grades from teachers whose duties include designing and conducting appropriate assessments and tests to monitor their students' progress in school. Finnish teachers have accepted curriculum development, experimentation with teaching methods, responsibility to engage in student welfare support, and collaboration with parents as important aspects of their work outside of classrooms. These are also some of the most essential elements of teacher leadership in Finnish schools.

Figure 3.2. Average Net Teaching Time in Hours per School Year in Finland, the United States, and in OECD Countries on Average in 2012

Average annual net teaching time in hours

■ United States   ▨ OECD average   ▨ Finland

Source: OECD (2014a).

Foreign visitors to Finnish schools often ask how teacher effectiveness is determined. They are also curious to know how administrators know which are effective teachers and where bad teachers are. The overall answer is simple: There are no formal teacher evaluation measures in Finland. Because there are no census-based standardized test data about student achievement available, it is not possible to compare school performance or teacher effectiveness in the same ways that it is measured in the United States or Australia. The only exception is the use of matriculation examination results by certain media every spring to rank Finnish high schools according to their students' grades on the exams. That annual early-summer news rarely gets any significant attention from parents or schools.

The questions of teacher effectiveness or the consequences of being an ineffective teacher are not relevant in Finland. As described earlier, teachers have time to work together during the school day and to understand how their colleagues teach. This is an important condition for reflecting on teachers' own teaching and also for building a sense of professional leadership and shared accountability between teachers. The school inspection system that previously provided external feedback and evaluation of how teachers taught and schools operated was abolished in the early 1990s. Today, school principals, aided by their own experience as teachers, are able to help their teachers recognize strengths and areas of work that need improvement. The basic assumption in Finnish schools is that teachers, by default, are well-educated professionals and are doing their best in schools. In real professional learning communities, teachers trust one another, communicate frequently about teaching and learning, and rely on their principals' guidance and leadership.

Internationally, identifying teacher effectiveness has become a new trend in finding ways to improve education. Novel statistical techniques, called value-added modeling (VAM), are intended to resolve the problem of socioeconomic and other differences by adjusting for students' prior achievement and demographic characteristics. Although VAM approaches are fairer comparisons of teachers than judgments of their students' test scores, closer analysis of VAM results has led researchers to doubt whether this methodology can identify good or bad teachers as well as its designers claim (Baker et al., 2010). It is safe to believe that such quantitative measures are rarely the sole or even the primary factor when it comes to identifying a good or poor teacher. Even some management experts from the business world warn against using such measures for making salary or bonus decisions, as has been done, for example, in paying teachers according to their performance merits (using student test scores as the main source of evidence). "In both the United States and Great Britain," reports a review of the problems with using student test scores to evaluate teachers by the Education Policy Institute, "governments have attempted to rank cardiac surgeons by their patients' survival rates, only to find that they had created incentives for surgeons to turn away the sickest patients" (Baker et al., 2010, p. 7). Paying teachers based on their students' standardized test scores is an alien idea in Finland. Authorities and most parents understand that caring for and educating children is too complex a process to be measured by quantitative metrics alone. In Finnish schools, the operational principle is that the quality of teaching and of the school is defined through the mutual interaction between the school and the students, together with their parents. These are also the essential ingredients of teacher leadership in Finland.

SCHOOL LEADERS ARE TEACHERS

Regardless of how well teachers are trained in any education system, consistent high educational performance requires good professional leadership at the school level. Some countries allow their schools to be led by noneducators, hoping that business-style management will raise efficiency and improve performance. Similarly, local education authorities and administrators are sometimes persons without experience in teaching or leading schools. In Finland, educational leadership in municipal education offices is without exception in the hands of professional educators who have experience in working in the field of education. This is an important factor in enhancing communication and building trust between schools and educational administration.

In Finland, school principals have to be qualified to teach in the schools that they lead, and they must have strong track records as teachers. They also must have successfully completed academic studies on educational administration and leadership offered by universities in Finland. This means that a corporate CEO or a retired military chief without these merits would not be qualified to lead a school in Finland. Without an exception the school principal is an experienced teacher with proven leadership competencies and a suitable personality. In many schools, principals also have a small number of classes that they teach themselves each week. According to TALIS 2013, three out of four lower-secondary school principals in Finland have teaching duties in school, compared to just one-third of principals with teaching responsibilities in TALIS countries on average (OECD, 2014b). Pedagogical leadership is one of the key areas of professional school leadership in Finland. Teachers rely on their leaders' vision and the principal understands and trusts teachers' work. Therefore, leadership and management in Finnish schools are informal but effective, as foreign observers have witnessed (Hargreaves, Halasz, & Pont, 2008).

Before the 1990s, becoming a school principal was often a reward for successful service as a teacher. In some cases, however, a rather young teacher was appointed as a school leader. Leadership experience or qualities were rarely examined when filling an open principal's post in schools. Nor did school principals need to be experts in administration, financial management, or political lobbying as they must today. In the early 1990s, this situation rapidly changed. One driver of this change was the sudden decentralization of public sector management and educational administration in Finland at that time. A new financing scheme that increased the autonomy of the municipalities immediately affected schools in most parts of the country. School principals offered to control their school budgets; in some cases, that included teachers' salaries and all recurrent costs.

Second, and a related driver of change, was an unexpected financial crisis that hit Finland harder than many other Western countries in the early 1990s. School principals became the operational arms of the municipalities in deciding how forthcoming budget cuts, which were typically double-digit in magnitude, would be managed. Finnish school principals found themselves in a situation similar to that of corporate CEOs who had to adjust their firms into shrinking markets. The nostalgic image of the head of the school had changed. Major educational changes—such as the curriculum reforms of 1994—have been implemented successfully primarily due to the professional attitude and pedagogical leadership of school principals. Ever since, this leadership community in Finland has served as a critical voice in shaping education policies and steering school improvement based on the needs of teachers, students, and society. Based on these experiences, it is difficult to imagine that market-based education reforms, which often undermine the central role of pedagogical leadership, could have been implemented in Finland. School principals have been the first to stand between these intentions and the well-being of schools.

GOOD TEACHERS, GREAT SCHOOLS

What else did OECD's TALIS 2013 reveal about Finland's lower-secondary teachers? The following are some of the main conclusions (OECD, 2014b). First of all, about three out of five teachers feel that their profession is valued in society, which is well above the average of 31% in the other 33 countries that took part in TALIS. Survey data show that when schools provide staff with the opportunity to participate in school decisionmaking, teachers are more likely to feel that teaching is a valued profession. Second, the vast majority of teachers in Finland report being satisfied with their work. More specifically, 95% of teachers report that the advantages of being a teacher outweigh the disadvantages; this is well above the average of 77% in the other countries surveyed. Similarly, 85% of Finnish lower-secondary school teachers would choose the profession again and just 5% of teachers regret becoming a teacher, compared with the averages of 78% and 9%, respectively, in other countries. Finally, 91% of teachers in Finland report that they are satisfied with their jobs.

However, TALIS 2013 also casts some worrying shadows on teachers and the teaching profession in Finland. First, 28% of lower-secondary school teachers in Finland said that they were not at all or only somewhat prepared for teaching the content of their subjects, while more than one-third reported being not at all or only somewhat prepared to teach their subjects' pedagogy or practical components. This is surprising and stands in contradiction with Finnish research on teachers' preparedness to work after their initial teacher education (Niemi, 2011). In these studies, Finnish teachers said they felt competent with planning, teaching methods, student assessment, and mastering the content. Conflict resolution, collaboration with parents, and teaching children with special needs are commonly viewed as weaker areas in new teachers' professional repertoires. Second, there is no common framework for teacher appraisal in Finland. Therefore, almost 28% of teachers in Finland teach in a school where the principal reports that teachers are not formally appraised by the principal. Instead, the main form of appraisal occurs through face-to-face and often informal dialogue with the school leader. Third, 37% of Finnish lower-secondary school teachers report that they have never received feedback on their teaching in school. Countries differ in the proportion receiving feedback and on the sources of feedback. The proportion of teachers who had never received feedback on their teaching was 7% in Alberta, 14% in Australia, and 1% in Singapore. In that context, 42% of teachers in Finland report having received feedback from their principal and 43% said they received feedback from other teachers in their schools.

These internationally low rates of formal teacher appraisal and feedback on teaching may partially be explained by rather informal collegial personal relations in Finnish schools. But if just 38% of teachers in Finland report a moderate or large positive change in teaching practices following the feedback—the lowest number of all surveyed countries— then this may point a chronic problem in Finland's lower-secondary schools. Designing appraisal and feedback systems could be an opportunity to speed up school improvement and the professional development of teachers in Finland. TALIS 2013 data suggest that teachers who think that appraisal and feedback positively influence their work report higher confidence in their teaching skills.

In summary, what are the relative strengths of teacher education in Finland, based on international perspectives? First, although the

Bologna Process directs overall European higher education structures and policies, it doesn't stipulate how signatory nations should design curricula or arrange their teacher education. There are, and will continue to be, significant differences in national teacher education policies and practices among European education systems. Within this mosaic of European teacher education systems, Finland has three peculiarities.

1. Talented and motivated individuals go into teaching. Since it shifted primary school teacher education to the universities and upgraded teacher diplomas to a required master's degree in the late 1970s, Finland has attracted some of its most talented and motivated youth to become teachers. As described earlier, there is a strong cultural influence in the career planning of young Finns, but that alone does not explain the sustained popularity of teaching. Two other salient factors may be identified. First, the required master's degree in educational sciences provides a competitive professional foundation, not only for becoming employed as a primary school teacher but also for many other careers, including education administration and work in the private sector. All graduating teachers are fully eligible to enroll in doctoral studies, which are still tuition-free in Finland. Second, many young Finns select teaching as their primary career because work in schools is perceived as an autonomous, independent, highly regarded profession, comparable to working as a medical doctor, lawyer, or architect, for example. Increased external control over teachers' work in schools through test-based accountability or centrally mandated regulation would likely deflect more bright young people to other professional careers where they have freedom to make use of their own creativity and initiative.

2. There is close collaboration between subject faculties and departments of teacher education in Finnish research universities. Subject teacher education is organized collaboratively and is coordinated to ensure both a solid mastery of the subjects to be taught and state-of-the-art pedagogical competences for all graduates. Faculties in Finnish universities perceive teacher education as an important component of their academic programs. Lecturers and some professors in the subject faculties have specialized in the teaching of their own disciplines, which has enhanced cooperation among teacher educators. Faculties of education and various subjects within the university are also positively interdependent: They can achieve sustainable success only when all of them do their best.

3. Teacher education is research-based. Teacher education in Finland is also recognized because of its systematic and research-based structure. All graduating teachers, by the nature of their degree, have completed research-based master's theses accompanied by rigorous academic requirements of theory, methodology, and critical reflection equal to any other field of study in Finnish universities at that level. Research orientation to teacher education prepares teachers, at all levels, to work in complex, changing societal and educational environments. Research-based academic training has also enabled the implementation of more radical national education policies. For example, enhanced professional competencies have led to putting increased trust in teachers and schools regarding curriculum planning, student assessment, reporting of student performance, and school improvement. Finland has successfully integrated research, knowledge of content and didactics, and practice into its teacher education programs.

Indeed, this research focus carries a twofold significance for teacher education. Research findings establish the professional basis for teachers to teach and work effectively within a complex knowledge society. Teacher education—within any society—has the potential to progress as an effective field of professional activity only through and from robust contemporary empirical, scientific inquiry. *Professionalism* as the main characteristic of teaching requires teachers to be able to access and follow ongoing developments in their own profession and to freely implement new knowledge within their own instructional work. Thus, further development of Finnish teacher education must necessarily be built upon ongoing, high-quality, internationally relevant research and development achievements.

What can we learn from Finland's teacher policies? Education reformers often argue that the way to improve schools is simply to have better teachers. The Finnish experience suggests that real life in schools is more complicated than that. Drawing from what Finland and other high-performing school systems have done to get the most out of their schools, two conditions must exist regarding teachers.

First, teachers and students must teach and learn in an environment that empowers them to do their best. When teachers have more control over curriculum design, teaching methods, and student assessment, they are more inspired to teach than when they are pressured to deliver prescribed programs and must submit to external standardized tests that determine progress. Similarly, when students are encouraged to find their own ways of learning without fear of failure, most will study and learn more than when they're driven to achieve the same standards under the pressure of regular testing.

I've argued elsewhere (Sahlberg, 2013a) that if education policies prevent teachers and students from doing what they think is necessary for good outcomes, even the best teachers will not be able to make significant improvements. Competition among schools over enrollment, standardized teaching and learning, and test-based accountability are the most common toxic aspects of today's school systems globally. These are the wrong means for sustainable improvement, and they are often the main reason why so many teachers leave the profession earlier than planned.

Second, teaching is a complex profession that requires advanced academic education. Current trends in many parts of the world suggest just the opposite: If you're smart, the thinking goes, you can teach because teaching is not rocket science; with clear guidelines and specific standards in hand, almost anyone can teach. In some countries, for example, retired military personnel are being converted into teachers and principals to address the teacher shortage caused by teachers who leave the profession early. In some other countries, teachers are licensed to teach through online courses or fast-track arrangements that give them only limited involvement in real classroom life or work in school prior to their employment.

Teaching will become a more popular career choice among young people if the basic qualification to become a teacher is elevated to a master's degree on a par with what is needed for other esteemed professions. Professional leadership will flourish among teachers only if they have the autonomy to influence what and how they teach and to determine how well their students are performing. Achieving these essential elements requires a scientific approach to teacher education, in which curriculum, pedagogy, assessment, school improvement, professional development, and systematic clinical practice play an integral part. This is the first lesson that can be learned from Finland.

Many visitors to Finland wonder why the Finnish education system hasn't been infected by the market-based reform ideas that are so prevalent around the world. The answer is simple: Teachers in Finland are prepared to resist these ideas because of their advanced academic education and the collaborative nature of their profession, just as medical doctors would reject any suggested cure for a disease if it were not based on reliable experiments and research. Not only are better-educated teachers more effective in the classroom, but they're also better equipped to keep their education systems healthy and free from reform ideas that are harmful to both teachers and children.

Finnish teacher education's greatest potential lies in the hundreds of talented and motivated young people who, year after year, seek enrollment in teacher education programs. This is a crucial factor for the continued and future success of teacher education in Finland. Young Finns gravitate toward teaching because they regard it as an independent, respected, and rewarding profession within which they will have freedom to fulfill their aspirations. However, general upper-secondary school graduates also weigh the quality of teacher education programs when they make decisions about their future career. It is therefore paramount that Finnish teacher education continues to develop in order to ensure that, in the future, it remains an attractive and competitive option for highly able young people.

Teachers' professional status in Finnish society is a cultural phenomenon, but how teachers become prepared to teach in classrooms and work collaboratively in professional communities is attributable to systematically designed and implemented academic teacher education. For other nations, imitating the Finnish curriculum system or organizational aspects of schools may not be a wise strategy. However, a positive lesson that Finns themselves have learned by raising the level of teacher education on par with other academic pursuits certainly merits closer examination. A critical condition for attracting the most able young people year after year to teacher education is that a teacher's work should represent an independent and respected profession rather than merely focusing on the technical implementation of externally mandated standards, endless tests, and administrative burdens. Indeed, teaching is not rocket science—it is much harder than that. This is the second lesson that Finland can offer to others.

WHAT IF FINLAND'S GREAT TEACHERS TAUGHT IN YOUR SCHOOLS?

I have been privileged to meet and host scores of foreign education delegations to Finland in recent years in their quest to build higher-performing school systems in their own countries. What most of these visitors take away is that Finland has a highly standardized teacher education system that requires all teachers to hold master's degrees that can be only earned in the country's research universities. Therefore, competition in these teacher education programs is tough. A visit to any of the Finnish universities reveals that Finland, just like Singapore, South Korea, and Japan, has strict control over the quality of applicants at their entry into teacher education and only the best candidates will be accepted. The number of accepted students accurately corresponds with the needs in the labor market after their graduation. Many guests realize that allowing "bad" teachers to enter teaching in Finnish schools rarely happens.

As a consequence of these lessons from Finland, I have often heard people wondering if the quality of their own schools and entire education system would improve if only they had teachers like the Finns have—just as having good teachers has improved schools in Finland, Singapore, and South Korea, for example. There has been a global movement to turn attention to teacher quality and how it might be improved. Indeed, the desire to enhance teacher quality comes from the lessons learned from education systems that score high on international student assessments. Each of these successful systems has managed to create a situation where teaching is regarding by young people as an interesting career choice. Most teachers in these countries spend most of their working lives serving schools. From the international perspective, however, there are three myths related to teacher quality and school improvement that often steer education policies in the wrong direction in countries where the teaching profession has declined in status (Sahlberg, 2013b).

The first myth is that *the most important single factor in improving quality of education is teachers.* This is what the former Washington, DC school chancellor Michelle Rhee said in *Waiting for "Superman"* in 2010 and what many other school "reformers" repeat in their change rhetoric. If this wasn't a myth, then the power of a school would indeed be stronger than children's family background or other out-of-school factors, and all children would achieve more if only there were good enough teachers in all schools. This myth has often led to the conclusion that what needs to be done first is to get rid of poorly performing teachers. However, there are two points of evidence that show this notion is indeed a myth.

First, since the Coleman Report in 1966, several studies have confirmed that a significant part of the variance in student achievement can be attributed to out-of-school factors such as parents' education and occupations, peer influence, and students' individual characteristics. Half a century later, research on what explains students' measured performance in school concludes that 10–20% of the variance in measured student achievement can be attributed to classrooms—that is, teachers and teaching—and a similar amount of the variance comes from factors within schools—that is, school climate, facilities, and leadership. In other words, up to two-thirds of what explains student achievement falls beyond the control of schools.

Second, over 30 years of systematic research on school effectiveness and school improvement reveals a number of characteristics that are typical of more effective schools (Teddlie, 2010). Although school effectiveness research shows mixed findings, most scholars agree that effective leadership is among the most important characteristics of effective schools, equally important as effective teaching. Effective leadership includes leader qualities, such as being firm and purposeful, having a shared vision and goals, promoting teamwork and collegiality, and frequent personal monitoring and feedback. Several other characteristics of more effective schools include features that are also linked to the culture of the school and leadership: maintaining focus on learning, producing a positive school climate, setting high expectations for all, developing staff skills, and involving parents. In other words, school leadership matters as much as teachers do.

The second myth is that *the quality of an education system cannot exceed the quality of its teachers*. This statement became known in education policies through the influential McKinsey & Company report titled *How the World's Best Performing School Systems Come out on Top* (Barber & Mourshed, 2007, p. 40). The same argument appears in the most recent and very influential PISA reports (OECD, 2013d, p. 96). Although these reports take a broader view on enhancing status of teachers by paying them better and by selecting initial candidates for teacher education programs more carefully, the impact of this statement is that the quality of an education system is a simple sum of the efforts of its individuals—in other words, of its teachers. By saying this, the authors assume that teachers work independently from one another and that what one teacher does doesn't affect the work of the others. This is a narrow human capital view to change. However, in most schools today, in Finland, the United States, and elsewhere, teachers work as teams and the outcome of their work is a joint effort of the whole school. This myth therefore undermines the impact of teamwork and the social capital that it creates in most schools today.

This myth has found its way into several national education policy documents and reform programs today. However, there are studies on team-based school culture and the role of collegiality in school that show how enhanced social capital through professional collaboration in school can increase teachers' effect on students' learning in school. This is the main principle of *Professional Capital* (2012), an award-winning book by Andy Hargreaves and Michael Fullan. The role of an individual teacher in a school is like that of a player on a football team: All teachers are vital, but the collegial culture and teachers' professional judgment in the school are even more important for the quality of the school. Team sports offer numerous examples of teams that have performed beyond expectations because of leadership, commitment, and spirit. Take the U.S. ice hockey team in the 1980 Winter Olympics, when a team of college kids beat both the Soviets and Finland in the final round to win the gold medal. The overall quality of the U.S. team certainly exceeded the quality of its individual players. The same can be said for schools in the education system.

The third myth is that *if any children had three or four great teachers in a row, they would soar academically, regardless of their socioeconomic background, while those who have a sequence of weak teachers will fall further and further behind.* This theoretical assumption appeared in an important policy recommendation called *Essential Elements of Teacher Policy in ESEA: Effectiveness, Fairness and Evaluation* (Center for American Progress & The Education Trust) presented to the U.S. Congress in 2011. Great teachers and great teaching here, again, are measured by the growth of students' test scores on standardized measurements.

The assumption that students would perform well if they simply had more great teachers presents a view that education reform alone could overcome the powerful influence of family and social environment mentioned earlier. It means that schools should get rid of low-performing teachers and hire only great ones. This myth has the most practical difficulties. The first one is related to what it means to be a great teacher. Even if this were clear, it would be difficult to know exactly who is a great teacher at the time of recruitment. Becoming a great teacher normally takes 5 to 10 years of systematic practice, and to reliably determine the "effectiveness" of any teacher would require at least 5 years of consistent, accurate data. This would, in general, be practically impossible.

Let's return to the question in the heading of this section. Imagine that we could transport Finnish teachers and school principals who all hold master's degrees and have been through highly regarded teacher preparation to teach in, say, Indiana in the United States. Indiana's own teachers and principals would go and work in Finnish schools. (Imagine that there would be no language barriers.) After 5 years—assuming that education policies in both Indiana and Finland would continue as they have been going—we would check what had happened to students' test scores on mandatory student assessments. I argue that if there were any gains in Indiana students' achievement, they would be only marginal. Why? Education policies in Indiana and in many other states in the United States create a professional and social context for teaching that would limit the Finnish teachers when it comes to using their knowledge, experience, and passion for the good of their students' learning. I have met some experienced Finnish teachers who teach in the United States, and they confirm my earlier hypothetical reasoning. Based on what I have heard from some of them, it is also probable that many of those transported Finnish teachers would already be doing something else other than teaching by the end of the 5th year—like their American peers. The other question is: Would Finnish school ratings collapse as a consequence of America teachers teaching in its schools? Most likely not. The educational culture in Finland would try to assist any teachers who cannot perform according to expectations. Less time in the classroom would provide these foreign teachers with more time to work with their colleagues and find better ways to help their students become successful.

Everybody agrees that the importance of the teaching profession and the quality of teaching in contributing to learning outcomes is beyond question. It is therefore understandable that teacher quality is often cited as the most important in-school variable influencing student achievement. But just having better teachers in schools will not automatically translate into better learning outcomes. Lessons from high-performing school systems, including Finland, suggest that we must reconsider the way we think about teaching as a profession and what the role of the school is in our society. Rather than dreaming about having teachers like those in Finland, Canada, or Singapore, national policymakers should consider the following three aspects affecting the teaching profession.

First, teacher education should be more standardized and at the same time teaching and learning should be less standardized. Singapore, Canada, and Finland all set high standards for their teacher preparation programs in academic universities. They don't allow fast-track pathways into teaching or alternative training that doesn't include studying theories of pedagogy and related clinical practice. All these countries make it a priority to have strict quality control before anybody will be allowed to teach.

Second, the toxic use of accountability for schools should be redesigned. Current practices in many countries that judge the quality of teachers by counting their students' measured achievement alone is in many ways inaccurate and unfair. It is inaccurate because most schools' goals are broader than just good performance in a few academic subjects. It is unfair because most of the variation in student achievement on standardized tests can be explained by out-of-school factors. In education systems that score high in international rankings, teachers feel that they are empowered by their leaders and other teachers. In Finland, the TALIS 2013 survey shows that teachers find their profession rewarding because of professional autonomy and the social prestige that comes with it.

Third, changing teacher policies is not enough to make the teaching profession attractive—other school policies must be changed, too. The experiences of those countries that do well in international rankings suggest that teachers should have autonomy in planning their work, freedom to use teaching methods that they know lead to best results, and authority to influence the assessment of the outcomes of their work. Schools and teachers must also be trusted in these key areas of teaching for the teaching profession to really become an attractive career choice for more young people.

CHAPTER 4

The Finnish Way

Competitive Welfare State

Real winners do not compete.

—Samuli Paronen, Finnish author, 1917–1974

What makes Finnish education unique is its steady progress from a system that was barely at international averages to one of the rare strong public educational performers today. Equally important, Finland has been able to create a network of schools where nearly everybody succeeds and failure is rare. Simultaneously, participation in and graduation from post-compulsory education in Finland—both upper-secondary and higher education—have increased significantly. The success of Finnish education has been frequently noted by global media and various education development agencies. This exceptional development was not accomplished by following the same education reform principles that are dominant in the United States, England, Australia, and much of the rest of the world.

Finland has a competitive national economy, low levels of corruption, good quality of life, a strong sustainable-development lifestyle, and gender equality. These qualities make Finland one of the most prosperous nations in the world. The success of Finland as a small, remote European nation has been built upon flexibility and a solution orientation in all aspects of society. In Finland's education system, these principles have enabled schools to experiment with creativity and take risks while seeking to reach set goals, whether these goals represent effective teaching or productive learning. This is in harmony with policies and strategies in other areas of the public sector. Especially interesting has been the close interplay between education policies and economic strategies since the early 1990s.

This chapter discusses in more detail how education policies in Finland have responded to international educational reform ideas and how they are linked to the overall development of the knowledge economy and welfare state. It describes the increased interdependency among public sector policies in Finland since 1970, and presents a tentative typology to compare education reform principles and economic development policies in Finland. The main point of this chapter is that education policies for system excellence need to be based on a systems view of policymaking and sustainable leadership that does not undermine complex relationships between different public sector policies in these societies.

THE POWER OF GLOBALIZATION

Internationalization has shaped Finland and the lives of its people during the past 2 decades. Membership in the European Union and an active role in the OECD have increased individual mobility and the exchange of policies between Finland and the rest of the developed world. Finnish people, however, remain divided regarding globalization. Many think that globalization is leading to a diminishing role for nation-states and the loss of their sovereignty, as a result of the emergence of global hegemony of transnational money, media, and entertainment corporations. Others argue that standardization in economies, policies, and cultures has become a new norm for competitive corporations and nations, thus diminishing Finnish customs and traditions. Changes in global culture also deeply affect educational policies, practices, and institutions. It is obvious that there is no straightforward view of the consequences of the globalization process on educational policies.

Globalization is a cultural paradox: It simultaneously unifies and diversifies people and cultures. It unifies national education policies by integrating them with broader global trends. Because problems and challenges are similar from one education system to the next, solutions and education reform agendas are also becoming similar. As a result of the international benchmarking of education systems by using common indicators and international comparisons of student achievement, the distinguishing features of different education systems are becoming more visible. For example, PISA has mobilized scores of politicians and education experts to visit other places, especially Finland, Canada, Singapore, Shanghai, and Korea, in order to learn how to redefine their own education policies and improve schools. As a consequence, globalization has also accelerated international collaboration, the exchange of ideas, and the transfer of education policies among education systems.

Analyzing global policy developments and education reforms has become a common practice in many ministries of education, development agencies, and consultant firms. Therefore, the world's education systems are beginning to share some core values, functions, and structures, and evidently they look alike. The question arises whether increased global interaction among policymakers and educators, especially the benchmarking of education systems through agreed-upon indicators and the borrowing and lending of educational policies, has promoted common approaches to education reform throughout the world.

Change knowledge in education has been created and disseminated predominantly by English-speaking countries. The United States, Canada, and the United Kingdom in the West and Australia, New Zealand and Singapore in the Asia-Pacific region have become the centers of gravity for research and debate on school improvement, school effectiveness, and educational change. Two academic journals, *School Effectiveness and School Improvement* (established in 1990) and the *Journal of Educational Change* (established in 2000), are the key forums within which contemporary knowledge is communicated.[1] Beyond the Anglo-Saxon world, the Netherlands, Sweden, Spain, and Norway have engaged most actively in international dialogue and research on educational change. Surprisingly, Finland, Korea, and Japan—all countries with high-performing and equitable education systems—have had only a modest role in the generation of global knowledge about change. Each of these countries has relied heavily on the research and innovation from the United States, United Kingdom, Australia, and Canada.

In the business of global education development, it is important to be a critical consumer of the available evidence and research. Indeed, rather than shifting emphasis toward standardized knowledge of content and mastery of routine skills, some advanced education systems are focusing on flexibility, risk taking, creativity, and problem solving through modern methods of teaching combined with community networks and smart technologies. The number of examples is increasing, including China, an economic power that is loosening its standardized control over education by gradually making school-based curriculum a national policy priority (Zhao, 2014). Japan and Singapore are adopting the idea of "less is more" in teaching in order to make room for creativity and innovation (OECD, 2011a). One of the highest-performing Canadian provinces, Alberta, is loosening its grip on schools by removing standardized provincial assessments and creating more intelligent accountability policies, which focus on authentic learning and variety of student assessment methods. Wales has done this already. Scotland is also building smarter curriculum and accountability practices by staying away from heavy-handed external testing and school inspection. Even in England, once the most test-intensive education system in the world, the government is putting an end to all standardized testing in primary schools.

As a reaction to the overemphasis on knowledge-based teaching and test-based accountability, authorities around the world are considering more dynamic forms of curriculum, introducing new forms of accountability, and enhancing leadership in education in order to find alternative instructional approaches that promote the productive learning required in knowledge economies. Instead of focusing on single institutions, education reforms are beginning to encourage networking of schools and communities. At the core of this idea is *complementarity*—that is, cooperation between schools and districts and striving for better learning in the network. Clustering and networking also appear to be core factors in nations' economic competitiveness and efforts to cope with globalization.

Although the improvement of education systems is a global phenomenon, there is no reliable, recent comparative analysis about how education reforms in different countries have been designed and implemented. However, the professional literature indicates that the focus on educational development has shifted from structural reforms to improving the quality of and access to education (Hargreaves, Lieberman, Fullan, & Hopkins, 2010). As a result, curriculum development, student assessment, teacher evaluation, integration of information and communication technologies into teaching and learning, and proficiency in basic competencies (that is, reading, writing, and arithmetic) and in scientific literacy have become common priorities in education reforms around the world. In order to bring about these changes in schools, governments employ often outdated and bad management models from the corporate world, such as competition between schools, standardization of teaching and learning, punitive test-based accountability, ill-informed performance-based pay, and data-driven decisionmaking. I call this the Global Educational Reform Movement (Sahlberg, 2006a, 2007, 2010a).

THE GLOBAL EDUCATIONAL REFORM MOVEMENT

The idea of the Global Educational Reform Movement, or simply GERM, evolves from the increased international exchange of policies and practices. It is not a formal global policy program, but rather an unofficial educational agenda that relies on a certain set of assumptions to improve education systems (Hargreaves, Earl, Moore, & Manning, 2001; Hargreaves & Shirley, 2009; Sahlberg, 2011). GERM has emerged since the 1980s and is one concrete offspring of globalization in education. It has become accepted as "a new educational orthodoxy" within many recent education reforms throughout the world, including reforms in the United States, many parts of Australia, Canada, the United Kingdom, some Scandinavian countries, and an increasing number of countries in the developing world.[2]

Tellingly, GERM is promoted through the strategies and interests of multinational private corporations, supranational development agencies, international donors, private foundations, and consulting firms through their interventions in national education reforms and policymaking processes around the world. In developing countries, global and regional development banks; in industrial nations, OECD and the International Monetary Fund (IMF); in the United States, wealthy corporations and their foundations as well as Pearson, McKinsey, and other influential companies have been the advocates of corporate models to national policymakers. Diane Ravitch (2013) has described how venture philanthropy injects billions of dollars into public education systems in the United States—and, to a lesser extent, in some other countries—and often insists on employing management concepts and principles borrowed from the business world in the school systems. By doing so, it promotes the viral spread of GERM not only within the United States but globally. There are only a small number of private foundations that provide funds to public education in Finland, and they have to operate under the close supervision of the authorities. Their influence on education policies or the direction of education reforms is next to none.

The inspiration for the emergence of GERM comes from three primary sources. The first is the new paradigm of learning that became dominant in the 1980s. The breakthrough of cognitive and constructivist approaches to learning gradually shifted the focus of education reforms from teaching to learning. According to this paradigm, the intended outcomes of schooling emphasize greater conceptual understanding, problem solving, emotional and multiple intelligences, and interpersonal skills, rather than the memorization of facts or the mastery of irrelevant skills. At the same time, however, the need for proficiency in literacy and numeracy has also become a prime target of education reforms.

The second inspiration is the public demand for guaranteed, effective learning for all pupils. The global campaign called Education for

All has been influential in shifting the policy focus in education from teaching of some to learning for all. Inclusive education arrangements and the introduction of common learning standards for all have been offered as means to promote the ideal of education for all. This has led, generally speaking, to raising expectations for all students through national curricula and common programs.

The third inspiration is the competition and accountability movement in education that has accompanied the global wave of decentralization of public services. Making schools and teachers compete for students and resources and then holding them accountable for the results (that is, student test scores), this movement has led to the introduction of education standards, indicators and benchmarks for teaching and learning, aligned assessments and testing, and prescribed curricula. As James Popham (2007) has noted, various forms of test-based accountability have emerged where school performance and raising the quality of education are closely tied to the processes of accreditation, promotion, sanctions, and financing. In other words, education has become a commodity where the efficiency of service delivery ultimately determines performance.

Since the 1980s, at least five globally common features of education policies and reform principles have been employed in attempts to improve the quality of education, especially in terms of raising student achievement. The first is increasing *competition* among schools. Almost all education systems have introduced alternative forms of schooling to offer parents more *choice* regarding their children's schooling (OECD, 2013d). The voucher system in Chile in the 1980s, free schools in Sweden in the 1990s, charter schools in the United States in the 2000s, and secondary academies in England in the 2010s are examples of faith in competition as an engine of betterment of education. At the same time, the proportion of more advantaged students studying in private schools or independent schools has grown (OECD, 2013d). In Australia, for example, nearly every third primary and secondary school student studies in nongovernmental schools (Jensen, Weidmann, & Farmer, 2013). Ranking schools based on their performance on national standardized assessments has further increased competition between schools. OECD data show that according to school principals across OECD countries, more than three-quarters of the students assessed by PISA attend schools that compete with at least one other school for enrollment (OECD, 2013d). Finally, students—especially in many Asian countries—experience stronger pressure to perform better against their peers due to tough competition for entry into the best high schools and universities (Zhao, 2014).

The second is *standardization* in education. Outcomes-based education reform became popular in the 1980s, followed by standards-based education policies in the 1990s, initially within Anglo-Saxon countries. These reforms, quite correctly, shifted the focus of attention to educational outcomes—that is, to student learning and school performance. Consequently, a widely accepted—and generally unquestioned—belief among policymakers and education reformers is that setting clear and sufficiently high performance standards for schools, teachers, and students will necessarily improve the quality of desired outcomes. The enforcement of external standardized testing and school evaluation systems to judge how these standards have been attained emerged originally from these standards-driven education policies. Standardization draws from an assumption that all students should be educated to the same, ambitious learning targets. This notion, in turn, has led to the prevalence of prescribed curricula and homogenization of curriculum policies worldwide. The National Curriculum in England in the 1990s, the New National Education Standards in Germany in the 2010s, and the Common Core State Standards in the United States are examples of attempts to bring coherence and quality to teaching and learning in all schools.

The third common feature of the global education reform movement is *focus on core subjects* in the curriculum, such as literacy and numeracy. Basic student knowledge and skills in reading, writing, mathematics, and natural sciences are elevated as prime targets and indices of education reforms. Due to the acceptance of international student assessments such as OECD's PISA and IEA's TIMSS and PIRLS as metrics of educational performance, these core subjects have now come to dominate what pupils study, teachers teach, schools emphasize, and national education policies prioritize in most parts of the world. According to the OECD and research in a number of countries, national education policies are increasingly being influenced by the international student assessments, especially PISA. Breakspear (2012) summarizes PISA's policy influence:

> The results make clear that PISA is becoming an influential element of education policymaking processes at the national level. Furthermore, the findings provide preliminary evidence that PISA is being used and integrated within national/federal policies and practices of assessment and evaluation, curriculum standards and performance targets. (p. 27)

Literacy and numeracy strategies that increased instruction time for so-called core subjects in England and Ontario are concrete programmatic examples of the global educational reform movement. In the United States, the No Child Left Behind legislation led most school districts to steal teaching time from other subjects—especially from social studies, arts, and music—and playtime from children by abolishing recess in many schools so students would be better prepared for state tests that measured student performance in literacy and mathematics (Jennings & Stark Rentner, 2006; Robert Wood Johnson Foundation, 2010). At the same time, however, to be successful in life and employment requires young people who are curious, who know how to work with other people, who can solve difficult problems, and who master leadership.

The fourth characteristic is *test-based accountability*—holding teachers and schools accountable for students' achievement through external standardized tests. School performance—especially raising students' measured achievement—is intimately tied to the processes of evaluating, inspecting, and rewarding or punishing schools and teachers. Performance-based pay, data walls in teachers' lounges, and school rankings in newspapers are examples of new accountability mechanisms that often draw their data primarily from external standardized student tests and teacher evaluations. The problem with test-based accountability is not that students, teachers, and schools are held accountable per se, but rather the way accountability mechanisms affect teachers' work and students' studying in school. Whenever school accountability relies on poor-quality and low-cost standardized tests, as is the case in many places, accountability becomes what is left when responsibility is subtracted.

The fifth globally observable trend in educational reform is *school choice*. Parental choice is an idea that became commonly known as a consequence of Milton Friedman's economic theories in the 1950s. Friedman and many of his disciples and advisees—including president Ronald Reagan—believe that parents must be given the freedom to choose their children's education, thereby encouraging healthy competition among schools so that they better serve families' diverse needs. Typically, school choice manifests itself through the emergence of private schools where parents pay tuition for their children's education. Today, there are scores of various types of alternative schools other than fee-based private schools to expand choice in education markets. Charter schools in the United States, free schools in Sweden, upper-secondary school academies in England, and religious schools in the Netherlands are examples of mechanisms to advance parental choice. School choice ideology maintains that parents should be able to use the public funds set aside for their children's education to choose the schools—public or private—that work best for them.

In 2009, the U.S. Department of Education launched a competitive grant program named Race to the Top (RTTT), which was intended to encourage and reward states that are creating conditions for innovation and reform. With its $4.35 billion budget, this program was designed to spur reforms in state and local district education by developing teacher and principal evaluation systems that substantially relied on measures of student achievement and growth. It encourages competition among states and also between districts as they seek more effective practices and practitioners. According to the Education Policy Institute's evaluation conducted by their partner organization Broader, Bolder Approach to Education in 2013, RTTT policies had fallen short in terms of teacher improvement and had failed to address the core drivers of opportunity gaps. Furthermore, RTTT's shortcomings have spurred state–district and union–management conflicts that hinder progress. The evaluation (Weiss, 2013, p. 8) concludes that "overall, this assessment finds that the key tenet of Race to the Top—that a state hold teachers and schools accountable before helping them establish foundations for success—is deeply flawed." Among other experts, Diane Ravitch (2013) has made similar conclusions about this federal reform program. Table 4.1 also illustrates how education policies in Finland since the 1980s have been almost the opposite those suggested by RTTT.

There are others who have analyzed global educational change efforts. Ben Levin (1998) has written about an epidemic of education policy and analyzed the condition in which educational ideas can and cannot be transported across the borders. Andy Hargreaves and Dennis Shirley (2009) have described global educational change by using the metaphor of "Ways" in their book *The Fourth Way*, to which I will return later in this chapter. Michael Fullan (2011) has used the term "drivers of change," such as education policy or strategy levers, which have the best chances of catalyzing intended change in education systems. "In the rush to move forward," writes Fullan (2011, p. 5), "leaders, especially from countries that have not been progressing, tend to choose the wrong drivers." These include accountability (versus professionalism), individual teacher quality (versus collegiality), technology (versus pedagogy), and fragmented strategies (versus systems thinking). These ineffective elements of education reform, which resonate closely with the aspects of GERM discussed above, have fundamentally missed the targets (see

Figures 2.5 and 2.12 in Chapter 2) and continue to do so, according to Fullan. In his analysis of whole-system reforms in the United States and Australia, he goes even further:

> There is no way that these ambitious and admirable nationwide goals will be met with strategies being used. No successful system has ever led with these drivers. They cannot generate on a large scale the kind of intrinsic motivational energy that will be required to transform these massive systems. The US and Australian aspirations sound great as goals but crumble from a strategy or driver perspective. (Fullan, 2011, p. 7)

None of the elements of GERM shown in Table 4.1 has been adopted in Finland in the ways that they have been within the education policies of many other nations. This, of course, does not imply that there is no educational standardization, learning of basic skills, or accountability in Finnish schools. Nor does it suggest that there is a black-and-white distinction between each of these elements in Finland vis-à-vis other countries. But, perhaps, it does imply that a good education system can be created using alternative policies that are the opposite of those commonly found and promoted in global education policy markets.

GERM has had significant consequences for teachers' work and students' learning in schools wherever it has been a dominant driver of change (Sahlberg, in press). The most notable impact is the standardization of educational and pedagogical processes. Performance standards set by educational authorities and consultants have been brought into the lives of teachers and students without a full understanding that most of what pupils need to learn in school cannot be formulated as a clear standard. New forms of student assessments and testing that have been aligned to these standards are often disappointments and even bring new problems to schools. However, because the standardization agenda promises significant gains in efficiency and quality of education, it has been widely accepted as a basic ideology of change, both politically and professionally.

The voices of practitioners are rarely heard in the education policy and reform business. The educational change literature is primarily technical discourse created by academics or change consultants. Therefore, I devote space here to a school improvement practitioner from Scotland. This example is particularly relevant because Scotland is currently recovering from a rather serious GERM infection that occurred a few years back. The symptoms included top-heavy planning, rigid curriculum, fixed measures

Table 4.1. Global Educational Reform Movement Vis-à-vis the Finnish Model of Educational Change

Global Education Reform Movement (GERM)	The Finnish Model
Competition between schools	*Collaboration among schools*
The basic assumption is that competition works as a market mechanism that will eventually enhance quality, productivity, and efficiency of service. When public schools compete over enrollment with charter schools, free schools, independent schools, and private schools, they will eventually improve teaching and learning.	The basic assumption is that educating people is a collaborative process and that cooperation, networking, and sharing ideas among schools will eventually raise the quality of education. When schools collaborate, they help one another and help teachers create a culture of cooperation in their classrooms.
Standardized learning	*Personalized learning*
Setting clear, high, and centrally prescribed performance targets for all schools, teachers, and students to improve the quality and equity of outcomes. This leads to standardized teaching through externally designed curriculum to ensure coherence and common criteria for measurement and data.	Setting a clear but flexible national framework for school-based curriculum planning. Encouraging school-based and individual solutions to national goals in order to find the best ways to create personalized learning opportunities for all. Using individualized learning plans for those who have special educational needs.
Focus on literacy and numeracy	*Focus on the whole child*
Basic knowledge and skills in reading, writing, mathematics, and the natural sciences serve as prime targets of education reform. Normally instruction time of these subjects is increased at the expense of other subjects (such as arts and music).	Teaching and learning focus on deep, broad learning, giving equal value to all aspects of the growth of an individual's personality, moral character, creativity, knowledge, ethics, and skills. Aim of schooling is to find each student's talent.
Test-based accountability	*Trust-based responsibility*
School performance and raising student achievement are closely tied to processes of promotion, inspection, and ultimately rewarding schools and teachers. Teacher pay and school budget are determined by students' test scores. Sanctions often include terminating employment or closing down the school. Census-based student assessment and data are used to inform policymaking.	Gradually building a culture of responsibility and trust within the education system that values teacher and principal professionalism in judging what is best for students. Targeting resources and support to schools and students who are at risk to fail or to be left behind. Sample-based student assessments and thematic research are used to inform policymaking.
School choice	*Equity of outcomes*
Basic premise is that parents must be given the freedom to choose their children's education, while encouraging healthy competition among schools to better serve families' needs. Ideally, parents should be able to use the public funds set aside for their children's education to choose the schools—public or private—that work best for them.	Basic premise is that all children should have equal prospects for educational success in school. Because school learning is strongly influenced by children's family background and associated factors, equity of outcomes requires that schools are funded according to their real needs to cope with these inequalities. School choice often leads to segregation that increases inequity of outcomes.

through audits, external snapshot inspection, and externally judged accountability. Many of these problems are now gradually fading away and giving room to more intelligent curriculum and evaluation policies. Niall MacKinnon (2011), who teaches at Plockton Primary School, makes a compelling appeal for "locally owned questions and purposes in realizing practice within the broader national policy and practice frameworks." He gets right to the point of how GERM affects teachers and schools:

> There is the real practical danger that without an understanding of rationale and theoretical bases for school development, practitioners may be judged by auditors on differing underlying assumptions to their own developmental pathways, and the universalistic grading schemas come to be applied as a mask or front giving pseudoscientific veneer to imposed critical judgments which are nothing more than expressions of different views and models of education. Through the mechanism of inspection, a difference of conceptual viewpoint, which could prompt debate and dialogue in consideration of practice, is eliminated in judgmental and differential power relations. One view supplants another. Command and control replaces mutuality, dialogue and conceptual exploration matched to practice development. Those who suffer are those innovating and bringing in new ideas. (p. 100)

GERM has gained global popularity among policymakers and change consultants because it emphasizes some fundamental new orientations to learning and educational administration. It suggests strong guidelines to improve quality, equity, and the effectiveness of education, such as putting making learning a priority, seeking high achievement for all students, and making assessment an integral part of the teaching and learning process. However, it also leads to the privatization of public schools. GERM assumes that external performance standards, describing what teachers should teach and what students should do and learn, lead to better learning for all. By concentrating on the basics and defining explicit learning targets for students and teachers, such standards place a strong emphasis on mastering the core skills of reading and writing and mathematical and scientific literacy. The systematic training of teachers and external inspection are essential elements of this approach.

Is there any evidence of how GERM has affected student learning? Evidence is found in Figures 2.5 and 2.12, which show how some of the GERM-infected school systems have performed on PISA since 2000. None of the countries that joined (or were infected by) the GERM—the United States, the United Kingdom, Canada, Australia, New Zealand, the Netherlands, or Sweden—has been able to improve students' learning as shown in the results of that international survey.

In 2012, when the OECD collected the data for that study from 65 education systems, the OECD (2013d) made this determination:

- Since the early 1980s, reforms in many countries have granted parents and students greater choice in the school the students will attend (p. 54).
- Between 2003 and 2012 there was a clear trend toward schools using student assessments to compare the school's performance with district or national performance and with that of other schools (p. 159).
- On average across OECD countries with comparable data from 2003 to 2012, students in 2012 were 20 percentage points more likely than their counterparts in 2003 to attend schools where the use of tests or assessments of student achievement are used to monitor teacher practice (p. 160).

Many countries have carried out their own studies to understand how market mechanisms affect the quality of their education systems. Wiborg (2010) studied the impact of 20 years of the free-school system (government-funded private schools) in Sweden and drew the following conclusion:

[T]he Swedish experiment (using for-profit private providers) has proved expensive and has not led to significant learning gains overall. At the same time the Swedish reforms, albeit on a small scale, appear to have increased inequality, even in the context of this very egalitarian system. (p. 19)

The Australian Grattan Institute examined how market mechanisms, especially school competition, choice, and autonomy, impact schools' performance. The conclusion was that relying on markets is not the best way to improve student learning. The report stated that

[b]y increasing competition, government policies have increased the effectiveness of many sectors of the economy. But school education is not one of them. (Jensen, Weidmann, & Farmer, 2013)

Do PISA data suggest that the notions behind GERM are correct? There are three distinct findings in PISA 2012 that are worth noting in order to see how the elements of GERM are associated with successful reforms worldwide.

The first finding is that education systems that give schools autonomy over their own curricula and student assessments often perform better than schools that do not (OECD, 2013d, p. 52). This contradicts the basic premise of GERM, which assumes that externally set teaching standards and aligned standardized testing are preconditions for success. PISA shows that success is often associated with balanced professional autonomy and a collaborative culture in schools. Evidence also shows that high-performing education systems engage their teachers in setting their own teaching and learning targets, crafting productive learning environments, and designing multiple forms of student assessments to best support learning and school improvement.

The second finding is that high average learning outcomes and system-wide equity are often interrelated (OECD, 2013b, p. 27). Equity of outcomes in education means that students' socioeconomic status has little impact on how well they learn in school. Equity is high on the agenda in all successful school systems. A focus on equity gives high priority to universal early childhood programs, comprehensive health and special education services in schools, and balanced curriculum that weighs arts, music, and sports, and academic studies equally. Fairness in resource allocation is important for equity, too. PISA 2012 (OECD, 2013b, p. 93) shows that fair resourcing is related to the success of the entire school system: High student performance tends to be linked to more equitable resource allocation between advantaged and disadvantaged schools.

The third finding is that school choice and competition do not improve the performance of education systems (OECD, 2013d, p. 133). In the OECD countries, school choice and competition between schools are related to greater levels of segregation in the education system. That, in turn, may have adverse consequences for equity in learning opportunities and outcomes. Indeed, successful education systems do better than those that have expanded school choice. All successful school systems have a strong commitment to maintain their public schools and local school control. The PISA 2012 data show that the prevalence of charter and free schools, and the related competition for students, has no discernible relationship to improving student learning.

Table 4.1 suggests that the Finnish model of educational change is radically different from GERM's. A typical feature of teaching and learning in Finland is high confidence in teachers and principals regarding curriculum, assessment, organization of teaching, and evaluation of the work of the school. Another feature is the way schools encourage teachers and students to try new ideas and approaches—in other words, to make school a creative and inspiring place to teach and learn. Moreover, teaching in schools aims to cultivate renewal while respecting schools' pedagogic legacies. This does not mean that traditional instruction and school organization are nonexistent in Finland; in fact, it is quite the opposite. What is important is that today's Finnish education policies are a result of 3 decades of systematic, mostly intentional development that has created a culture of diversity, trust, and respect within Finnish society in general and within the education system in particular.

I have named this alternative approach to the global educational reform movement the *Finnish Way*. A similar attempt in the development of an information society and economic system is called the *Finnish Model* (Castells & Himanen, 2002; Dahlman, Routti & Ylä-Anttila, 2006). What distinguishes Finland from most other nations is the proven level of performance of the education system that has occurred simultaneously in learning outcomes and equity in education. These are both the next-generation applications of the Third Way, or radical centrism, which became well known in the 1990s through the leadership of Tony Blair, Bill Clinton, and Gerhard Schröder. In education, the Finnish Way seems to have strongly inspired the Fourth Way (2009):

> The Fourth Way is a way of inspiration and innovation, of responsibility and sustainability. The Fourth Way does not drive reform relentlessly through teachers, use them as final delivery points for government policies, or vacuum up their motivations into a vortex of change that is defined by short-term political agendas and the special interests with which they are often aligned. (Hargreaves & Shirley, 2009, p. 71)

The Finnish Way is a professional and democratic path to improvement that grows from the bottom, steers from the top, and provides support and pressure from the sides. "Through high quality teachers committed to and capable of creating deep and broad teaching and learning," as Hargreaves and Shirley describe the Fourth Way, "it builds powerful, responsible and lively professional communities in an increasingly self-regulating but not self-absorbed or self-seeking profession" (Hargreaves & Shirley, 2009, p. 107). In the Finnish Way, teachers design and pursue high standards and shared targets, and improve their schools continuously through professional collaboration and networks, from evidence, and from literature in their trade.

AN INNOVATION ECONOMY

The major economic transformation and need for sophisticated knowledge and skills in new high-tech industries provided the Finnish education system with unique opportunities for radical renewal in the 1990s. This happened at the same time that three significant economic and political processes were unfolding: the collapse of the Soviet Union (1989–1991), a deep and severe economic recession triggered by a Finnish banking crisis (1990–1993), and integration with the European Union (1992–1995). Each of these changes influenced the Finnish education sector either directly or indirectly. By the middle of the 1990s, a clear Finnish consensus emerged that mobile communication technologies would eventually foster the transformation to a knowledge economy and that this was perhaps the best way out of the economic crisis and into the heart of European power (Halme et al., 2014). It was also realized that the knowledge economy is not only about preparing human capital for higher know-how; it is also about having highly educated and critical consumers who are able to benefit from innovative technological products in markets that require better technological literacy.

At the beginning of 1993, Finland was in the most severe economic recession since the 1930s. Unemployment was reaching 20%, Gross Domestic Product volume had declined 13%, the banking sector was collapsing, and public debt had gone through the roof. The government led by the new, young prime minister Esko Aho responded to this national crisis in an unexpected way. First, investments were heavily targeted toward innovation instead of toward promoting a range of traditional activities. The survival strategy addressed diversification away from timber and conventional industries and toward high-technology and mobile communication. It introduced a new national competitiveness policy and accelerated the privatization of government-owned companies and public agencies. It also accelerated the liberalization of fiscal markets and foreign ownership in Finland. The key assumption was that the facilitation of private sector innovation and reciprocal collaboration between public and private actors would be superior to traditional direct intervention and investment in broader research and development policy. Overcoming the crisis was mainly a result of the strong concentration on the telecommunication industry, and the support of the Nokia Corporation in particular. Nokia gave birth to a completely new electronics industry in Finland, which was an essential part of the successful Finnish economic comeback in the 1990s.

Second, knowledge accumulation and development became the key turnaround feature in pulling Finland up from depression. Without many natural resources to rely on, Finland's main determinants for growth strategies became knowledge and the active internationalization of its economy and education. In 1998, the World Economic Forum (WEF) ranked Finland 15th in its global economic competitiveness index. By 2001, Finland had climbed to the top position in this influential ranking that covers more than 130 economies of the world (Alquézar Sabadie, & Johansen, 2010; Sahlberg, 2006a). Gross expenditure on research and development, commonly used as a proxy for competitiveness in knowledge-based economies, increased from 2.0% in 1991, to 3.5% in 2003, and to 3.9% in 2010, at the same time that the OECD average was fluctuating between 2.0% and 2.3% (Statistics Finland, n.d.b). The number of knowledge workers in the Finnish labor force also increased significantly. The total research and development labor force in 1991 was exactly at the OECD average at that time—slightly more than 5 per 1,000 workers. By 2003, this number had climbed to 22 per 1,000, almost three times higher than the concurrent OECD average.

The transformation of the Finnish economy into a knowledge-economy is described as "remarkable, not only in light of its earlier economic difficulties . . . [but because] it is interesting to see that a knowledge economy can be built successfully in a small and comparably peripheral country" (Dahlman, Routti & Ylä-Anttila, 2006, p. 4). Trust and increased investment in innovation resulted in education policies in the 1990s that focused on better knowledge and skills, along with creativity and problem solving. The strong focus on mathematics, science, and technology contributed markedly to the growth of Nokia as a world leader in mobile communications and Stora Enso in paper manufacturing. Several Finnish universities were closely connected to research and development in these firms. Indeed, governmental innovation agencies actively facilitated innovation as a third element in the Finnish knowledge and innovation triangle. Finnish economists who endorsed the importance of innovation and education in national development policy also played an important role. Education was seen as necessary and as a potential investment—not just an expenditure—in helping to develop innovation and adopting more innovation throughout the economy. Highly educated people are certainly "irreplaceable for the implementation of new technologies from home and abroad" (Asplund & Maliranta, 2006, p. 282).

The information society and knowledge economy have been important contextual factors for educational change in Finland since the 1970s. The economic sector in Finland has expected the education system to provide skilled and creative young people who have the competencies businesses need to deal with rapidly changing economic and technological environments. In their call for raising standards of knowledge and skills, Finnish employers, for example, were reluctant to advocate for narrow specialization and early selection to schools, unlike many other countries at that time. While Finnish industry actively promoted better learning of mathematics, sciences, and technology, it also supported rather innovative forms of school–industry partnerships as part of the formal curriculum. The rapid emergence of innovation-driven businesses in the mid-1990s introduced creative problem solving and innovative cross-curricular projects and teaching methods to schools.[3] Some leading Finnish companies reminded education policymakers of the importance of keeping teaching and learning creative and open to new ideas, rather than fixing them to predetermined standards and accountability through national testing.

Membership in the European Union in 1995 marked a mental challenge and change for, and within, Finland. The Soviet Union had disappeared only a few years earlier, an event that boosted the consolidation of Finland's identity as a full member of Western Europe. The accession process of becoming a European Union member state was as important as attaining actual membership in 1995. As a new Finnish identity emerged during the years of accession to the European Union, the Finnish people were motivated to ensure that they and their institutions, including schools, were up to the level of other European nations. In fact, the poor reputation of mathematics and sciences in Finnish schools, compared with their European peers in the 1970s and 1980s, became a reason to try harder to improve Finnish educational performance to the European level. Although education is not included in formal European Union membership requirements or common policies, the accession process nonetheless had a tangible positive impact on strengthening public institutions, including the education system in Finland, especially in the midst of the worst economic recession, described earlier in this chapter. Moreover, Finnish educators became increasingly aware of various European education systems. This certainly drove the ongoing education reform and the adoption of new ideas as more information became readily available about practices within other systems.

History and the personal mindset of Finns suggest that they are at their best when faced with these kinds of global challenges. For example, experiences such as the war against the Soviet Union (1939–1944), the 1952 Olympics, and the deep economic recession of the early 1990s provide good evidence of the competitive and resilient Finnish spirit, or *sisu*, as the Finns say. These educational and cultural attitudes were complemented by key economic, employment, and social policies that evolved since the 1970s, while the establishment of a welfare state and its institutions and policies was completed by the end of the 1980s. Survival has always been the best source of inspiration and energy for the Finns to go beyond expectations.

Analysis of educational change often includes speculation about the basic nature of change—that is, whether it is evolutionary or revolutionary. These terms refer to change as being either continuous, with smooth development from one stage to another, or a radical transition, where entirely new institutions and rules are created. Educational change in Finland has displayed periodic evolution, meaning that the nature of educational change has changed during these times. What is important to realize, as shown in Table 4.2, is that 1990 marks an important watershed in history that distinguishes two periods in Finnish education. The time prior to 1990 was characterized by the creation of institutions and frameworks for a welfare-based education system. The years since 1990 have been more concerned with interests, ideas, and innovations that have formed the education system as an integral part of a complex social, economic, and political system. Part of the success of the Finnish Way emerges from an ability to create punctuated equilibrium between these two periods of educational change.

Two simultaneous processes have played an important role in developing the education system in Finland since 1970. On the one hand, increased interaction among various public sector policies has strengthened the coherence of economic and social reforms and, therefore, created conditions for what Hargreaves and Fink (2006) term "sustainable leadership" in education. This increased coherence enables a systematic commitment to longer-term vision and intersector cooperation among different policies and strategies. On the other hand, internationalization and Finland's integration into the European Union have harmonized and intensified the consolidation and development of public institutions and their basic functions. In this light, three conclusions can be drawn

Table 4.2. Increased Interdependency Among Public Sector Policies in Finland Since 1970

Strategy	Economic Policies	Employment Policies	Social Policies	Education Reform Principles
1970s: Institutionalization. Consolidation of the pillars of welfare state and strengthened state-driven social capital. Fostering conventional industrial production structures.	Small, open economy that depended on exports and was state-regulated. Investments mainly in physical capital.	Establishing active employment policies and unemployment benefit system. Strengthening direct training for labor markets.	New risk-management systems for adults. Systems for unemployment, work–life balance, access to further education and housing.	Emphasis on equity and equal access to good primary and secondary education for all. Securing public provision of education.
1980s: Restructuring. Welfare state completed. Restructuring economic regulations, information technology infrastructure, and public administration.	Rapid public sector growth. Industrial production concentrates on metal and wood sectors.	Restructuring unemployment benefit system. Using early retirement as part of new employment policies.	Student welfare services and medical care system. Student loan and social benefit systems. Restructuring unemployment legislation.	Restructuring upper-secondary education to increase access for all students. Transferring upper-secondary schools to municipal authority.
1990s: Ideas and Innovation. Public sector liberalization. Diversification of exports through innovation-driven markets and dissemination of ideas through a network society.	Public sector growth halts and starts to decline. Private service sector starts to grow and new ICT industries emerge. Investments in R&D increased. Restructuring of banking sector.	Recession cuts employment benefits. New labor market benefit system to encourage employment. Employment policy system reform.	Fixing social consequences of Big Recession, especially for in-debt and long-term unemployed. Retraining and further education of unemployed.	Empowering teachers and schools through school-based curricula, coordinated innovations, and networking schools and municipalities for sharing ideas and change. Expansion of higher education sector.
2000s: Renewal. Strengthening well-performing parts of economy and renewing social policies (further privatization) to match financial realities.	Focus on services increases. Central administration loses its role and productivity of public sector is emphasized.	Aging population casts a shadow on employment. Accent on rights and obligations of unemployed. Cross-sector approach emphasized.	Renewing immigration legislation. Adapting social system for further diversification.	Renewing education legislation, strengthening evaluation policies, and tightening state control over schools and productivity in education sector. Sizes of schools increase.

Establishment of institutions

Interests, ideas, and innovations

Interdependency between public sector policies strengthens

Source: Sahlberg (2010b).

regarding how Finnish educational success can be understood from an economic and political perspective:

1. The success of Finnish education reform is mainly based on institutions and institutional structures established in the 1970s and 1980s, rather than on changes and improvements implemented from the 1990s. The state-generated social capital that is created through government regulations and motivated by the responsibility to provide basic conditions of well-being for all has provided a favorable social context for educational achievement.
2. Changes in Finnish primary and secondary education after 1990 have been more about interests, ideas, and innovations than about new institutional structures. Institutional changes in the 1990s have been smaller, except in higher education, where a new polytechnic system was introduced. Nonetheless, directions remain clear and are based on earlier policies.
3. The emphasis on national competitiveness that has been a key driving force in most public sector policies in the European Union has not been converted to clear targets or operations in Finnish public policy sectors during the 1990s and 2000s. At the same time, equality and equity principles promulgated in the early 1970s have gradually lost influence in these policies.

To sum up, since 1970 there have been two differing yet interconnected educational change periods, which are distinguished in terms of the theories of change and sources of ideas and innovation that drive them. On one hand, education reform principles have increasingly been created interdependently with other public policy sectors, following a *complementarity* principle. On the other hand, ideas for educational change—particularly for improving teaching and learning in schools—have been built upon past good practices and traditions in Finland. This has sometimes been labeled *pedagogical conservatism* and has created a pedagogical equilibrium between progressivism and conservatism through learning from the past and teaching for the future (Simola, 2005, 2015). A common conclusion about the role of social and economic policies in building the education system in Finland since the 1970s is that it demonstrates how context makes a difference in educational achievement. In other words, it shows that individual well-being, equitable distribution of income, and social capital can explain student learning in international comparisons.

Let's take a closer look at how social policies and the welfare state are linked to performance in Finland's education system.

WELFARE, EQUALITY, AND COMPETITIVENESS

Social policy decisions in the 1950s and 1960s in Finland underscored the economic importance of farms run by families. However, the general perceived image of Finland remained agrarian despite rapid industrialization and agriculture's declining contribution to the GDP over the second half of the 20th century. Regardless of drastic changes in the way of life and emerging cosmopolitanism among Finnish people, traditional social values endured. According to Richard Lewis (2005), who has studied the Finnish culture closely, these values included such cultural hallmarks as a law-abiding citizenry, trust in authority including schools, commitment to one's social group, awareness of one's social status and position, and a patriotic spirit. Policies that guided education reforms since the 1970s relied on these cultural values and principles of consensus-building that have been distinguishing characteristics of Finnish society.

Finland followed the main postwar social policies of other Nordic countries. This led to the creation of a type of welfare state where basic social services, including education, became public services for all citizens, particularly for those most in need of support and help. It increased the level of social capital, as did national government policies that affected children's broader social environment and improved their opportunities and willingness to learn. Martin Carnoy (2007) calls this "state-generated social capital"—that is, the social context for educational achievement created by government social policies. The influence of social restructuring and educational reform in Finland was profound and immediate. Eager to improve their children's economic and social opportunities, Finnish parents turned to the education system, which has served as an equalizing institution in Finnish society.

Income inequality is often claimed to affect people's lives in more ways than just how much they can afford to spend on their living. Are education systems in more equal societies performing better than elsewhere? Richard Wilkinson and Kate Pickett (2009) argue in their book *The Spirit Level* that indeed these systems are doing better in more ways than one. Actually, Wilkinson and Pickett show how income inequality is related to many other issues in our societies as well. Income inequality, which can be measured in different ways, calculates the gap between the wealthiest and poorest quintile in each country. In Figure 4.1, I use the data from the OECD's Income Distribution Database and PISA Database to construct a relationship between income inequality and mathematics learning in OECD countries. It appears that there is a not strong but still recognizable relationship between wealth distribution and student learning: In more equal societies, pupils seem to do better in school. Wilkinson and Pickett show how more equitable countries (statistically) have more literate citizens, rarer school dropout, less obesity, better mental health, and fewer teenage pregnancies than those countries where the income gap between the poor and wealthy is wider. All these inequalities are closely linked to teaching and learning in school.

It is understandable that income inequality, child poverty, and lack of appropriate pupil welfare in schools all play an important part in improving the quality of education systems. This has been well understood

Figure 4.1. Income Inequality (Gini) and Mathematics Learning Outcomes (PISA) in OECD Countries in 2012

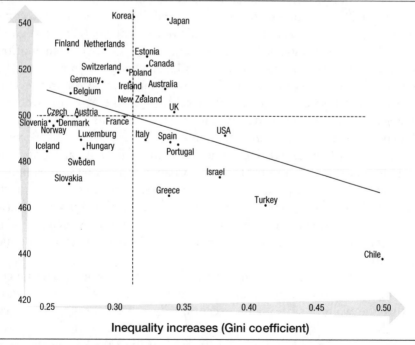

Source: OECD (2013a) and OECD Income Distribution Database (www.oecd.org/social/income-distribution-database.htm).

in Finland during the past half-century. Complimentary school lunches, comprehensive welfare services, and early support to those who are in need have been made available for all children in all Finnish schools— free of charge. Every child has, by law, a right to these welfare services in their school.

This chapter suggests that educational progress in Finland should be viewed within the broader context of economic and social development and renewal, both nationally and globally. Interestingly, the growth of the Finnish education sector coincided with an impressive economic trans- formation from an agrarian, production-driven economy to a modern in- formation society and knowledge-driven economy. Indeed, Finland has transformed itself into a modern welfare state with a dynamic knowledge economy in a relatively short time. The Finnish experience of the 1990s represents one of the few documented examples of how education and therefore knowledge can become driving forces of economic growth and transformation. During that decade, Finland became the most specialized economy in the world in telecommunications technology and thus com- pleted its transition from being a resource-driven country to a knowledge- and innovation-driven economic and educational system.

In the 2000s, Finland consistently scored high in international com- parisons of national economic competitiveness, transparency and good governance, technological advancement, innovation, implementation of sustainable development policies, and, surprisingly, happiness of the people. Finland was ranked as the most competitive economy several times in the first decade of the 21st century by the World Economic Forum's Global Competitiveness Index.[4] This is significant, given that Finland experienced a severe economic crisis in the early 1990s. Becom- ing a competitive knowledge economy, a leader in innovation and re- search, and the first country to make broadband Internet connection a human right for all citizens required a major restructuring of the Finnish economic system. Moreover, Finland has a reputation for rule of law and, as a consequence, enjoys a low level of corruption, which plays an important role in economic development and the performance of public institutions.

After the historic economic crisis of the 1990s, good governance, strong social cohesiveness, and an extensive social safety net provid- ed by the welfare state made exceptionally rapid economic recovery possible. A similar turnaround of Finnish economic progress was re- corded after the global financial crisis in 2008. One of the strategic principles used in pulling the Finnish economy out of downturn has been continuous high levels of investment in research and development, as described earlier in this chapter. Despite severe cuts in public spending, both in the early 1990s and after the most recent fiscal crisis, the Finnish belief in knowledge generation and innovation has remained strong. In 2013, regardless of stagnated economic growth, Finland spent 3.6% of its GDP on research and development—one of the highest of all the OECD countries.

As noted, this chapter asserts that education system performance has to be seen within the context of other systems in the society—for example, health, environment, rule of law, governance, economy, and technology. Not only does the education system operate well in Finland, but it is part of a well-functioning democratic welfare state. Attempts to explain the success of the education system in Finland should be put in the wider context and seen as a part of the overall function of democratic civil society. Economists have been interested in finding out why Finland has been able to become the most competitive economy in the world. Educators are trying to figure out the secret of Finland's high educational performance. The quality of a nation or its parts is rarely a result of any single factor. The entire society needs to perform harmoniously. This can be called system excellence.

Four common features are often mentioned as contributing factors for positive educational and economic progress. First, policy development has been based on integration rather than exclusive subsector policies. Education sector development is driven by medium-term policy decisions that rely on sustainable basic values, such as equal opportunities for good education for all, the inclusion of all students in mainstream publicly financed education, and strong trust in public education as a civil right rather than an obligation. These medium-term policies integrate education and training, and involve the private sector and industry in the creation and monitoring of their results. Similarly, economic and industrial policies have integrated science and technology policies and innovation systems with industrial clusters. Integrated policies have enhanced systemic development and the interconnectedness of these sectors and have thus promoted more sustainable and coherent political leadership for their successful implementation.

Second, strategic framework development and change have been built upon a longer-term vision. National development strategies, such as the Information Society Program in 1995, the National Lifelong Learning Strategy in 1997, and the Ministry of Education Strategy 2020, have served as overarching frameworks for the sector strategies. These and other strategies have emphasized increasing flexibility, coherence among various sectors, and the development of local and regional responsiveness and creativity in institutions.

Third, the roles of government and public institutions have been central in policy developments and the implementation of both education and economic reforms. Good governance, high-quality public institutions, and the rule of law play important roles in policy development and the implementation of planned changes. Evaluation approaches in both sectors are development-oriented, and various players in the system are held accountable for process and outcomes. Specific institutions, such as the Parliamentary Committee of the Future, are shared by private and public representatives as well as by the key stakeholders of the society for consensus-building purposes.

Fourth, a highly educated labor force and broad participation in education at all levels guarantee the stock of *human capital* that is necessary for both a good education system and economic growth. For instance, all teachers are required to hold a master's degree, and most workers are encouraged to participate in continuous professional development as part of their work. Teachers are considered professionals in their schools and are therefore actively involved in planning and implementing changes in their work.

Flexibility is one of the key denominators of education and economic development in Finland. The education system went through a major transformation in the early 1990s when most state regulations were abolished and pathways to education opportunities were dramatically increased. Similarly, private sector regulations were loosened and more flexible standards were introduced, especially to foster networking among private companies, universities, public research, and development institutions.

Strong integrated policy frameworks and longer-term strategic visions have enhanced sustainable leadership in education and private sector developments. Because of this sustainability factor, the education system has been resistant to the market-oriented principles of the Global Education Reform Movement. Frequent and open dialogue between private business leaders and the public education sector has increased mutual understanding of what is important in achieving the common good and promoting the development of a knowledge economy. Indeed, active cooperation between education and industry has encouraged schools to experiment with creative teaching and learning practices, especially in nurturing entrepreneurship and building positive attitudes toward work. Most important,

BOX 4.1: LEADERSHIP IN FINNISH SCHOOLS

School sizes in Finland are increasing. One hundred fifty years ago, when the Finnish public school was born, most schools had only one teacher. Today, these schools do not exist. In today's schools, teachers have to be able to work together in shared spaces and also educate students together. Each teacher has to adjust his or her pedagogical thinking and principles to those of other teachers. It is therefore essential that the school has a common culture that enables consistent teaching and learning for shared purposes. This is why a principal is needed in each school.

The Finnish school principal is always also a teacher. Almost all Finnish principals teach some classes each week. Finnish school principals have an increasing amount of administrative duties. Many complain that the workload is becoming too heavy. The principal needs a good theory of leadership in order to cope successfully with all tasks and responsibilities in school. I would say that principals should also have a vision of what a good school is and should know how leadership can help achieve that vision.

In my work as a principal, I make basic values the foundation on which I lay my leadership. In good schools, daily routines work well and teaching is effective. My task is to help my teachers do their best, and I make the necessary decisions so that my school operates well. I work hard to create a good atmosphere in school and to inspire teachers and students. As a leader of my own school and as part of the network of other public schools in my district, I must know national and local-level policies. It is important to guarantee that public money is wisely spent in all schools, including mine. That's what makes a good school principal.

I strive to be a good principal in my school. It means that I have to do my best as a manager, leader, director, and pedagogic guide for teachers and students: In other words, I want to be a good and trusted person. The biggest challenge for me is to combine all these aspects of my work. Being a school principal is not like being an administrator or the coach of a sports team. A school principal is in charge of the part of a complex social system that is continuously changing. Without experience as a teacher, this work would be very difficult to carry out successfully.

—Martti Hellström, School Principal Emeritus of Aurora School, City of Espoo

the main principle in the development of Finnish society has been encouraging intellectual growth and the learning of each individual. Developing cultures of growth and learning in education institutions as well as in workplaces has proved to be one of the key success factors.

FOREIGN INNOVATION, FINNISH IMPLEMENTATION

Many foreign observers have been surprised that they see only a few originally Finnish innovations practiced in classrooms. A closer look at the origin of Finland's current pedagogical models, school improvement practices, and education innovation in general reveals another intriguing characteristic of Finland's schools: Many of the innovations that have made Finnish schools blossom can be traced back to other countries, often to the United States. This is surprising given Finland's strong position as one of the most innovative societies and knowledge economies in the world.

Another observation is that all successful education systems have derived critical lessons and practical models from abroad. Singapore, one of the most successful reformers and highest performers in education, has been sending students to study education in American and British universities and encouraged their own university professors to collaborate in teaching and research with foreign colleagues. Japan, Hong Kong, and South Korea have done the same. More recently China has also benefited from education innovation imported from the United States and other Western education systems.

Finland is no exception to this trend. The most successful practices in pedagogy, student assessment, school leadership, and school improvement in Finland are predominantly foreign. Finnish students and principals study educational psychology, teaching methods, curriculum theories, assessment models, and classroom management researched and developed in U.S. universities and research institutions. Primary school teacher education curriculum (presented in Table 3.2) in Finnish universities includes textbooks and research articles with models, methods, and theories written by international scholars. Professional development and school improvement courses and longer programs often include guest speakers from abroad to share their knowledge and experience with Finnish educators. So common is the reliance on U.S. ideas in Finland that some have come to call the Finnish school system a large-scale laboratory of American education innovation.

The relatively low overall rating of "innovation in education" in the United States in the OECD's innovation-in-education ranking (in which Finland did not participate) in 2014 (OECD, 2014c) raises an interesting question: Why don't current education reformers in the United States make better use of the American education innovations that other countries have been able to utilize to improve the performance of their school systems during the last century? According to the OECD, the United States exhibits only modest innovation in its education system, but, at the same time, it is the world leader in producing research, practical models, and innovation for other countries. The following five American educational ideas have been instrumental in accelerating Finland's success in education.

1. John Dewey's Philosophy of Education. The roots of Finland's pedagogical ideas date back to the 1860s when Uno Cygnaeus, who is sometimes referred as the father of basic education in Finland, said that in an ideal classroom, pupils speak more than the teacher. He was also a proponent of practical aspects of education and insisted that both boys and girls must learn all the practical skills that people need in everyday lives. It is understandable that the pragmatic, child-centered educational thinking of John Dewey has been widely accepted among Finnish educators. Dewey's philosophy of education forms a foundation for academic, research-based teacher education in Finland and influenced also the work of the most influential Finnish scholar, Matti Koskenniemi, in the 1940s. All primary school teachers read and explore Dewey's and Koskenniemi's ideas as part of their courses leading to the master's degree. Many Finnish schools have adopted Dewey's view of education for democracy by enhancing students' access to decision-making regarding their own lives and studying in school.

2. Cooperative Learning. Unlike in most other countries, cooperative learning has become a pedagogical approach that is widely practiced throughout the Finnish education system. Finland's 9-year comprehensive school, launched in the early 1970s, was built on an idea of regular small-group learning of students with diverse backgrounds. But it was the national curriculum reform in 1994 that brought cooperative learning as it is known now to all Finnish schools. Before that, cooperative learning researchers and trainers, including David Johnson, Roger Johnson, and Elizabeth Cohen (and Yael and Shlomo Sharan), had visited Finland to train trainers and teachers on their methods of teaching.

Their books and articles were translated into Finnish and shared with all schools. The 1994 National Curriculum included a requirement that all schools design their own curricula in a way that would enhance teaching and learning according to constructivist educational ideas. Although cooperative learning was not mentioned as an obligatory pedagogical practice in schools, there were several recommendations for teachers to include elements of cooperative learning into their regular teaching. Ever since, cooperative learning has become an integral part of initial teacher education in Finland and one of the most popular themes in professional development of teachers and school leaders in Finland.

   3. Multiple Intelligences. The spirit of the 1970s school reform in Finland included another idea that derives from U.S. universities and scholars: development of the whole child. The overall goal of schooling in Finland was to support a child's holistic development and growth by focusing on different aspects of talent and intelligence. After abolishing all streaming and tracking of students in the mid-1980s, both education policies and school practices adopted the principle that all children can learn, that children have different kinds of intelligences, and that schools must find ways to cultivate these different individual aspects in balanced ways. Howard Gardner's theory of multiple intelligences (Gardner, 1983) became a leading idea in transferring these policy principles to school practice. Again, the 1994 National Curriculum emphasizes that school education must provide all students with opportunities to develop all aspects of their minds. As a consequence, that curriculum framework required that all schools have a balanced program, blending academic subjects with art, music, crafts, and physical education. This framework, moreover, mandated that all schools provide students with sufficient time for their self-directive activities. Gardner's influence has also been notable in the Finnish system by conferring a broader definition of "talent." Today, Finnish teachers believe that over 90% of students can learn successfully in their own classrooms if given the opportunity to evolve in a holistic manner.

   4. Alternative Classroom Assessments. Without a system of frequent standardized and census-based testing, the Finnish education system relies on local monitoring and teacher-made student assessments. A child-centered, interaction-rich, whole-child approach in the national curriculum requires that different student assessment models be used in schools. Furthermore, primary school pupils don't get any grades in their assessments before they are in 5th grade. It was natural that Finnish teachers found alternative student assessment methods attractive. And it is ironic that many of these methods were developed at U.S. universities and yet are far more popular in Finland than in the United States. These methods include portfolio assessment, performance assessment, self-assessment and self-reflection, and assessment for learning methods. Teacher education programs in Finland include elements of study of educational assessment and evaluation theories and also provide all students with practical knowledge and skills for how to use alternative student assessment methods in the classroom.

5. Peer Coaching. Another surprising aspect of Finnish education is that it lacks much of the change knowledge that is normally expected to guide policymakers and education authorities in planning and implementing desired reforms in education. Research and development of system-wide educational reform and change hasn't belonged to the repertoire of Finnish academia. The number of research papers related to that field has therefore remained minimal. Instead, Finnish education experts have relied on foreign sources of expertise and knowledge. A good example of an innovation designed in the United States is peer coaching, which evolved in the 1980s and 1990s as a result of the research and development work of Bruce Joyce and his colleagues (Joyce & Showers, 1995). Bruce Joyce also visited Finland in the 1980s to train trainers and education leaders on how the impact of professional development for teachers can be enhanced. Peer coaching—that is, a confidential process through which teachers work together to reflect on current practices; expand, improve, and learn new skills; exchange ideas; conduct classroom research; and solve problems together in school—have become normal practice in school improvement programs and professional development in Finland since the mid-1990s.

For many educators, including me, the United States is home to a great deal of educational change knowledge, research, and innovation. The question of why this doesn't show in international comparisons, like international student assessments or the recent review of innovation in education by the OECD, is an important one. Indeed, visitors to the United States often wonder why innovations that have brought improvement to all successful education systems in the world have not been practiced on a large scale in the U.S. school system. Lessons from Finland suggest that it may be that the work of the school in the United

States is so much steered by bureaucracies, test-based accountability, and competition that schools are simply doing what they are forced to do in this awkward situation. Many visitors from the United States often note that what they see in Finnish schools reminds them of practices they had seen in many schools in the United States in the 1970s and 1980s.

THE FINNISH DREAM CHALLENGED

It would be a mistake to think that the education reforms of the 1970s that created Finland's *peruskoulu* were supported by all business leaders, politicians, and educators. The campaign against *peruskoulu* was particularly harsh from some parts of the business community. Finnish business leaders followed closely the way *peruskoulu* was implemented. Most of the privately governed grammar schools were amalgamated into the public school networks of the municipalities and all school fees were abolished. The Finnish Business and Policy Forum (EVA), a policy and pro-market think tank, gave funding to a foundation that was opposed to this ongoing school reform and wanted to see private schools as alternatives to these new schools. The Parliament's conservative right accused advocates of *peruskoulu* of being socialist, warning that the model would jeopardize the steady economic progress and prosperity of Finnish society. The other side of the aisle defended the reforms by saying they would secure a good education for every child in Finland and thereby raise the well-being and prosperity of Finnish society. There was also a debate in the 1970s about the ability of the new *peruskoulu* to keep up with the international race for a knowledgeable and skilled labor force. These critics feared that *peruskoulu* would not allow the most able and talented to progress as far as they should in school.

In the late 1980s, when opposition to ongoing education reform was particularly strong, some parents as well as politicians and business leaders voiced their criticism and dissatisfaction with *peruskoulu*, where all streaming and tracking had been abolished a few years earlier. According to these critics, the emphasis on social equality had led to a suppression of individuality. This concern was, in fact, voiced by the prime minister at the Finnish School Principals' Annual Meeting in November 1987:

> When believing that anyone can learn everything, the goals of the comprehensive school are set too high. When trying to educate the whole population to the unattainable comprehensive school level, the financial and

mental resources of a small nation are being wasted on a hopeless task. These same educational resources would be badly needed to educate those who have proven to be talented in different areas to international high standards. Only that way can we maintain Finland's position in the hard international competition in science and the economy. (Aho, Pitkänen, & Sahlberg, 2006)

Triggered by this perception of the political leadership, Finnish business leaders launched a survey in 1988 to find out the actual state of *peruskoulu* as the main medium of education in Finland. The grim conclusion was that *peruskoulu* was killing talent. In other words, it wasn't allowing able and gifted pupils to progress to their full potential because it insisted on social equality by employing a unified curriculum in all classrooms. This coincided with the deregulation of the economy. The education system had to support the transition of Finnish society into a more liberal and competitive market economy. There were those— including the then–prime minister of Finland—who argued that the economic transformation from postindustrial to knowledge economy requires that able and talented students should be offered opportunities to progress freely and not to "wait for the mediocre students," especially in mathematics and science.

The campaign to reform the Finnish education system according to the models of the emerging New Public Management movement continued into the 1990s. The Education Reform Act of 1988 in England with the first national curriculum and common attainment targets for all, the outcome-based education policies of New Zealand, and the standards-based model of the United States were all seen by some Finns as suitable alternatives to the new Finnish Way in education. Increasing choice, competition, and specialization were cited as a way to improve education. National assessments and regular testing of student achievement were promoted as the necessary way to catch up to other education systems that seemed to be increasing the gap between them and Finland in education.

Criticism continued and sharpened until the end of the 1990s, although research findings did not support the contention that students were learning less because of *peruskoulu* (Linnakylä & Saari, 1993). Shifting the responsibility of curriculum planning, school improvement, and student assessment to municipalities and schools in the mid-1990s had strengthened support from teachers and principals to develop the Finnish school system without using models of marketplace management.

The critical voices were suddenly muted in early December 2001 when news of the first PISA study was published in the global media: Finland had outperformed all other OECD countries in reading, mathematics, and science when measured at the end of *peruskoulu*. Indeed, the Finnish Way was validated, and as many have said, PISA had saved Finnish *peruskoulu* from the toxic influences of the Global Educational Reform Movement.

CHAPTER 5

Is the Future Finnish?

A good hockey player plays where the puck is. A great hockey player plays where the puck is going to be.

—Wayne Gretzky, Hall of Fame Canadian hockey player

Finland has been engaged in comprehensive school reform since the 1970s. Research on specific features of *peruskoulu* led to the development of applied educational sciences, or subject didactics, in Finnish universities. However, more generic understandings of educational change remained relatively untouched. Even today, research on educational change, school improvement, and school effectiveness in Finland is modest by international standards. Much more analytical and research work on the Finnish educational system is conducted on the country's educational policies at different phases of its history. It is somewhat paradoxical that even with undeveloped domestic educational change knowledge, Finland has been able to transform its education system in only about 2 decades, as this book describes. Models of change in Finland have often been borrowed from abroad, but educational policies, as discussed earlier, were crafted and then implemented according to the principles of the Finnish Way.

Now Finland is at a fork in the road. Until the end of the 20th century, Finland had been following other countries, learning from them and sometimes adapting their good ideas for its own restructuring and development. Indeed, it is easier to walk the paths that others have traveled than to be in the lead. But the future requires new ways of thinking. Finland has shown that in the past it has been able to be innovative when needed and has used its past experience as a basis for new policies and practices. The Country Brand Delegation—the Finnish government's taskforce to uplift the international image of the nation—crystallized Finland's greatest strength as "the unbiased, solution-focused approach to problems, which derives from our history and culture. When faced with an impossible situation, we roll up our sleeves and double our efforts" (Ministry of Foreign Affairs, 2010, p. 3). Therefore, this final chapter argues first that educational excellence has been attained because Finland has chosen an alternative way in its educational reform, often almost in opposition to the Global Educational Reform Movement (GERM). Finland's approach reflects a particular winning strategy: Achieving system excellence that includes strong equity at the same time as high quality of outcomes is indeed possible by doing things differently from others. The chapter next discusses some of the factors behind the educational success in Finland since the 1970s. It then suggests that Finland needs to work out a shared vision of the future that will inspire practitioners and communities to continuously renew teaching in schools and education in the communities. Ultimately, the core question considered is this: Will Finland be able to maintain its educational success in the future?

SUCCESS BY BEING DIFFERENT

In this book I have conveyed my concern that an insistence on following the Global Educational Reform Movement may jeopardize schools' efforts to teach children to live a good life that contributes to a sustainable future. It is common that district and whole system–level education reform interventions rely on strategic priorities for setting higher expectations, strengthening accountability, increasing autonomy, expanding learning time, intensifying data use, and investing more heavily in human capital in schools. Evidence suggests that GERM is the wrong way to improve educational performance—in other words, the quality and equity of educational outcomes—and there is no reason to believe that the system-wide change would succeed by relying on these principles anywhere. Forgoing the tenets of GERM, Finland has demonstrated sustained educational improvement and strong overall performance since the early 1970s. Finnish schools operate in congruence with an inclusive welfare state and a competitive knowledge economy, as was described in previous chapters. It is therefore useful to look at how that society has responded to the global challenge to transform national education systems to increase their overall effectiveness and relevance for 21st-century knowledge and skills that are required for a good life.

Finland's success as a nation owes much to being courageously different from most others. Whereas others have desired individual excellence, Finland has worked toward equity. Many countries allow anybody into the teaching profession, but Finnish schools require higher professionalism from their teachers. When others have invested in having costly educational data systems, the Finns have focused on teaching and learning. Finnish educational reform principles since the early 1990s—when much of the public sector administration went through a thorough decentralization—have relied on developing professional responsibility by educators and encouraging learning among teachers and schools, rather than by applying bureaucratic, top-down accountability policies. Therefore, sample-based testing of students, thematic assessments of schools, reflective self-evaluations by teachers, and an emphasis on creative learning have established a culture of mutual trust and respect within the Finnish education system. As this book has described, before the end of upper-secondary school in Finland no external high-stakes tests are employed. There is no inspection of teachers, and only loose external teaching and learning standards to steer the schools. These practices leave teachers with the opportunity to focus on learning rather than be concerned about frequent testing and the public rankings of their schools. Some policymakers predicted in the mid-1990s that Finland would follow the school accountability policy models emerging in many other European countries. But in a review of policy development in Finland 20 years later, test-based accountability was not even mentioned (Laukkanen, 1998, 2008). Other Nordic countries have moved to adopt policies that are closer to GERM, and thus they have distanced themselves from their eastern neighbor and more Nordic traditions of trust-based responsibility and other forms of collaborative school cultures.

Explaining the educational success of nations or schools is by no means easy. Finland is said to have well-prepared teachers, pedagogically designed schools, good school principals, a relatively homogeneous society, an inclusive national educational vision, and an emphasis on special education needs—each of these separately and collectively certainly help the Finnish educational system to perform well (Hargreaves, Halasz, & Pont, 2008; Hautamäki et al., 2008; Kasvio, 2011; Matti, 2009; Sahlberg, 2010a; Simola, 2015; Välijärvi et al., 2007). Critics claim that because Finland doesn't have the very diverse ethnic population that characterizes many other nations, its schools perform better. Others suggest that low levels of child poverty and a socially cohesive society can explain the good educational performance of Finnish students. I argue, however, that because Finland has established universal early childhood education and care for all children, and because it has kept its schools as centers of learning and caring, teachers can concentrate on what is most important and what they can do best: helping children learn. They are not disturbed by frequent testing applied to schools, competition against other schools, or performance targets imposed by administrators. Since the beginning of the 1990s, Finnish schools have been systematically encouraged by educational authorities to explore their own conceptions of learning, develop teaching methods to match their own learning theories in action, and craft pedagogical environments to meet the needs of all their students. This is why many Finnish students learn well in all schools.

The National Board of Education's (1999) *A Framework for Evaluating Educational Outcomes in Finland* and the national Law on Education in 1998 stipulate the requirements and basic principles of student assessment and school evaluation. Teachers are responsible for the overall assessment of their students, using a mix of diagnostic, formative, performance, and summative assessments. The municipality's responsibility is to plan and implement any necessary evaluations within and of their schools, based on their own and nationally expressed needs. Thus, current education policies encourage cooperation between schools and try to protect schools, teachers, and children from unhealthy competition. Education policies in Finland encourage collaboration and friendly rivalry, not competition and choice.

Finland is the land of nongovernmental organizations. There are 130,000 registered nongovernmental groups or societies in Finland with a total of 15 million members. On average, each citizen belongs to three associations or societies. Young Finns are also actively involved in sports and youth associations that normally have clear educational aims and principles. They learn social skills, problem solving, and leadership when they participate in these associations. It is commonly accepted in Finland that these associations give a positive added value to the formal education offered by schools.

Finland's recipe for improving learning for all students differs from those found in many other countries:

1. Guarantee equal opportunities for good public education for all.
2. Strengthen the professionalism of and trust in teachers.
3. Engage teachers and principals in all central aspects of planning, implementation, and evaluation of education, including curriculum, assessment, and policy.

4. Facilitate network-based school improvement collaboration between schools and nongovernmental associations and local communities.

The key message of this book is that schools in competition-rich environments are stuck in a tough educational dilemma. The way forward requires brave, new thinking about the process of schooling. The current culture of toxic accountability in the public sector, as it is employed in England, North America, and many other parts of the world, often threatens school and community social capital; it damages rather than supports trust.[1] As a consequence, teachers and school leaders are no longer trusted; there is a crisis of suspicion, as O'Neill (2002) has observed. Although the pursuit of transparency and accountability provides parents and politicians with more information, it also builds suspicion, low morale, and professional cynicism.

SUCCESSFUL EDUCATIONAL REFORM

A typical feature of education in Finland is the way teachers and students are encouraged to try new ideas and methods, learn from innovations, and cultivate creativity in schools. At the same time, many teachers respect the traditions of good teaching. Education policies today are a result of 3 decades of systematic, mostly intentional, development that has created a culture of diversity, trust, and respect within Finnish society in general and within its education system in particular.

OECD's education chief Andreas Schleicher (2006) suggests that one element of Finland's success has been "the capacity of policy makers to pursue reform in ways that went beyond optimising existing structures, policies and practices, and moved towards fundamentally transforming the paradigms and beliefs that underlay educational policy and practice until the 1960s" (p. 9). Although education policy discourse in Finland changed dramatically during the 1990s as a consequence of new public sector management and other neoliberal policies, Finland has remained rather immune to market-based educational reforms. Instead, education sector development has been built upon values grounded in equity and the equitable distribution of resources rather than on competition and choice. Importantly, the Trade Union of Education in Finland (OAJ), which represents more than 95% of all teachers in Finland, has consistently resisted adopting business management models in the education sector. Moreover, Finland is a society where achieving consensus on important social and political issues is not rare. Although education is politicized in Finland as it is everywhere, Finns have been able to get together across political party lines and reach agreements. *Peruskoulu* is a good example of that.

A question asked repeatedly is this: Why are Finnish schools and students doing better in international comparison studies than most others? This book describes how Finland, by employing alternative approaches in education policies, has been able to improve student achievement.[2] Jouni Välijärvi (2002), who has worked with colleagues for several decades on international student assessments, observes that

> [F]inland's high achievement seems to be attributable to a whole network of interrelated factors in which students' own areas of interest and leisure activities, the learning opportunities provided by school, parental support and involvement as well as social and cultural context of learning and of the entire education system combine with each other. (Välijärvi et al., 2002, p. 46)

One accomplishment of the Finnish education system that is often overlooked is the especially high level of reading literacy that Finnish children already possess at an early age. There are both educational and sociocultural reasons for this: Reading instruction in schools is based on individual development and pace rather than on standardized instruction. Finnish parents read a lot, books and newspapers are easily available through a dense library network, and children are exposed to subtitled television and movies at an early age. Good reading comprehension and the ability to understand texts fast is a great advantage in the mathematics and science sections of PISA tests, which are based on being able to understand descriptive tasks in all measured areas.

Another overlooked direction of Finnish educational development is the reform of school architecture along the guidelines set out by the National Curriculum Framework and its pedagogical and philosophical principles. New school buildings are always designed in collaboration with teachers and architects, and they are thereby adapted to the teaching and learning needs of specific communities. The physical environment provides an important context for both students and teachers. "If the building is consciously viewed as an instrument of learning," reasons Kaisa Nuikkinen (2011, pp. 13-14), "the architecture itself can serve as an inspirational, tangible teaching tool, offering a living example of such things as good ergonomic design and the principles of sustainable development." The school building can create a sense of well-being, respect, and happiness—all hallmarks of Finnish schools.

The following five interrelated factors are often mentioned when Finnish experts explain the reasons behind good educational performance. All are related to education or school and should not suggest that social, community, physical environment, or family factors would not have important roles to play.

Peruskoulu offers equal educational opportunities for all. All Finnish children start their formal schooling in August of the year they turn 7. Normally, class-based primary school lasts 6 years and is followed by 3-year lower-secondary school, although today *peruskoulu* is formally a unified 9-year school. Today it is widely recognized that the 6-year primary school provides a solid basis for the high-quality education system. Finnish experience and international research show that investment in early childhood development and primary education pays off in later grades through better aptitude and learning skills, as well as through positive overall outcomes (Cunha & Heckman, 2010). Schools are typically small, with class sizes ranging from 15 to 25 students. In 2014, 23% of Finnish comprehensive schools had fewer than 50 pupils; just 7% of schools had more than 500 pupils. In other words, Finnish schools are rather small by international standards. Primary schools (grades 1 to 6) typically have fewer than 300 pupils and often operate separately from the upper grades (7 to 9), although the unified *peruskoulu* is gradually bringing these two schools under the same roof. As a consequence of tightening financial conditions in Finnish municipalities, about 1,000 comprehensive schools have been shut down during the first decade of this century. Many of them were small rural schools.

Teaching is an inspiring profession that attracts many young Finns. In Finnish society, the teaching profession has always enjoyed great public respect and appreciation, as explained in Chapter 3. Classroom teaching is considered an independent, respected profession that attracts some of the best upper-secondary school graduates each year. The main reason for the strong appeal of teaching as a career is the fact that a master's degree is the basic requirement for permanent employment as a teacher in Finnish schools, and having a master's degree opens the door to other future employment options. Therefore, individuals who choose teaching as their first career do not feel that their lives are limited to working in a school. Indeed, teachers with a master's degree often find interest in their credentials from human resource departments within the Finnish private sector and third-sector organizations. They also have access to doctoral studies in Finnish universities. During the past decade, Finnish schools have noted an upsurge in school principals and teachers who possess a PhD in education.

Westbury and colleagues point out that preparing teachers for a research-based profession has been the central idea of teacher education development in Finland since the mid-1970s (Westbury et al., 2005). Teachers' higher academic qualifications have enabled schools to play an increasingly active role in curriculum planning, evaluating education outcomes, and leading overall school improvement. The OECD (2005) review on equity in education in Finland describes how Finland has created a virtuous circle surrounding teaching:

> High status and good working conditions—small classes, adequate support for counselors and special needs teachers, a voice in school decisions, low levels of discipline problems, high levels of professional autonomy—create large pools of applicants, leading to highly selective and intensive teacher preparation programs. This, in turn, leads to success in the early years of teaching, relative stability of the teacher workforce, and success in teaching (of which PISA results are only one example), and a continuation of the high status of teaching. (p. 21)

Today, the Finnish teaching profession is on par with other highly regarded professions; teachers can diagnose problems in their classrooms and schools, apply evidence-based and often alternative solutions to them, and evaluate and analyze the impact of implemented procedures. Parents trust teachers as professionals who know what is best for their children.

Finland has a smart policy for accountability. Finland has not followed the educational accountability movement that assumes that making schools and teachers more accountable for their performance is the key to raising student achievement. Traditionally, the evaluation of student outcomes has been the responsibility of each Finnish teacher and school. Due to the absence of national standardized tests, student assessment is based on teacher-created tests at the school level and on sample-based national assessments. Normally, Finnish pupils are not assessed using numerical grades that would enable a direct comparison of pupils with one another before 5th grade in primary school. Only descriptive assessments and feedback are employed, depending on how student assessment is described in the school curriculum or municipal education plan. Primary school is, to a large extent, a "standardized testing-free zone," and pupils are allowed to focus on learning to know, to create, and to sustain natural curiosity. Fear of learning and anxiety are not common in Finnish schools.

Educational accountability in the Finnish education context preserves and enhances trust among teachers, students, school leaders, and education authorities, and it involves them in the process, offering them a strong sense of professional responsibility and initiative. Shared responsibility for teaching and learning characterizes the way educational accountability is arranged in Finland. Parents, students, and teachers prefer smart accountability that enables schools to keep the focus on learning and that permits greater freedom in curriculum planning, compared with the external standardized-testing culture that prevails in some other nations.

Enhancing equity of outcomes has been the key education policy. The Finnish Dream was built on the idea that all children can learn and that they must be given equal opportunities to succeed in school. In the 1970s and the 1980s, many people in Finland feared that when equality and equity are the primary goals of education, the quality of learning outcomes suffer. The Finnish Way to enhance equity included adjusting school funding to the real needs of each school; making special education universal and flexible so that help is available early on; embedding health and well-being services in every school, for every child, every day; ensuring balanced curriculum throughout school system that will serve multiple intelligences and different personalities evenly; and making sure that good teachers are employed in all schools. Only after the first PISA results became public in late 2001 did many admit that this Finnish strategy of driving quality gains by investing in equity in education was correct. Indeed, the most successful education systems are those that combine quality with equity. OECD (2012) concluded in its report _Equity and Quality in Education_ that

> [s]chool choice advocates often argue that the introduction of market mechanisms in education allows equal access to high quality schooling for all. Expanding school choice opportunities, it is said, would allow all students—including disadvantaged ones and the ones attending low

performing schools—to opt for higher quality schools, as the introduction of choice in education can foster efficiency, spur innovation and raise quality overall. However evidence does not support these perceptions, as choice and associated market mechanisms can enhance segregation. (p. 64)

Figure 5.1 shows how equity (the strength of the relationship between students' family background and their measured achievement in school) and quality (measured learning outcomes in reading, mathematics, and science) are associated with one another. Following the OECD definition of a successful (i.e., high achievement and high equity) education system, Figure 5.1 illustrates that the most successful school systems in 2012 were Canada, Estonia, Finland, Japan, and Korea (in alphabetical order).

The association between students' family background and their measured achievement in school has been the subject of thousands of studies since the Coleman Report was released in the 1960s. Equity of outcomes in education systems diminishes as this association becomes more uncertain. In other words, when students' socioeconomic background doesn't determine their school performance, the education system is more equitable. In Figure 5.1 equity is determined by calculating the economic, social, and cultural status (ESCS) index and then by linking it to individual students'

Figure 5.1. Relationship Between Quality of Learning Outcomes (in Mathematics) and Equity (ESCS) in Education in OECD Countries in 2012

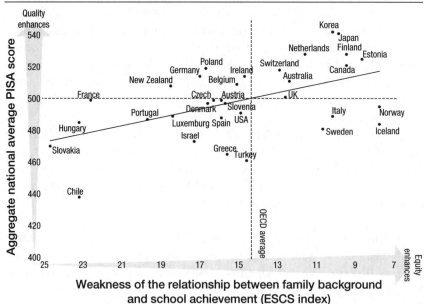

Weakness of the relationship between family background and school achievement (ESCS index)

measured achievement in school. Another way to estimate the equity of education systems is to look at students' performance variance within and between schools in measured subjects, as we see in Figure 2.2. A third way to evaluate the equity of education systems is to see how many students who come from disadvantaged home backgrounds can "beat the odds" and exhibit high levels of achievement in school. These students are called *resilient* because they overcome adversity and achieve academic success.

The share of resilient students among all students can be calculated in different ways. OECD's PISA 2012 (OECD, 2013b, p. 194) survey classifies a student as resilient if "he or she is in the bottom quarter of the PISA index of economic, social and cultural status (ESCS) in the country of assessment and performs in the top quarter of students among all countries, after accounting for socio-economic status." By calculating the share of resilient students among all students in the education system, we'll get another indication of the equity of that education system. Across all OECD countries, 6.5% of the entire student population is resilient; in other words, they beat the socioeconomic odds that are stacked against them when compared with similar students in other countries. As Figure 5.2 shows, Sweden has 4.3%, the United States 5.2%, Finland 8.1%, and Canada 8.3% resilient students.

Figure 5.2. Percentage of Resilient Students Among All Students in Selected Countries in 2012

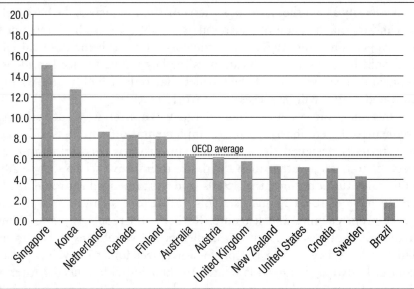

Source: OECD, 2013b.

OECD (2011b) data suggest that "resilience does not appear to be a domain-specific characteristic but rather a general feature of some disadvantaged students, their communities or the schools they attend that help them overcome their social disadvantage and become high performers" (p. 33). The percentage of resilient students among all students therefore indicates the equity of education outcomes. All these different equity indices show that Finnish education policies have been successful in offering a good school for all students. Strong equity in the Finnish school system is associated with universal access to early childhood education; comprehensive special-needs education; a systematic focus on students' health, well-being, and happiness in school; a whole-child approach through balanced curriculum; and research-based education for all teachers. In other words, Finland has achieved great system excellence by creating individual opportunity.

The Finnish education system has sustainable leadership and political stability. The success of Finnish education is not the result of any major national education reform per se. Instead, education development in Finland has been based on the continual adjustment of schooling to the changing needs of individuals and society. Risto Rinne and colleagues (2002) claim that although the emergence of the new public sector management meant revolutionary changes in Finnish educational discourse, the new rhetoric and practices have not been able to take root in education as easily as in other parts of society. As a consequence, the basic values and the main vision of education as a public service have remained unchanged since the 1970s. Governments from both the political left and right have respected education as the key public service for all citizens and have maintained their belief that only a highly and widely educated nation will be successful in world markets.

In education systems that undergo wave after wave of reforms, frequently the emphasis is on the implementation and consolidation of externally designed changes. The main result is frustration and resistance to change rather than the desire to improve schools. A steady political situation since the 1980s and sustained educational leadership have enabled Finnish schools and teachers to concentrate on developing teaching and learning. Rather than repeatedly allocating financial resources and time to implement new reforms, teachers in Finland have been given the professional freedom to develop pedagogical knowledge and skills related to their individual needs. After a decade of centralized inservice teacher education, following the launch of comprehensive school reform in the 1970s, the focus of professional development programs has shifted to meet the authentic demands and expectations of schools and individuals.

THE TRANSFER OF CHANGE KNOWLEDGE

Today, Finland is often used as a model of successful educational change. "As societies move beyond the age of low-skill standardization," writes Andy Hargreaves and colleagues (2008, p. 92), "Finland contains essential lessons for nations that aspire, educationally and economically, to be successful and sustainable knowledge societies." However, reform ideas and policy principles that have been employed in Finland since the 1970s will not necessarily work in other cultural or social contexts. For example, in Finland, as in other Nordic countries, people trust one another and therefore also trust their teachers and principals more than is the case in many other countries (OECD, 2008). Similarly, there are other sociocultural factors that have been mentioned by some external observers, such as social capital, ethnic homogeneity, and the high professional status of teachers, that may play a key role when considering the transferability of education models and policies.[3]

Indeed, many want to learn how to develop a good education system from the Finns (Barber & Mourshed, 2007; Darling-Hammond & Lieberman, 2012; Hargreaves et al., 2008; Mortimore, 2013; OECD, 2011a, 2013g; Ofsted, 2010). Since the early 2000s tens of thousands visitors have traveled from great distances to learn Finnish lessons about successful educational improvement. Understanding Finnish educational success, however, needs to include an awareness of the sociocultural, political, and economic perspectives. I call them invisible factors because they often remain hidden due to visible factors, such as school environment, teachers, curricula, technology, and so on.

There is more to the picture than meets the eye. An external OECD expert review team that visited Finland observed that "it is hard to imagine how Finland's educational success could be achieved or maintained without reference to the nation's broader and commonly accepted system of distinctive social values that more individualistic and inequitable societies may find it difficult to accept" (Hargreaves et al., 2008, p. 92). Another visiting OECD team confirmed that the Finnish approaches to equitable schooling rely on multiple and reinforcing forms of intervention with support that teachers can get from others, including special education teachers and classroom assistants (OECD, 2005). Furthermore, Finland has shown that educational change should be systematic and coherent, in contrast with the current haphazard intervention efforts of many other countries. The conclusion was that "developing the capacities of schools is much more important than testing the hell out of students, and that some nonschool policies associated with the welfare state are also necessary" (Grubb, 2007, p. 112). Scores of news articles on Finnish education have concluded that trust, teacher professionalism, and taking care of those with special needs are the main (visible) factors that distinguish Finnish schools from most others.[4] There are also theories of change that represent very different paradigms from that of the Finnish Way.

These observations about the problem of the transferability of educational change knowledge contradict the thinking of those who claim that context, culture, politics, or governance are not very important to a school system and its leaders when seeking real improvement in educational outcomes. International consulting corporation McKinsey & Company analyzed education policies and practices in 25 countries hoping to find out how the world's best-performing school systems come out on top. While acknowledging that the context determines the course the system leaders must follow for achieving real improvement in outcomes, McKinsey argues that culture, politics, or governance will not be as important to the school system and its leaders as the following educational reform principles:

1. The quality of an education system cannot exceed the quality of its teachers;
2. The only way to improve outcomes is to improve instruction; and
3. Achieving universal high outcomes is only possible by putting in place mechanisms to ensure that schools deliver high-quality instruction to every child (Barber & Mourshed, 2007, p. 40).

McKinsey's view of educational improvement belongs to a mechanistic and reductionist paradigm that is built on a classical theory of human capital. Each of the three elements of McKinsey's theory of change is fragile in light of contemporary conceptions of systemic educational change. I already pointed out the weakness of McKinsey's first reform principle in Chapter 3. The second and third principles undermine the power of social capital and influence of out-of-school factors in explaining educational outcomes. Interestingly, the Finnish experience does not confirm the findings and recommendations of McKinsey & Company.

Another example of educational change in contrast to the Finnish Way is the U.S. education reform known as No Child Left Behind. This reform, which was approved by both major political parties in 2002, requires states, school districts, and schools to ensure that all students are proficient in grade-level math and reading by 2014. Due to the fact that the federal role in education in the United States is limited, the states define what grade-level performance means. According to this federal law, however, schools must make "adequate yearly progress" so that proficiency rates increase in the years leading up to 2014. If one child in school doesn't meet the proficiency target, the school will be labeled as a "low-performing school." The main mechanisms for achieving the intended change are accountability, standardized testing, school improvement, corrective actions, and restructuring. Failure to meet the adequate yearly progress goal may lead to losing students or closing down the school. This legislation, according to many teachers and scholars, has led to fragmentation in instruction, further interventions that were uncoordinated with the basic classroom teaching, and a larger number of poorly trained tutors working with students and teachers (Darling-Hammond, 2010; Ravitch, 2010c). As a consequence, schools have experienced too many instructional directions for any student, with an increase in unethical behaviors such as students cheating on tests and administrators manipulating student assessment protocols, as well as a loss of continuity in instruction and in systematic school improvement.

The perverse nature of NCLB became evident in Vermont, a small U.S. state in northern New England. In August 2014, the year when the reform should have led all students to be proficient in reading and mathematics, Vermont's secretary of education Rebecca Holcombe sent a letter to all parents and caregivers in her state. She wanted to inform citizens about the fact that in that year, every school whose students took the New England Common Assessment Program (NECAP) tests in the previous year was now considered a "low-performing" school by the U.S. Department of Education. Vermont is one of the highest-performing states in the U.S. in National Assessment of Educational Progress, has the best graduation rate in the nation, and is ranked second in child well-being. In her letter the secretary also wrote that the Vermont Agency of Education does not agree that all of their schools were low-performing schools. It is difficult to imagine an education reform that would be more distant from the Finnish Way—or education policies in any other high-performing country—than NCLB.

The differences between these approaches to educational change and the Finnish Way described in this book are indeed notable: Rather than relying on data-driven bureaucratic delivery of education policies and reforms with detailed target-setting, the Finns have gradually built trust in schools and strengthened professional responsibility among teachers and leaders so that the education system works as a self-improving organization. Rather than believing that standardized instruction and related testing can be brought in at the last minute to improve student learning and turn around failing schools, the Finns have worked systematically over the past 30 years to make sure that competent professionals who can craft the best learning conditions for all students are working in all schools. The rational and bureaucratic approaches to educational change above resonate with the key ideas of GERM and can be found in the educational policies of numerous nations and jurisdictions around the world, but not in Finland.

Importing specific aspects of the education system from Finland—whether those include curricula, teacher training, special education, or school leadership—is probably of little value to those who hope to improve their own education systems. The Finnish welfare system guarantees all children the safety, health, nutrition, and moral support that they need to learn well in school. As the passage from the novel *Seven Brothers* at the beginning of Chapter 1 illustrates, literacy and education in general have historically played a central role in what it means to be a full member of Finnish society. One lesson we can learn from Finland is, therefore, that successful change and good educational performance often require improvements in social, employment, and economic sectors. As described by Stuart Kauffman (1995), the separate elements of a complex system rarely function adequately in a new environment and in isolation from their original system. Therefore, rather than only specific aspects or innovations from other education systems, it may be the features and policy principles of a larger, complex system—in this case, the Finnish Way—that should be borrowed. In a complex system, interactions among elements of the system determine the behavior of that system as much as its individual elements alone. Some issues that should be considered when contemplating the transfer of ideas from the Finnish education system to other countries include:

1. *Technical drivers of good educational performance.* These include common comprehensive school for all, research-based teacher education, professional support for teachers, smart

accountability policies, relatively small schools, and good educational leadership, especially within schools.

2. *Sociocultural factors.* These include a long reliance on the social value of literacy and education, strong professional ethics, trust in public institutions (including schools), and state-driven social capital created by a welfare state.

3. *Links to other public policy sectors.* The success of one sector depends on the success of all others. Therefore, good educational performance may only be explained through larger policy principles, including other public policies, such as health, youth, and employment policies.

Finnish people also need to be careful to avoid the illusion that the current methods of measuring the performance of education systems will last forever. Although there are clear advantages to relying on global education indicators—especially those that are related to the economics of education—and student achievement numbers produced by PISA and other surveys, there will be a growing pressure in the coming years to develop educational units of measurement that better cover a broader range of learning and acknowledge the changing face of future societies. PISA looks at just one part of the desired outcome of education. At the same time, as Peter Mortimore (2009) writes:

> PISA also suffers some limitations: It assesses a very limited amount of what is taught in schools; it can adopt only a cross-sectional design; it ignores the role and contribution of teachers; and the way its results are presented—in some, at least, of its tables—encourages a superficial, "league table" reading of what should be a more interesting but essentially more complex picture. (p. 2)

Many teachers and principals in Finland hold a skeptical view of international measurements and benchmarking tools. They perceive teaching and learning as complex processes and are aware that quantifying their effectiveness is difficult.

Is there anything we can learn from the Finns? I am not suggesting that other nations should adopt the Finnish education system or even its elements, such as *peruskoulu* or academic teacher education, as I have clearly pointed out above. However, there are many things that we can learn from one another in education. Although sensitivity to the problems of transferring educational ideas from one place to another is essential, I would propose that there are three main lessons from Finland that are relevant in trying to improve quality and equity of education in other places.

First, we should reconsider those education policies that advocate choice, competition, and privatization as the key drivers of sustained educational improvement. None of the best-performing education systems today currently rely primarily on them. Indeed, the Finnish experience shows that a consistent focus on equity and shared responsibility—not choice and competition—can lead to an education system in which all children learn better than they did before.

Second, we should reconsider teacher policies by giving teachers a government-paid master's degree–level university education, providing better professional support in their work, and making teaching a respected profession. As long as teachers' practice is not trusted and they are not respected as professionals, talented young people are unlikely to consider teaching as their lifelong career. Even if they do, they will likely leave teaching early because of the lack of a respectful professional working environment. The experience of Finland and other successful education systems speaks clearly to this fact.

Finally, thanks to international student assessment studies and educational indicators, the differences between high-performing education systems and those that are struggling are becoming more visible. The secret of Finland's steady improvement and overall high educational performance is the result of a smart combination of national traditions and foreign influence. In international education, being a forerunner and a shining star is not necessarily the best position to hold when transforming education systems to meet the needs of the future. Therefore, aiming merely to be close to the leaders is probably the best plan.

THE FUTURE OF FINNISH EDUCATION

In the first decade of this millennium, Finland established a global reputation as a model educational nation. International media played a key role in promoting Finland's new position in the global limelight. *Newsweek* titled its May 24, 1999, article about Finland "The Future Is Finnish." The article praised the smart way Finland has been able to create a national vision for an innovation-based society that combines mobile communications and information technologies unlike any other (*Newsweek*, 1999). This book has described how Finland's education system has progressed steadily since the early 1970s until the mid-2000s. Mobile phone makers, symphony orchestra conductors, game designers, and Formula 1 drivers are symbols of what a Finnish culture and society that values ingenuity, creativity, and risk taking is able to nurture. But will the Finnish education system continue to be a model in the future?

On the one hand, Finland's systemic educational leadership since the 1970s, its stable political structure, and its established complementarity among public policy sectors suggest that its educational performance will remain good. On the other hand, PISA survey results, in particular, have created a feeling of complacency among education policymakers, politicians, and the public at large regarding the status of Finnish education. This may lead to a condition that favors the status quo, where education policies and the leaders of a high-performing system are motivated more by a desire to maintain the current situation than to see what possible reforms the future might require of the Finnish education system. Only now, after international student assessments have sent worrying signals of declining student performance, have Finnish authorities listened more carefully to calls for renewal of the education system.

Finland has done little to improve its schools since the first PISA results were released in 2001. Many of us in Finland have noted that other countries have continued to improve their school systems, but Finland did not follow suit. At the same time, when the financial situation in many municipalities significantly worsened, authorities and many educators spent time and intellectual effort to figure out how Finland's international reputation as an education leader could be converted into commercial products and economic profit. The education situation in Finland appears to be similar to the situation in 2013 when Nokia sold its mobile phone business to Microsoft. It is telling that when Apple came out with the iPhone, Nokia held the dominant position in the cellphone industry and, blinded by its success, failed to recognize the challenge. Nokia had invented the touch screen, but failed to take the next step. Apple did take that step, and, as a result, leapfrogged over Nokia. What happened there is similar to the situation in Finnish education at the moment. The huge flow of foreigners from all over the world who come to visit the remarkably successful Finnish schools have made the authorities afraid to change anything. The drive for change led by education activists in the 1990s has been extinguished. Although the Finnish education system still performs well internationally, there are some signs that parts of the strong and equitable education system may be breaking down. A large majority of school expenditures are covered by local taxes. Catastrophic economic situations in many municipalities, as Peter Johnson describes in Box 5.1, have lowered teacher morale and jeopardized many support functions for students at a time when the need for help and counseling is even greater than before. History may one day show that Finland has failed to learn from its own lessons and thus became lost in the journey toward educational change.

Educational change in Finland has been driven by culture and emotion in the context of social, political, and economic survival. Finland has shown that there is an alternative way of change to the process many other countries have employed. Finns themselves have learned that technical knowledge and political interests are not enough to renew society without emotional engagement. Indeed, global educational reforms show that too rational an approach to change does not work. Renewal requires energy, and energy is driven by emotion. In an era of big changes, emotional passion often emerges from crisis—or a sense of survival—as it did in Finland. But it can also come from recognizing new economical, technological, or cultural opportunities and innovation.

At the beginning of the 21st century, Finland has become a model nation for other reasons: It built a competitive knowledge economy while maintaining much of the social justice of the Nordic welfare state model. A high-level think tank called the New Club of Paris considered possible futures for Finland and stated that survival is no longer the impetus for maintaining all the good that Finland has built. In its recommendations to the Finnish government, the New Club of Paris suggested that

> Other drivers with emotional effect need to be identified. The question is how to broaden the scale of emotional recognition and exploitation. Instead of survival the driver for change could be a powerful vision, or the Big Dream of Finland. If people do not love the idea, it is futile to publish new strategies. The new strategy with cultural and emotional dimensions should be simple; a couple of words that people can immediately and emotionally relate to. This is currently missing. (Ståhle, 2007, p. 2)

Some Finns are concerned about how the country is seen by other nations in this competitive, globalized world. Several international comparisons indicate that Finland has become one of the most functional and attractive countries in many ways—including well-being, governance, economic performance, sustainable development, education, and happiness. For a rather small and young nation, that seems to be good

BOX 5.1: LEADING A LOCAL SCHOOL DISTRICT

The development of the education system is based on systematic and sustainable fiscal policies. Finnish education depends heavily on public funding. As a result of the global financial crisis, the Finnish public sector has been hit hard. Municipalities are experiencing rapidly tightening budgets. During the last decade, the debt burden of Finnish municipalities has tripled and the Finnish national debt is bigger than ever before. Increasing productivity and cutting public spending are now common public policies in Finland. Merging or closing down small schools is one result of these policies.

From an international perspective, Finland is still a country of small schools. The average size of a comprehensive school in Finland is 200 students. In 2008, there were 2,988 comprehensive schools. Since 2004, that number has decreased by 14%. A total of 1,900 comprehensive schools have disappeared since 1990. This has radically changed the density and nature of the comprehensive school network in Finland. More students now travel longer distances to school. Many small villages are affected when their school closes down. Much of this structural change has been steered by economic rather than educational considerations.

The worsening situation of the Finnish public sector has also caused many municipalities to use temporary layoffs of teachers as a cure for their chronic financial crisis. Teachers have been sent home without pay for a few days or, in some cases, weeks. While teachers are on this forced unpaid leave, other teachers have to take care of their classes and students. Savings have often been minor, but the negative implications of this practice for the schools have been severe.

I am concerned about the longer-term effects of these public sector policies. Economic forecasts in Finland do not promise better times ahead. On one hand, we know from experience that simply increasing financial resources does not solve the daily problems of schools. But sustained shrinking of education budgets creates a situation in which some essential structures will be jeopardized. Will schools and municipalities be able to achieve more with less in the future? I think it is possible, but it will require a careful analysis of current structures and practices. We need to be clear about where the savings can be made and where resources can be transferred toward development and renewal. However, without a sufficient slice from the overall public budget to education, this renewal will be very difficult. Cutting budgets and making high-quality education less likely is not a smart way to reward people for their good work.

—Peter Johnson, Director of Education, City of Kokkola

enough. In 2008 the Ministry of Foreign Affairs invited an influential delegation of thought leaders to think about how to insure this positive situation—or even strengthen it—in the future. The group's final report suggested that functionality, nature, and education are seen as the key themes on which the future of Finland should be built. It also insisted that—despite or perhaps because of the current positive situation—Finland must continue to ask itself "what shall we do next" in all fields of operations (Ministry of Foreign Affairs, 2010).

The spirit of these general recommendations should also be considered when it comes to education. The chief instrument that guides Finnish education policies and educational renewal today is the Development Plan for Education and Research for 2011–2016. Like the previous document for 2007–2012, this plan continues earlier policies and development principles. These documents emphasize securing equal opportunities, improving the quality of education, preparing skilled workers, developing higher education, and dignifying teachers as the main resources for a good education. Furthermore, these documents place a strong emphasis on the *complementarity* principle by developing the education system as a whole. All this assumes that the Finnish education system will continue to perform well in the coming years. However, there are some trends within the governance of the education system and within Finnish society in general that seem to be cause for concern.

First, national education authorities have tightened their control over schools. This shift signals that confidence in schools' ability to judge what is best for their own pupils and parents is declining. For example, the National Curriculum Frameworks of 2004 reduced schools' role in curriculum planning. The New National Curriculum Frameworks of 2016 are not going to change the traditional organization of work in schools; it merely adds new expectations on the top of the old structure.

Second, the governmental Education Sector Productivity Program for 2006–2010 and the new government program for 2011–2015 call for municipalities and schools to do more with fewer resources, which often leads to school mergers and increasing school sizes. In some cases, productivity gains are sought by reducing after-school activities, special education, and student counseling services. This may turn out to be harmful for the development of social capital in Finnish schools. Moreover, there is no clear idea within the Finnish education system about what direction public education should take in the future.

Third, Finland is slipping away from its top position as the most transparent nation, the country with the most competitive economy, and a socially equal society, according to the most recent international indices. PISA 2012 data show that part of Finland's decline is happening because poorly performing students and schools have been declining to become notably worse than they were before. In the 2003 PISA survey, the Finnish sample showed 6.8% poor-performing students (below level 2) and 6.7% highest-performing students in mathematics (level 6) (OECD, 2004). Nine years later, when mathematics was again the main focus of the PISA survey, Finland had 12.2% poor performers and 3.5% highest performers. This is a significantly negative change but keeps Finland still above the averages. In 2012, OECD averages were 23.0% and 3.3%, respectively (OECD, 2013a). OECD's TALIS 2013 also showed some alarming trends among Finnish lower-secondary school teachers: Participation in professional development is low, teachers rarely receive feedback on their teaching, and many teachers feel unprepared to teach in today's schools. Perhaps the most troublesome finding is the overly traditional nature of teaching and learning in Finnish lower-secondary classrooms. Only lower-secondary school teachers in Japan and Croatia report lower rates of using technology, small-group learning, and projects that take longer than 1 week.

Other indicators also suggest that inequalities in Finnish society and in its education system are increasing. Figure 4.1 suggested that when income equality in a country diminishes, there is bad news on the horizon. In terms of income equality, Finland has been among the top countries in the world, together with other Nordic countries. Figure 5.3 shows how income inequality has changed in Finland over the past 2 decades. Increasing inequality is often related to growing social problems, such as increasing violence, diminishing social trust, worsening child well-being, increased poverty, and declining educational attainment. Therefore, the challenge for Finland—where income inequality has increased faster than in other OECD countries—is not just to try to maintain high student performance but to strive to keep the country an equal society and to hold onto its leading position as the most equitable education system in the world.

In reforming its education system Finland has actively listened to other countries' advice about what is necessary for raising the quality of student learning and meeting new challenges in education. Finnish education authorities have been particularly attentive to what supranational organizations—the OECD, the European Commission, and United Nations agencies—have considered the necessary steps for Finland's educational policies. The educational research community in Finland has adopted models and ideas from their foreign colleagues. In Finland's current

Figure 5.3. Income Inequality in Finland Using Gini (%) Coefficient for 1991–2012

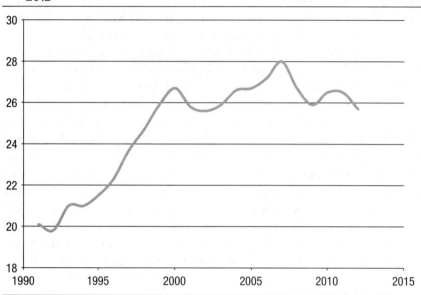

Source: Statistics Finland (n.d.c).

situation, a new orientation is needed. It is still important to maintain ongoing, active communication and collaboration with international partners. Today, however, Finland has become more of a giving partner than a receiving one. As a result, Finland needs to be prepared to collaborate and exchange experiences with other education systems that are trusted sources of inspiration, ideas, and innovation. I have suggested that a *new global partnership* for the leadership of educational change is needed. This partnership should be based on systems excellence and good practices, and a willingness to move fearlessly to implement innovative ideas and solutions for the future of education. Finland holds a place in this league of new education leaders. But it can't hold that position without an inspiring vision for education. To date, Finnish education authorities have invested more time in thinking about how to turn Finland's global educational fame into a profitable business rather than building real international partnerships that might have been helpful in shaping a much-needed vision. After PISA 2000 made Finnish education an international poster boy, education policies have brought fragmented projects and pieces of new legislation that municipalities have been obliged to implement without a shared view of the overall direction.

Any movement needs a foundation that draws from a core set of values, philosophies, and a commonly shared vision. As I see it, *Finnish school 2.0* should be based on a community of learners where learning sparks from individual interests, passion, and creativity and aims to help each learner to find his or her own talent. Whatever the vision is, completely new forms of school have to be considered. The new global partnership in educational change should kick off from this starting point.

The inspiring idea—or Big Dream—has often united the Finnish people and provided them with a source of emotional energy that they can use to make changes. After World War II, the idea was to give all Finns an equal opportunity for a good public education regardless of their domicile, socioeconomic status, or other life conditions. This became the main principle behind building *peruskoulu* in the early 1970s. The first PISA survey in 2000 proved that the Finnish Dream was fulfilled. The fifth PISA study in 2012 insists that a new Finnish dream is urgently needed.

In the midst of one of the worst post–World War II economic crises in the early 1990s, Finland turned again to education and insisted that nothing less than becoming the leading and most competitive knowledge economy of the world was enough to bring Finland back to the trajectory of other advanced economies. The dream then was to make the education system bring about the social cohesion, economic transformation, and innovation that would help Finland become a full member of the European Union and remain a fully autonomous nation. The education system was, as has been discussed in previous chapters, the key driver that raised the nation out of the economic crisis. The past visions of education have been accomplished, and now it is time to form a new vision that is capable of steering educational change in Finland over the next few decades. In conclusion, I offer some seeds for creating this new vision for the future of education in Finland.

The Finnish Dream for the future of Finnish education should be something like this: *Help all students find their talent and passion in school.* That talent might be academic, artistic, creative, kinesthetic, or something else. Passion sparks when curiosity drives the discovery of each person's unique talent. Every school needs to be a safe learning community for all students to engage, explore, and interact with other people. School should teach knowledge and skills as they've always done, but they must prepare young people to be wrong, too. If people are not prepared to be wrong, as Sir Ken Robinson (2009) says, they will not come up with any valuable new ideas. Being willing to take risks and to tolerate being wrong are the only ways the Finns can make the best use of our scarce human resources.

The existing format of schooling requires radical changes. First and foremost, Finnish schools must restore the student engagement that was once a hallmark so that more personalized learning occurs in school. Personalization doesn't mean replacing teachers with technology and individualized study. The new Finnish school must be a socially inspiring and safe environment where all pupils can learn the social skills that they will need in their lives. Personalized learning and social education lead to more specialization but build on the stronger common ground of knowledge and skills. In this new vision for schools, the following themes of change would emerge.

1. Less classroom-based teaching. Developing customized and activity-based learning eventually leads to a situation where people can learn most of what is now taught in schools through digital devices, anytime and anyplace. Handheld portable devices will provide online access to knowledge and other learners. Shared knowledge and competencies that are becoming an integral part of modern expertise and professional work will also become part of schools and traditional classrooms. Finland and some other countries have shown that it is not the length of the school year or school day that matters most. Less teaching can actually lead to more student learning if the circumstances are right and the solutions are smart. Those correct circumstances include trust in schools, adequate support and guidance for all students, and curriculum that can be locally adjusted to meet the interests and requirements of local communities.

Instead of continuing to think of future schooling in terms of allocating time to subjects, right now we should make a bold move and rethink the way time is organized in schools. This would mean devoting less time to conventional subjects, such as mother tongue, mathematics, and science, and more time to integrated themes, projects, and activities. Naturally, organized lessons should be more available in the lower grades of primary school, and then should gradually decrease as pupils' ability to manage their own behavior and learning develops. This would also mean making a shift from common curriculum-based teaching to a system based on individual learning plans. Doing so would give all students extended time to spend engaged in personally meaningful workshops, projects, and the arts.

2. More personalized learning. It is important for each young person to acquire certain basic knowledge, such as reading, writing, and using mathematics. In the future, it will be important for students to have alternative ways to learn these basic things. Children will learn more and more of what we used to learn in school out of school, through media, the Internet, and different social networks to which they belong. As a result, an increasing number of students will find teaching in school irrelevant because they have already learned what is meaningful for them elsewhere.

A common trend in most OECD countries is a steadily weakening engagement and declining interest among young people in school learning. Finland is no exception. Some suggest that the older our children get, the less motivated they are when it comes to what goes on in their schools. My own observation after visiting schools and classrooms around the world is that what is most often missing is a real spirit of curiosity—among both children and adults. If curiosity is related to exploration, investigation, and learning, then it should be a central element of school learning for children at all ages. Curiosity represents a thirst for knowledge and is therefore a major force behind learning and achievement.

We need to rethink schools so that learning relies more on customized individual learning plans and less on teaching drawn from a standardized curriculum. The art of education in the future will be to find a balance between these two. Because of the expanding educational possibilities in our digital world, young children enter schools with huge differences between them in what they already know and are able to do. This also means that young people are interested in a great variety of issues that may be completely foreign to teachers in their schools. Customized study plans or personalized learning must not mean that students will study alone with tools and information from the Internet only. Instead, they should have well-prepared, rich, and educationally justified individual plans for learning that are jointly designed and agreed upon by teachers, parents, and the students themselves.

3. Focus on social skills, empathy and leadership. In the future, people will spend more time on and give more personal attention to media and communication technologies than they do today. From an educational point of view, this means two things. First, people will generally spend less time together in a concrete social setting. Social interaction will be based on using social networking and other future tools that rely on digital technological solutions. Second, people will learn more about the world and other people through media and communication technologies. Expanding engagement in social media and networks will create a whole new source of learning from other people who have similar interests. By default, these new social tools will increase opportunities for creative action, as people can become part of open source projects designing games or digital solutions in collaboration with others in these networks.

Schools need to rethink what their core task should be when it comes to educating people. The point of school cannot remain what it is today: to provide the minimum basic knowledge and skills that young people will need in the future. The future is now, and many young people are already using those skills in their lives today. Schools need to make sure that all students become fluent in reading, mathematics, and science concepts, and possess the core of cultural capital that is essential. Equally important, however, is for all students to develop the attitudes and skills they need to use the available information and opportunities. They will also need to develop better skills for social interaction—both virtual and real—learn to cooperate with people who are very different from themselves, and learn to cope in complex social networks. What most people in the future will need that they are not likely to learn anywhere other than school is real problem solving in cooperation with other people. This will become one of the basic functions of future schools: to learn empathy, cooperation, and creative problem solving in small groups of diverse individuals.

4. The purpose of schooling is to find your talent. Current education systems judge individual talent primarily through standardized knowledge tests. At worst, these tests include only multiple-choice tasks. At best, they expand beyond routine knowledge and require analysis, critical thinking, and problem-solving skills. However, they rarely cover nonacademic domains that include creativity, artistic skills, complex handling of information, or communicating new ideas to others. It is not only important to assess how students learn the basic knowledge and skills in school, but also to know how they develop their communication, problem-solving skills, and creativity.

Conventional knowledge tests as we know them now will gradually give way to new forms of assessment in schools. As schools move to emphasize teaching skills that everybody needs in a complex and unpredictable world, the criteria of being a successful school will also have to change. People will learn more of what they need through digital tools and media, and therefore it will become increasingly difficult to know exactly what role schools have played in students' learning (or *not* learning, if you wish). Two themes will be important as we move toward the end of this decade.

First, curiosity in school will be more important than ever, serving as an engine of learning and thereby engaging all students in intellectual, social, cultural, and physical activities. A lack of engagement is the main reason for the challenges that teachers face in schools and classrooms today. By the end of *peruskoulu*, a growing number of young people find school learning irrelevant, and are seeking alternative pathways to fulfill their interests. Therefore, curiosity and engagement in productive learning in school should become an important criterion for judging the success or failure of schools in the future.

Second, students' ability to create something valuable and new in school will be more important than ever—not just for some students, but for all of them. If creativity is defined as coming up with original ideas that have value, then creativity should be just as important as literacy and should be treated with the same status. Finnish schools have traditionally encouraged risk taking, creativity, and innovation. These traditions need to be strengthened. When the performance of students or the success of schools is measured, the creative aspect of both individual learning and collective behavior should be valued highly. In other words, a successful school is one that is able to take every individual—both students and teachers—further in their development than they could have gone by themselves.

Is Finland now on the right course toward the new kind of school described by these four themes of change? The country's declining position in OECD's PISA rankings since 2009 has forced Finnish policymakers to do something. Worsening mathematics and reading literacy skills that were exposed by a large-scale national research study comparing Finnish lower-secondary school students' learning-to-learn skills between 2001 and 2012 was an alarming signal and the first wakeup call for Finnish authorities and politicians (Hautamäki, Kupiainen, Marjanen, Vainikainen, & Hotulainen, 2013). Three weeks after this study was released, the 2012 PISA results confirmed these disappointing trends in student achievement. Education authorities decided to announce a national campaign to turn around negative development. It is called "The Future of *Peruskoulu*." This campaign is led by the minister and steered by two task forces. The rather conservative working methods of this campaign beg the question of whether the Finns could have learned something from Alberta and Ontario, where similar initiatives have been successfully designed and implemented by engaging large numbers of teachers and principals in educational renewal.

However, the Trade Union of Education in Finland (OAJ) had already invited its members and the wide stakeholder community to think about the future of education in Finland in 2012. This was Finnish teachers' reaction to the leadership vacuum and the lack of systematic dialogue about the direction Finnish education should be taking. OAJ has mobilized teachers and citizens all over Finland to share their views on how education should be handled in the future. Neither of these two initiatives suggests any radical changes to the current structure or logic of schooling in Finland. Moreover, they will not bring any significant new resources or investments that would speed up the renewal at the time of deep economic crisis in Finland.

Twenty-three hundred years ago, Aristotle said that happiness is the ultimate purpose of human existence. Happiness has indeed become one of the indices used to measure the success of nations. Some education systems, like Finland's, view children's well-being and happiness as integral goals of schools. I believe that happiness occurs when people can do the things they like and that they find meaningful and rewarding. Happiness flourishes when we get closer to our element, which Sir Ken Robinson (2009) says is "about discovering yourself, and you can't do this if you're trapped in a compulsion to conform. You can't be yourself in a swarm" (p. 148). Today, our education systems are becoming obsolete and they need not more reform but a total redesign.

What we need to turn my suggested four change themes into reality in Finland is not just another educational reform but a renewal, a continuous and systemic transformation of teaching and learning, moving step-by-step toward the new big dream. Finland has what it takes to make that happen. It requires a new global partnership and leadership in educational change. An important lesson from Finland is that there are different pathways to educational excellence. These paths differ from the Global Educational Reform Movement discussed in the previous chapter. One way of increasing productivity and improved efficiency may lead to financial savings and perhaps temporarily better services, but, as Finnish futurologists Pirjo Ståhle and Markku Wilenius (2006) point out, shrinking budgets will never create sustainable improvements unless there are simultaneous investments in something new. Forecasts for the Finnish economy and society in general suggest that more investments are needed to bring about new ideas and innovations in both education and economic development, and to maintain the high level of social capital that has traditionally been the driver of strong educational performance in Finland.

At the end of the 1990s, Finland was able to benefit from one of the most competitive national economies. Experimentation, creativity, and networking were seen as the heart of school improvement, and trust in teachers and schools was endorsed as a key principle of education management. Educational change should provide encouragement and support for risk taking so that creativity will flourish in classrooms and schools, leading to new ideas and innovation. This is possible only with continuous renewal of Finnish education, guided by wise educational leadership in close relation with other public sector policies.

What many countries are looking for now is a socially just education system with schools that inspire teachers and students alike to do their best. Seymour Sarason (1996) reminded educational reformers that "teachers cannot create and sustain contexts for *productive learning* unless those conditions exist for them" (p. 367). Finnish educational policy fits precisely with this conviction. The Finnish government understands the importance of teachers and accordingly invests heavily not only in teacher education and professional development but also in work-conducive environments so that the teaching profession attracts and retains talent.

Well before the surge in attention to Finnish education following the publication of the PISA 2000 results, I had the privilege to host Seymour Sarason in Helsinki for a week in 1995. He was finalizing the revision of his book *The Culture of the School and the Problem of Change*, from which the observation above is drawn. I took Seymour to visit schools, talk to professors, and tell senior education authorities about the laws of school change as he saw them. He also read the Finnish 1994 National Curriculum Frameworks for comprehensive and upper-secondary schools and the education development plans we had prepared for the future of schooling. In our final meeting, I asked Seymour to summarize his findings. He said: "Why did you bring me here? Your school system to me looks very close to what John Dewey had in mind and what I have been writing about teaching and schools for the last three decades."

Indeed, John Dewey dreamed of the teacher serving as a guide to help children formulate questions and devise solutions. Dewey saw the pupil's own experience, not information imparted by the teacher, as the critical path to understanding. Dewey also contended that democracy must be the main value in each school, just as it is in any free society. The education system in Finland is, as Sarason pointed out, shaped by these ideas of Dewey's and flavored with Finnish principles of practicality, creativity, and common sense. What the world can learn from educational change in Finland is that creating a good and equitable education system for all children is possible, but it takes the right mix of ingenuity, time, patience, and determination.

The Finnish Way of educational change should be encouraging to those who have found the path of competition, choice, test-based accountability, and performance-based pay to be a dead end. Moreover, the future of Finnish education described above can offer an alternative means to customized learning. For the Finns, personalization is not about having students work independently at computer terminals. The Finnish Way is to address the needs of each child with flexible arrangements and different learning paths. The wisdom of Finnish education is simple: The teacher's task is to help students to do their best.

As a countervailing force against the Global Education Reform Movement that is driving school systems around the world, the Finnish Way reveals that creative curricula, autonomous teachers, courageous leadership, and high performance go together. The Finnish Way makes plain that collaboration with teachers, not confrontation, is the path to better results. The evidence is clear—and the road ahead should be, too.

Afterword

I am often asked if there are any countries that are providing nationally for the sorts of education that I advocate. Finland, I say, and over the past 204 pages, Pasi Sahlberg has clearly explained why that might be. He has described how and why the Finnish system has evolved as it has, how it works now, the principles on which it is based, and the challenges it faces in future. Is education in Finland perfect? Of course not. Will it stay as it is forever? How could it?

Like all human systems, Finnish education is in a constant process of becoming. It is embedded in the numerous economic, social, and cultural changes that are affecting Finland's overall way of life. And they, in turn, are part of larger global trends that are affecting all of us, wherever we are. National systems of education have to evolve for precisely that reason. How they should evolve is exactly what this book is about.

The main theme of *Finnish Lessons* is that transforming education is about creating the best conditions for young people to become engaged learners, fulfilled individuals, and compassionate, productive citizens. The Global Education Reform Movement (or GERM, as Pasi so deftly puts it) may declare this intention, but the practices it has promoted in schools have largely had the opposite effects. In country after country, the standards movement has narrowed curricula, dampened morale, lowered aspirations, heightened anxiety, and hampered achievement among students and teachers alike. The countries that have done well on the standards agenda are often paying a heavy price in a loss of creativity, innovation, and engagement in students, the very qualities on which personal, cultural, and economic vitality now depend.

In recent years, my own work has focused on the importance of creativity in schools and on enabling students to develop their personal talents and passions. In his final chapter, Pasi argues that these must be priorities in the next phase of evolution in Finnish education. What does that involve?

I define creativity as the process of having original ideas that have value. There are various misconceptions about creativity. One is that it is a special power that only a few people have. It is not. It is a process that draws on a wide range of capacities that we all have. Another is that creativity is limited to certain sorts of activities, especially the arts. It is not. As essential as they are in education, creativity is not just about the arts. We can be creative in any activity that involves our intelligence, including mathematics, sciences, technology, and whatever else you might do.

I make a distinction between *general* and *personal* creativity (Robinson, 2011). One of the obstacles to original thinking is conventional patterns of thought that we take for granted: we can all be too easily entrapped in "common sense." There are techniques of general creative thinking that anyone can learn and practice for challenging accepted habits of thought and for generating new ideas and perspectives. These techniques should be taught routinely in schools like other core skills. They should also be part of the professional development of teachers so that they can use them for themselves and help their students to do the same.

In *The Element: How Finding Your Passion Changes Everything*, I look more closely at *personal* creativity (Robinson, 2009). We all have unique patterns of aptitudes and interests. Being in your Element is partly about finding what those are. It's not enough to know what you're good at. Many people are good at things they don't care for. You may have an aptitude for music or math or design or cooking, but not enjoy it. To be in your Element, you have to love it. If you do love something that you're good at, it never feels like work. On the contrary, you get energy from doing it and often a new sense of purpose, too.

There are some things that we want all students to know, understand, and be able to do. But they also need to discover and develop their unique interests and abilities. When they do, they are much more likely to face their lives with confidence and enthusiasm and to meet the challenges they face with resilience and resourcefulness.

Helping all students to find their Element has implications for the structure of the school curriculum, for methods of teaching and learning, and for assessment and accreditation. It is also at the heart of what it means to personalize education. As Pasi argues, doing that in a full-blooded and determined way is now the leading challenge for education systems that are serious about helping young people succeed in a world that is changing more rapidly than ever before.

For the past 15 years, Finland has been well ahead of the curve in education. The rest of the world has much to learn from these Finnish Lessons. One of the most important lessons is that this story is still evolving and is far from over.

—Sir Ken Robinson
Los Angeles, September 2014

Notes

Introduction

1. The World Bank and OECD have used Finland as an example in Aho, Pitkänen, and Sahlberg (2006) and OECD (2011a). The McKinsey Company refers to Finland as a global benchmark of good practice in Barber and Mourshed (2007) and Auguste, Kihn, and Miller (2010).

2. There was a public debate in the Finnish media soon after the first OECD PISA results were published. Several members of the Finnish academic community rejected the results by arguing that the tests didn't measure "pure" mathematics or physics, but rather some forms of common everyday knowledge that are irrelevant for further studies in these subjects.

3. Howard Gardner visited Finland in May 2010, and his interview was published in *Helsingin Sanomat* on May 28, 2010 (p. B9).

Chapter 1

1. *Peruskoulu* is the Finnish term that refers to 9-year compulsory school, which consists of six grades of lower comprehensive school (primary school) and three grades of upper comprehensive school (lower-secondary school).

2. The Second Republic refers to the period of 1946–1994 in Finnish history in Alasuutari (1996).

3. Tenth grade is a voluntary additional year following the completion of compulsory education. Students have personalized learning plans that are typically blended with academic and practical subjects or themes. One of the key purposes of 10th grade is to provide young people with a second chance to improve their knowledge and skills so that they will be successful in upper-secondary school. Tenth grade is arranged as part of normal *peruskoulu* and is taught by their teachers.

4. www.washingtonpost.com/blogs/answer-sheet/wp/2014/03/20/weird-list-of-topics-avoided-on-california-high-school-exit-exam/

5. The Aquarium Project was a government-funded school improvement initiative to support the shift from a centrally steered system of management to

local leadership and continuous improvement. A good description can be found (in Finnish) in the doctoral thesis of Hellström (2004).

6. The National Institute for Health and Welfare (THL; www.thl.fi/en/web/thlfi-en) is a research and development institute under the Finnish Ministry of Social Affairs and Health. THL seeks to serve the broader society in addition to the scientific community, actors in the field, and decisionmakers in central government and municipalities. The aim is to promote health and welfare in Finland.

Chapter 2

1. The International Association for the Evaluation of Educational Achievement conducts PIRLS and TIMSS studies in 4-year or 5-year cycles. TIMSS (Trends in International Mathematics and Science Study) measures trends in mathematics and science achievement at the 4th and 8th grades. It has been conducted on a regular 4-year cycle since 1995, making TIMSS 2011 the fifth assessment of mathematics and science achievement trends. PIRLS (Progress in International Reading Literacy Study) measures trends in reading comprehension at the 4th grade. First assessed in 2001, PIRLS has been on a regular 5-year cycle since then. Both TIMSS and PIRLS were assessed in 2011, when the cycles of both studies came into alignment. More information and results are available at timssandpirls.bc.edu.

Chapter 3

1. The Bologna Process is an intergovernmental initiative that currently has 46 signatories. It aims at creating a European Higher Education Area with harmonized degree systems and the European Credit Transfer System (ECTS). Teacher education is described in Pechar (2007) and Jakku-Sihvonen and Niemi (2006).

2. Pan-European collaboration in teacher education has increased due to the Bologna Process and specific exchange programs in Europe, but strong and active research links have remained between Finnish universities and their North American, British, and Australian counterparts.

3. There has been continuous debate over whether the matriculation examination negatively affects the way that teachers teach in upper-secondary schools. Some of the empirical research findings are reported in Häivälä (2009).

Chapter 4

1. These are the two main academic journals dedicated to school improvement and educational change.

2. The initial idea of "a new educational orthodoxy" comes from Andy Hargreaves. See Sahlberg (2011).

3. I was leading a national project called Creative Problem-Solving in Schools that had close links to Finnish innovation enterprises such as Nokia, Kone, and Vaisala. It was administrated and funded by the National Board of General Education. Part of the inspiration for this project was the Creative Problem Solving initiative based in Buffalo, New York.

4. The World Economic Forum (WEF) is a Switzerland-based international organization that coordinates research on economics. Similar comparisons of national economic competitiveness are done by the International Institute for Management Development (IMD). In the European Union's internal ranking of its member states' economic competitiveness, Finland ranked at the top with Sweden in 2010.

Chapter 5

1. A salient example of this accountability culture is the well-known and controversial "deliverology" approach, which relies on targets, measuring, and accountability to manage and monitor the implementation of education reform policies and strategies. For a pro-deliverology perspective, see Barber, Moffit, and Kihn's (2011) "field guide." For a critical perspective, see Seddon's (2008) critique.

2. For example, Hargreaves (2003), Schleicher (2007), and Grubb (2007) have underscored the importance of alternative education policies in transcending the conventional educational reforms.

3. Cultural factors have been discussed by external observers of Finnish education. See Hargreaves et al. (2008), Schleicher (2006), and Grubb (2007).

4. An archive of media coverage of Finnish education since the 2000 PISA survey can be found online at www.pasisahlberg.com.

References

Adams, R. J. (2003). Response to "Cautions on OECD's recent educational survey (PISA)." *Oxford Review of Education, 29*(3), 377–389.

Aho, E. (1996). *Myrskyn silmässä* [In the eye of the storm]: *Kouluhallituksen pääjohtaja muistelee.* Helsinki, Finland: Edita.

Aho, E., Pitkänen, K., & Sahlberg, P. (2006). *Policy development and reform principles of basic and secondary education in Finland since 1968.* Washington, DC: World Bank.

Alasuutari, P. (1996). *Toinen tasavalta: Suomi 1946–1994.* Tampere, Finland: Vastapaino.

Allerup, P., & Mejding, J. (2003). Reading achievement in 1991 and 2000. In S. Lie, P. Linnakylä, & A. Roe (Eds.), *Northern lights on PISA: Unity and diversity in Nordic countries in PISA 2000* (pp. 133–146). Oslo, Norway: University of Oslo, Department of Teacher Education and School Development.

Alquézar Sabadie, J., & Johansen, J. (2010). How do national economic competitiveness indices view human capital? *European Journal of Education, 45*(2), 236–258.

Amrein, A. L., & Berliner, D. C. (2002). High-stakes testing, uncertainty, and student learning. *Education Policy Analysis Archives, 10*(18).

Asplund, R., & Maliranta, M. (2006). Productivity growth: The role of human capital and technology in the road to prosperity. In A. Ojala, J. Eloranta, & J. Jalava (Eds.), *The road to prosperity: An economic history of Finland* (pp. 263–283). Helsinki, Finland: SKS.

Atjonen, P., Halinen, I., Hämäläinen, S., Korkeakoski, E., Knubb-Manninen, G., Kupari, P., . . .Wikman, T. (2008). Tavoitteista vuorovaikutukseen. Perusopetuksen pedagogiikan arviointi [From objectives to interaction: Evaluation of the pedagogy of basic education]. *Koulutuksen arviointineuvoston julkaisuja, 30,* 197. Jyväskylä, Finland: Koulutuksen Arviointineuvosto.

Au, W. (2009). *Unequal by design: High-stakes testing and the standardization of inequality.* New York, NY: Routledge.

Auguste, B., Kihn, P., & Miller, M. (2010). *Closing the talent gap: Attracting and retaining top third graduates to a career in teaching.* London, England: McKinsey & Company.

Baker, E., Barton, P., Darling-Hammond, L., Haertel, E., Ladd, H., Linn, R., . . . Shepard, L. (2010). *Problems with the use of student test scores to evaluate teachers: Briefing paper 278*. Washington, DC: Education Policy Institute.

Barber, M., Moffit, A., & Kihn, P. (2011). *Deliverology 101: A field guide for educational leaders*. Thousand Oaks, CA: Corwin.

Barber, M., & Mourshed, M. (2007). *The McKinsey report: How the world's best performing school systems come out on top*. London, England: McKinsey & Company.

Bautier, E., & Rayon, P. (2007). What PISA really evaluates: Literacy or students' universes of reference? *Journal of Educational Change, 8*(4), 359–364.

Berry, J., & Sahlberg, P. (2006). Accountability affects the use of small group learning in school mathematics. *Nordic Studies in Mathematics Education, 11*(1), 5–31.

Bracey, G. (2005). Research: Put out over PISA. *Phi Delta Kappan, 86*(10), 797.

Breakspear, S. (2012). *The policy impact of PISA: An exploration of the normative effects of international benchmarking in school system performance* (OECD Education Working Papers, No. 71). OECD Publishing. Retrieved from dx.doi .org/10.1787/5k9fdfqffr28-en

Brophy, J. (2006). *Grade repetition. Education policy series 6*. Paris, France: International Institute for Educational Planning.

Campbell, D. T. (1976). *Assessing the impact of planned social change*. Paper #8. Hanover, NH: Dartmouth College, The Public Affairs Center.

Carnoy, M. (with A. Gove & J. Marshall). (2007). *Cuba's academic advantage: Why students in Cuba do better in school*. Palo Alto, CA: Stanford University Press.

Castells, M., & Himanen, P. (2002). *The information society and the welfare state: The Finnish model*. Oxford, England: Oxford University Press.

Center for American Progress & The Education Trust. (2011). *Essential elements of teacher policy in ESEA: Effectiveness, fairness, and evaluation*. Retrieved from www.americanprogress.org/issues/education/report/2011/02/23/9167 /essential-elements-of-teacher-policy-in-esea-effectiveness-fairness-and -evaluation/

Coleman, J., Campbell, E., Hobson, C., McPartland, J., Mood, A., Weinfeld, F., & York, R. (1966). *Equality of educational opportunity*. Washington, DC: U.S. Government Printing Office.

Cunha, F., & Heckman, J. (2010). *Investing in our young people* (NBER working paper 16201). Cambridge, MA: National Bureau of Economic Research. Retrieved from www.nber.org/papers/W16201.pdf

Dahlman, C., Routti, J., & Ylä-Anttila, P. (2006). *Finland as a knowledge economy: Elements of success and lessons learned*. Washington, DC: World Bank.

Darling-Hammond, L. (2006). *Powerful teacher education: Lessons from exemplary programs.* San Francisco, CA: Jossey-Bass.

Darling-Hammond, L. (2010). *The flat world and education. How America's commitment to equity will determine our future.* New York, NY: Teachers College Press.

Darling-Hammond, L., & Lieberman, A. (Eds.). (2012). *Teacher education around the world: Changing policies and practices.* New York, NY: Routledge.

Department for Education. (2010). *The importance of teaching: The schools white paper.* London, England: Department for Education.

Dohn, N. B. (2007). Knowledge and skills for PISA. Assessing the assessment. *Journal of Philosophy of Education, 41*(1), 1–16.

Elley, W. B. (Ed.). (1992). *How in the world do students read?* Hamburg, Germany: Grindeldruck.

Fullan, M. (2010). *All systems go: The change imperative for whole system reform.* Thousand Oaks, CA: Corwin.

Fullan, M. (2011). *Choosing wrong drivers for whole system reform* (Seminar series 204). Melbourne, Australia: Centre for Strategic Education.

Gameran, E. (2008, February 29). What makes Finnish kids so smart? *Wall Street Journal.* Retrieved from online.wsj.com/article/SB120425355065601997.html

Gardner, H. (1983). *Frames of minds: The theory of Multiple Intelligences.* New York, NY: Basic Books.

Gardner, H. (2010, January 10). The ministers' misconception. Retrieved from www.thegoodproject.org/the-ministers-misconceptions/

Goldstein, H. (2004). International comparisons of student attainment: Some issues arising from the PISA study. *Assessment in Education: Principles, Policy and Practice, 11*(3), 319–330.

Grek, S. (2009). Governing by numbers: The PISA "effect" in Europe. *Journal of Education Policy, 24*(1), 23–37.

Grubb, N. (2007). Dynamic inequality and intervention: Lessons for a small country. *Phi Delta Kappan, 89*(2), 105–114.

Häivälä, K. (2009). *Voice of upper-secondary school teachers: Subject teachers´ perceptions of changes and visions in upper-secondary schools.* Annales Universitatis Turkuensis, C 283 (in Finnish). Turku, Finland: University of Turku.

Halme, K., Lindy, I., Piirainen, K., Salminen, V., & White, J. (2014). Finland as a knowledge economy 2.0: Lessons on policies and governance. Washington, DC: World Bank.

Hargreaves, A. (2003). *Teaching in the knowledge society. Education in the age of insecurity.* New York, NY: Teachers College Press.

Hargreaves, A., Crocker, R., Davis, B., McEwen, L., Sahlberg, P., Shirley, D., & Sumara, D. (2009). *The learning mosaic: A multiple perspectives review of the Alberta initiative for school improvement.* Edmonton, Alberta, Canada: Alberta Education.

Hargreaves, A., Earl, L., Moore, S., & Manning, M. (2001). *Learning to change: Teaching beyond subjects and standards.* San Francisco, CA: Jossey-Bass.

Hargreaves, A., & Fink, D. (2006). *Sustainable leadership.* San Francisco, CA: Jossey-Bass.

Hargreaves, A., & Fullan, M. (2012). *Professional capital. Transforming teaching in every school.* New York, NY: Teachers College Press.

Hargreaves, A., Halasz, G., & Pont, B. (2008). The Finnish approach to system leadership. In B. Pont, D. Nusche, & D. Hopkins (Eds.), *Improving school leadership, volume 2: Case studies on system leadership* (pp. 69–109). Paris, France: OECD.

Hargreaves, A., Lieberman, A., Fullan, M., & Hopkins, D. (Eds.). (2010). *Second international handbook of educational change.* New York, NY: Springer.

Hargreaves, A., & Shirley, D. (2009). *The Fourth Way: The inspiring future of educational change.* Thousand Oaks, CA: Corwin.

Hargreaves, A., & Shirley, D. (2012). *The Global Fourth Way: The quest for educational excellence.* Thousand Oaks, CA: Corwin.

Hautamäki, J., Harjunen, E., Hautamäki, A., Karjalainen, T., Kupiainen, S., Laaksonen, S., . . . Jakku-Sihvonen, R. (2008). *PISA06 Finland: Analyses, reflections and explanations.* Helsinki, Finland: Ministry of Education.

Hautamäki, J., Kupiainen, S., Marjanen, J., Vainikainen, M-P., & Hotulainen, R. (2013). *Oppimaan oppiminen peruskoulun päättövaiheessa. Tilanne vuonna 2012 ja muutos vuodesta 2001.* [Learning to learn at the end of basic education. Results in 2012 and changes from 2001.] Faculty of Behavioral Sciences, Department of Teacher of Education Research Report No 347. Helsinki, Finland: University of Helsinki.

Hellström, M. (2004). *Muutosote. Akvaarioprojektin pedagogisten kehittämishankkeiden toteutustapa ja onnistuminen* [The way of change—The implementation and success of pedagogical development projects at the experimental schools of the Aquarium Project]. Helsinki, Finland: University of Helsinki.

Itkonen, T., & Jahnukainen, M. (2007). An analysis of accountability policies in Finland and the United States. *International Journal of Disability, Development and Education, 54*(1), 5–23.

Jakku-Sihvonen, R., & Niemi, H. (Eds.) (2006). *Research-based teacher education in Finland: Reflections by Finnish teacher educators.* Turku, Finland: Finnish Educational Research Association.

Jennings, J., & Stark Rentner, D. (2006). *Ten big effects of the No Child Left Behind Act on public schools*. Washington, DC: Center on Education Policy.

Jensen, B., Weidmann, B., & Farmer, J. (2013). *The myth of markets in school education*. Melbourne, Australia: Grattan Institute.

Jimerson, S. (2001). Meta-analysis of grade retention research: Implications for practice in the 21st century. *School Psychology Review, 30*, 420–437.

Jokinen, H., & Välijärvi, J. (2006). Making mentoring a tool for supporting teachers' professional development. In R. Jakku-Sihvonen & H. Niemi (Eds.), *Research-based teacher education in Finland: Reflections by Finnish teacher educators* (pp. 89–101). Turku, Finland: Finnish Educational Research Association.

Joyce, B., & Showers, B. (1995). *Student achievement through staff development: Fundamentals of school renewal* (2nd ed.). White Plains, NY: Longman.

Joyce, B., & Weil, M. (1986). *Models of teaching* (3rd ed.). Englewood Cliffs, NJ: Prentice Hall.

Jussila, J., & Saari, S. (Eds.). (2000). *Teacher education as a future-moulding factor: International evaluation of teacher education in Finnish universities*. Helsinki, Finland: Higher Education Evaluation Council.

Kangasniemi, S. (2008, February 27). Millä ammatilla pääsee naimisiin? [With which profession to get married?] *Helsingin Sanomat Koulutusliite*, pp. 4–6.

Kasvio, M. (Ed.). (2011). *The best school in the world: Seven Finnish examples from the 21st century*. Helsinki, Finland: Museum of Finnish Architecture.

Kauffman, S. (1995). *At home in the universe: The search for the laws of self-organization and complexity*. Oxford, England: Oxford University Press.

Kets De Vries, M. (2006). *The leader on the couch*. San Francisco, CA: Jossey Bass.

Kiuasmaa, K. (1982). *Oppikoulu 1880–1980: Oppikoulu ja sen opettajat koulujärjestyksestä peruskouluun* [Grammar school 1880–1980: Grammar school and its teachers from school order to comprehensive school]. Oulu, Finland: Kustannusosakeyhtiö Pohjoinen.

Kivi, A. (2005). *Seven brothers* [*Seitsemän veljestä*, R. Impola, Trans.]. Beaverton, ON: Aspasia Books. (Original work published 1870)

Koskenniemi, M. (1944). *Kansakoulun opetusoppi* [Didactics of primary school]. Helsinki, Finland: Otava.

Kreiner, S., & Christensen, K. B. (2013, June). Analyses of model fit and robustness: A new look at the PISA scaling model underlying ranking of countries according to reading literacy. *Psychometrika*, 1–22.

Kupari, P., & Välijärvi, J. (Eds.). (2005). *Osaaminen kestävällä pohjalla. PISA 2003 Suomessa* [Competences on the solid ground. PISA 2003 in Finland]. Jyväskylä, Finland: Institute for Educational Research, University of Jyväskylä.

Kuusi, P. (1961). *60-luvun sosiaalipolitiikka* [Social politics of the 1960s]. Porvoo, Finland: WSOY.

Laukkanen, R. (1998). Accountability and evaluation: Decision-making structures and the utilization of evaluation in Finland. *Scandinavian Journal of Educational Research, 42*(2), 123–133.

Laukkanen, R. (2008). Finnish strategy for high-level education for all. In N. C. Sognel & P. Jaccard (Eds.), *Governance and performance of education systems* (pp. 305–324). Dordrecht, The Netherlands: Springer.

Lavonen, J., Krzywacki-Vainio, H., Aksela, M., Krokfors, L., Oikkonen, J., & Saarikko, H. (2007). Pre-service teacher education in chemistry, mathematics and physics. In E. Pehkonen, M. Ahtee, & J. Lavonen (Eds.), *How Finns learn mathematics and science* (pp. 49–68). Rotterdam, The Netherlands: Sense Publishers.

Lehtinen, E. (2004). *Koulutusjärjestelmä suomalaisen yhteiskunnan muutoksessa* [Education system in the changing Finnish society]. Helsinki, Finland: Sitra.

Lehtinen, E., Kinnunen, R., Vauras, M., Salonen, P., Olkinuora, E., & Poskiparta, E. (1989). *Oppimiskäsitys* [Conception of knowledge]. Helsinki, Finland: Valtion painatuskeskus.

Levin, B. (1998). An epidemic of education policy: (What) can we learn from each other? *Comparative Education, 34*(2), 131–141.

Lewis, R. (2005). *Finland, cultural lone wolf.* Yarmouth, ME: Intercultural Press.

Liiten, M. (2004, February 11). Ykkössuosikki: Opettajan ammatti [Top favorite: Teaching Profession]. *Helsingin Sanomat.* Retrieved from www.hs.fi/artikkeli /Ykk%C3%B6ssuosikki+opettajan+ammatti/1076151893860

Linnakylä, P. (2004). Finland. In H. Döbert, E. Klieme, & W. Stroka (Eds.), *Conditions of school performance in seven countries: A quest for understanding the international variation of PISA results* (pp. 150–218). Munster, Germany: Waxmann.

Linnakylä, P., & Saari, H. (1993). *Oppiiko oppilas peruskoulussa? Peruskoulu arviointi 90 -tutkimuksen tuloksia* [Does the pupil learn in peruskoulu? Findings of the Peruskoulu 90 reserach]. Jyväskylä, Finland: Jyväskylän yliopiston kasvatustieteiden tutkimuslaitos.

MacKinnon, N. (2011). The urgent need for new approaches in school evaluation to enable Scotland's Curriculum for Excellence. *Educational Assessment, Evaluation and Accountability, 23*(1), 89–106.

Martin, M. O., Mullis, I. V. S., Gonzales, E. J., Gregory, K. D., Smith, T. A., Chrostowski, S. J., . . . O'Connor, K. M. (2000). *TIMSS 1999 international science report: Findings from IEA's repeat of the third international mathematics and science study at the eighth grade.* Chestnut Hill, MA: Boston College.

Matti, T. (Ed.). (2009). *Northern lights on PISA 2006. Differences and similarities in the Nordic countries*. Copenhagen, Denmark: Nordic Council of Ministers.

Meyer, H-D., & Benavot, A. (2013). PISA and the globalization of education governance: Some puzzles and problems. In H-D. Meyer & A. Benavot (Eds.), *PISA, power, and policy the emergence of global educational governance* (pp. 9-26). Oxford, England: Symposium Books.

Miettinen, R. (1990). *Koulun muuttamisen mahdollisuudesta* [About the possibilities of school change]. Helsinki, Finland: Gaudeamus.

Ministry of Education. (2004). *Development plan for education and research 2003–2008*. Helsinki, Finland: Author.

Ministry of Education. (2007). *Opettajankoulutus 2020* [Teacher Education 2020]. Committee Report 44. Helsinki, Finland: Author.

Ministry of Education. (2009). *Ensuring professional competence and improving opportunities for continuing education in education* (Committee report 16). Helsinki, Finland: Author.

Ministry of Foreign Affairs. (2010). *How Finland will demonstrate its strengths by solving the world's most intractable problems: Final report of the country brand delegation*. Helsinki, Finland: Author.

Mortimore, P. (2009). *Alternative models for analysing and representing countries' performance in PISA*. Paper commissioned by Education International Research Institute. Brussels, Belgium: Education International.

Mortimore, P. (2013). *Education under siege. Why there is a better alternative*. Bristol, England: Policy Press.

Mourshed, M., Chijioke, C., & Barber, M. (2010*). How the world's most improved school systems keep getting better*. London, England: McKinsey.

Murgatroyd, S. (2007). *Accountability project framework—Developing school based accountability*. Unpublished report. Edmonton, Alberta, Canada: The Innovation Expedition Inc.

National Board of Education. (1999). *A framework for evaluating educational outcomes in Finland*. Helsinki, Finland: Author.

National Board of Education. (2010). *National Core Curriculum for Pre-primary Education 2010*. Helsinki, Finland: Author. Retrieved from www.oph.fi /english/

National Board of Education. (2013). *Korkeakouluun hakeneet, hyvaksytyt ja opiskelupaikan vastaanottaneet*. Helsinki, Finland: Author. Retrieved from https://opintopolku.fi/wp/wp-content/uploads/2014/01/YO-Hakeneet-hyväksytyt-ja-paikanvastaanottaneet.pdf

National Board of Education. (2014). *Opettajat Suomessa 2013* [Teachers in Finland 2013]. Helsinki, Finland: Author.

National Youth Survey. (2010). *KNT 2010*. Helsinki, Finland: 15/30 Research.

Newsweek. (1999, May 24). *The future is Finnish*. Retrieved from www.newsweek .com/1999/05/23/the-future-is-finnish.html

Nichols, S. L., & Berliner, D. C. (2007). *Collateral damage: How high-stakes testing corrupts America's schools*. Cambridge, MA: Harvard Education Press.

Niemi, H. (2008). Research-based teacher education for teachers' lifelong learning. *Lifelong Learning in Europe, 13*(1), 61–69.

Niemi, H. (2011). Educating student teachers to become high quality professionals: A Finnish case. *CEPS Journal 1*(1), 43–66.

Nuikkinen, K. (2011). Learning spaces: How they meet evolving educational needs. In M. Kasvio (Ed.), *The best school in the world: Seven Finnish examples from the 21st century* (pp. 10–19). Helsinki, Finland: Museum of Finnish Architecture.

OECD. (2001). *Knowledge and skills for life: First results from PISA 2000*. Paris, France: Author.

OECD. (2004). *Learning for tomorrow's world: First results from PISA 2003*. Paris, France: Author

OECD. (2005). *Equity in education: Thematic review of Finland*. Paris, France: Author.

OECD. (2007). *PISA 2006: Science competencies for tomorrow's world* (Vol. 1). Paris, France: Author.

OECD. (2008). *Trends shaping education*. Paris, France: Author.

OECD. (2010). *PISA 2009 results: What students know and can do. Student performance in reading, mathematics and science* (Vol. 1). Paris, France: Author.

OECD. (2011a). *Strong performers and successful reformers in education: Lessons from PISA for the United States*. Paris, France: Author.

OECD. (2011b). *Against the odds: Disadvantaged students who succeed in school*. Paris, France: Author.

OECD. (2012). *Equity and quality in education*. Paris, France: Author.

OECD. (2013a). *PISA 2012 results: What students know and can do. Resources, policies and practices* (Vol. 1). Paris, France: Author.

OECD. (2013b). *PISA 2012 results: Excellence through equity. Resources, policies and practices* (Volume 2). Paris, France: Author.

OECD. (2013c). *PISA 2012 results: Ready to learn. Resources, policies and practices* (Vol. 3). Paris, France: Author.

OECD. (2013d). *PISA 2012 results: What makes schools successful? Resources, policies and practices* (Vol. 4). Paris, France: Author.

OECD. (2013f). *Education at a glance: Education indicators*. Paris, France: Author.

OECD. (2013g). *Lessons from PISA 2012 for the United States: Strong performers and successful reformers in education.* Paris, France: Author.

OECD. (2013h). *OECD skills outlook: First results from the survey of adult skills.* Paris, France: Author.

OECD. (2014a). *Education at a glance: Education indicators.* Paris, France: Author OECD.

OECD. (2014b). *TALIS 2013 results: An international perspective on teaching and learning.* Paris, France: Author.

OECD. (2014c). *Measuring innovation in education: A new perspective.* Paris, France: Author.

Ofsted (Office for Standards in Education, Children's Services and Skills). (2010). *Finnish pupils' success in mathematics: Factors that contribute to Finnish pupils' success in mathematics.* Manchester, England: Author.

O'Neill, O. (2002). *A question of trust.* Cambridge, England: Cambridge University Press.

Pechar, H. (2007). "The Bologna Process": A European response to global competition in higher education. *Canadian Journal of Higher Education, 37*(3), 109–125.

Piesanen, E., Kiviniemi, U., & Valkonen, S. (2007). *Opettajankoulutuksen kehittämisohjelman seuranta ja arviointi. Opettajien täydennyskoulutus 2005 ja seuranta 1998–2005 oppiaineittain ja oppialoittain eri oppilaitosmuodoissa* [Follow-up and evaluation of the teacher education development program: Continuing teacher education in 2005 and its follow-up 1998–2005 by fields and teaching subjects in different types of educational institutions]. Jyväskylä, Finland: University of Jyväskylä, Institute for Educational Research.

Popham, J. (2007). The no-win accountability game. In C. Glickman (Ed.), *Letters to the next president. What we can do about the real crisis in public education* (pp. 166–173). New York, NY: Teachers College Press.

Prais, S. J. (2003). Cautions on OECD's recent educational survey (PISA). *Oxford Review of Education, 29*(2), 139–163.

Prais, S. J. (2004). Cautions on OECD's recent educational survey (PISA): Rejoinder to OECD's response. *Oxford Review of Education, 30*(4), 569–573.

Ravitch, D. (2010a, June 22). Obama's awful education plan. *Huffington Post.* Retrieved from www.huffingtonpost.com/diane-ravitch/obamas-awful-education -pl_b_266412.html

Ravitch, D. (2010b, July 6). Speech to the Representative Assembly of the National Education Association, New Orleans, LA.

Ravitch, D. (2010c). *The death and life of the great American school system: How testing and choice are undermining education.* New York, NY: Basic Books.

Ravitch, D. (2013). *Reign of error: The hoax of the privatization movement and the danger to America's public schools.* New York, NY: Alfred A. Knopf.

Riley, K., & Torrance, H. (2003). Big change question: As national policy-makers seek to find solutions to national education issues, do international comparisons such as TIMSS and PISA create a wider understanding, or do they serve to promote the orthodoxies of international agencies? *Journal of Educational Change, 4*(4), 419–425.

Rinne, R., Kivirauma, J., & Simola, H. (2002). Shoots of revisionist education policy or just slow readjustment? *Journal of Education Policy, 17*(6), 643–659.

Robert Wood Johnson Foundation. (2010). *The state of play: Gallup survey of principals on school recess.* Princeton, NJ: Author.

Robinson, K. (with L. Aronica). (2009). *The element: How finding your passion changes everything.* New York, NY: Viking Books.

Robinson, K. (2011). *Out of our minds: Learning to be creative.* Chichester, England: Capstone Publishing.

Robitaille, D. F., & Garden, R. A. (Eds.). (1989). *The IEA study of mathematics II: Context and outcomes of school mathematics.* Oxford, England: Pergamon Press.

Saari, S., & Frimodig, M. (Eds.). (2009). Leadership and management of education. Evaluation of education at the University of Helsinki 2007–2008. *Administrative Publications 58.* Helsinki, Finland: University of Helsinki.

Sahlberg, P. (2006a). Education reform for raising economic competitiveness. *Journal of Educational Change, 7*(4), 259–287.

Sahlberg, P. (2006b). Raising the bar: How Finland responds to the twin challenge of secondary education. *Profesorado, 10*(1), 1–26.

Sahlberg, P. (2007). Education policies for raising student learning: The Finnish approach. *Journal of Education Policy, 22*(2), 173–197.

Sahlberg, P. (2009). Ideat, innovaatiot ja investoinnit koulun kehittämisessä [Ideas, innovation and investment in school improvement]. In M. Suortamo, H., Laaksola, & J. Välijärvi (Eds.), *Opettajan vuosi 2009–2010* [Teacher's year 2009–2010] (pp. 13–56). Jyväskylä, Finland: PS-kustannus.

Sahlberg, P. (2010a). Rethinking accountability for a knowledge society. *Journal of Educational Change, 11*(1), 45–61.

Sahlberg, P. (2010b). Educational change in Finland. In A. Hargreaves, A. Lieberman, M. Fullan, & D. Hopkins (Eds.), *Second international handbook of educational change* (pp. 323–348). New York, NY: Springer.

Sahlberg, P. (2011). The fourth way of Finland. *Journal of Educational Change, 12*(2), 173–185.

Sahlberg, P. (2012). The most wanted: Teachers and teacher education in Finland. In L. Darling-Hammond & A. Lieberman (Eds.) *Teacher education around the world: Changing policies and practices* (pp. 1–21). New York, NY: Routledge.

Sahlberg, P. (2013a). Teachers as leaders in Finland. *Educational Leadership*, *71*(2), 36–40.

Sahlberg, P. (2013b, May 15). What if Finland's great teachers taught in U.S. schools? *Washington Post*. Retrieved from www.washingtonpost .com/blogs/answer-sheet/wp/2013/05/15/what-if-finlands-great-teachers -taught-in-u-s-schools-not-what-you-think.

Sahlberg, P. (in press). The Global Educational Reform Movement and its impact on schooling. K. Mundy, A. Green, R. Lingard, & A. Verger (Eds.), *The handbook of global policy and policy-making in education* (pages not available). New York, NY: Wiley-Blackwell.

Sarason, S. B. (1996). *Revisiting "the culture of the school and the problem of change."* New York, NY: Teachers College Press.

Schleicher, A. (2006). *The economics of knowledge: Why education is key for Europe's success*. Brussels, Belgium: The Lisbon Council.

Schleicher, A. (2007). Can competencies assessed by PISA be considered the fundamental school knowledge 15-year-olds should possess? *Journal of Educational Change, 8*(4), 349–357.

Schulz, W., Ainley, J., Fraillon, J., Kerr, D., & Losito, B. (2010). ICCS 2009 International Report: Civic knowledge, attitudes and engagement among lower-secondary school students in thirty-eight countries. Amsterdam, The Netherlands: IEA.

Seddon, J. (2008). *Systems thinking in the public sector: The failure of the reform regime . . . and a manifesto for a better way*. Axminster, England: Triarchy Press.

Sellar, S., & Lingard, B. (2013). The OECD and the expansion of PISA: New global modes of governance in education. *British Educational Research Journal*. doi:10.1002/berj.3120

Simola, H. (2005). The Finnish miracle of PISA: Historical and sociological remarks on teaching and teacher education. *Comparative Education, 41*(4), 455–470.

Simola, H. (2015). *The Finnish education mystery. Historical and sociological essays on schooling in Finland*. London, England: Routledge.

Ståhle, P. (Ed.). (2007). *Five steps for Finland's future*. Helsinki, Finland: TEKES.

Ståhle, P., & Wilenius, M. (2006). *Luova tietopääoma: Tulevaisuuden kestävä kilpailuetu* [Creative intellectual capital: Sustainable competitive advantage of the future]. Helsinki, Finland: Edita.

Statistics Finland. (2011). *Population structure*. Retrieved from www.stat.fi/til /vaerak/2010/vaerak_2010_2011-03-18_tie_001_en.html

Statistics Finland. (2014a). *Nearly every fifth Finn is aged 65 or over*. Retrieved from tilastokeskus.fi/til/vaerak/index_en.html

Statistics Finland. (2014b). *Discontinuation of education*. Retrieved from www
.stat.fi/til/kkesk/index_en.html

Statistics Finland. (n.d.a). *Education*. Retrieved from www.stat.fi/til/kou_en.html

Statistics Finland. (n.d.b). *Research and development*. Retrieved from www.stat.fi
/til/tkke/index_en.html

Statistics Finland. (n.d.c). *Income and consumption*. Retrieved from www.stat.fi/til
/tul_en.html

Spieghalter, D. (2013, December 3). East Asian countries top global league
tables for educational performance. Retrieved from www.theguardian.com
/world/2013/dec/03/east-asian-top-oecd-education-rankings

Teddlie, C. (2010). The legacy of the school effectiveness research tradition. In
A. Hargreaves, A. Lieberman, M. Fullan, & D. Hopkins (Eds.), *The second
international handbook of educational change* (pp. 523–554). Dordrecht,
Netherlands: Springer.

Toom, A., Kynäslahti, H., Krokfors, L., Jyrhämä, R., Byman, R., Stenberg, K.,
... Kansanen, P. (2010). Experiences of a research-based approach to teacher education: Suggestion for the future policies. *European Journal of Education, 45*(2), 331–344.

Tucker, M. (2011). *Surpassing Shanghai: An agenda for American education built
on the world's leading systems*. Cambridge, MA: Harvard Education Press.

UNICEF. (2012). *Measuring child poverty: New league tables of child poverty
in the world's richest countries*. Florence, Italy: Innocenti Research Centre
Report Card #10.

Välijärvi, J. (2004). Implications of the modular curriculum in the secondary
school in Finland. In J. van den Akker, W. Kuiper, & U. Hameyer (Eds.),
Curriculum landscapes and trends (pp. 101–116). Dordrecht, Netherlands:
Kluwer.

Välijärvi, J. (2008). Miten hyvinvointi taataan tulevaisuudessakin? [How to
guarantee welfare also in future?]. In M. Suortamo, H., Laaksola, & J.
Välijärvi (Eds.), *Opettajan vuosi 2008–2009* [Teacher's year 2008–2009]
(pp. 55–64). Jyväskylä, Finland: PS-kustannus.

Välijärvi, J., Kupari, P., Linnakylä, P., Reinikainen, P., Sulkunen, S., Törnroos,
J., & Arffman, I. (2007). *Finnish success in PISA and some reasons behind
it II*. Jyväskylä, Finland: University of Jyväskylä.

Välijärvi, J., Linnakylä, P., Kupari, P., Reinikainen, P., & Arffman, I. (2002).
Finnish success in PISA and some reasons behind it. Jyväskylä, Finland:
Institute for Educational Research, University of Jyväskylä.

Välijärvi, J., & Sahlberg, P. (2008). Should "failing" students repeat a grade? A
retrospective response from Finland. *Journal of Educational Change, 9*(4),
385–389.

Voutilainen, T., Mehtäläinen, J., & Niiniluoto, I. (1989). *Tiedonkäsitys* [Conception of knowledge]. Helsinki, Finland: Kouluhallitus.

Weiss, E. (2013). *Mismatches in Race to the Top limit educational improvement: Lack of time, resources, and tools to address opportunity gaps puts lofty state goals out of reach.* Washington, DC: Broader, Bolder Approach to Education/Education Policy Institute.

Westbury, I., Hansen, S-E., Kansanen, P., & Björkvist, O. (2005). Teacher education for research-based practice in expanded roles: Finland's experience. *Scandinavian Journal of Educational Research, 49*(5), 475–485.

Wiborg, S. (2010). *Swedish free schools: Do they work?* London, England: Centre for Learning and Life Chances in Knowledge Economies and Societies, www.llakes.org.

Wilkinson, R., & Pickett, K. (2009). *The spirit level: Why more equal societies almost always do better.* New York, NY: Allen Lane.

World Bank. (2011). *Learning for all: Investing in people's knowledge and skills to promote development.* Washington, DC: World Bank.

Zhao, Y. (2009). *Catching up or leading the way: American education in the age of globalization.* Alexandria, VA: ASCD.

Zhao, Y. (2013, December 2). Reading the PISA tea leaves: Who is responsible for Finland's decline and the Asian magic? Retrieved from zhaolearning.com/2013/12/02/reading-the-pisa-tea-leaves-who-is-responsible-for-finland's-decline-and-the-asian-magic/

Zhao, Y. (2014). *Who's afraid of the big bad dragon: Why China has the best (and worst) education system in the world.* San Francisco, CA: Jossey Bass.

Index

f or *t* following a page number refers to a figure or table, respectively. *n* refers to a note.